Cousins

Cousins

Our primate relatives

Robin Dunbar and Louise Barrett

London, New York, Sydney, Dehli, Paris,
Munich, and Johannesburg

Publisher: Sean Moore
Editorial director: LaVonne Carlson
Project editor: Barbara Minton
Editor: Jennifer Quasha
Editorial assistance: Alison Marra
Art editors: Gus Yoo, Megan Clayton
Production director: David Proffit

This book is published to accompany the TV series *Cousins*,
first broadcast on BBC1 in 2000.
Series producer: Bernard Walton
Producer: Miles Barton

First published 2000 by BBC Worldwide Ltd
Woodlands, 80 Wood Lane, London W12 0TT

Library of Congress Cataloguing-in-Publication Data

Dunbar, R.I.M. (Robin Ian MacDonald), 1947-
    Cousins : our primate relatives / Robin Dunbar and Louise Barrett.-- 1st American ed.
        p.cm.
    Includes bibliographical references (p.).
    ISBN 0-7894-7155-8 (alk. paper)
        1. Primates. I. Barrett, Louise. II. Title.

QL737.P9D75 2001
599.8--dc21   00-058930

Commissioning editors: Sheila Ableman and Shirley Patton
Project editor: Susan Watt
Text editor: Ben Morgan
Design concept: The Attik
Art direction: Pene Parker and Lisa Pettibone
Design: Philip Lewis
Picture research: Frances Abraham
Maps: Olive Pearson
Illustrations: Annabel Milne
Graphics: Martin Lubikowski

Printed and bound in the UK by Butler & Tanner Ltd., Frome, Somerset
Color origination by Radstock Repro, Midsomer Norton, Somerset
Jacket printed by Lawrence Allen Ltd., Weston-super-Mare, Somerset

Contents

THE PRIMATE WORLD   **10**

The primates are one of the most ancient of the mammal families, with an ancestry dating back
to the age of the dinosaurs. With the demise of these huge reptiles 65 million years ago, the
primates began to flourish, moving out of the shadows and successfully diversifying into a wide
variety of species and lifestyles. Today, the primates found throughout the world represent only
a fraction of the species that once existed – and many of these are now under threat.

THE PROSIMIANS   **48**

The prosimans are the most unusual of the modern-day primates. Although most species are
solitary and live in the dark, they nevertheless have active social live in which scents and sounds
play a very important role. The island of Madagascar is the domain of the lemurs, and here
another unusual feature of prosimian life is found: females are often dominant to males;
is they who call the shots.

THE MONKEYS

Sociability is the hallmark of monkey life. All species of monkey live in groups of one kind or another. But while group living is an ideal solution to the problem of avoiding predators, it also creates problems of its own as animals are forced to compete for food. Good social skills are essential under these circumstances. Keeping track of dominance hierarchies and navigating their way through complex networks of relationships means that the monkeys need to keep their wits about them at all times.

THE APES

Gorillas, chimpanzees, and humans belong to the same primate group: the apes. Like their monkey cousins, apes are highly social creatures with a diversity of lifestyles, but with more refined social and intellectual skills and larger brains. In just a few million years, humans have evolved to become the dominant ape species. What separates us from – and unites us with – the other apes? Are we as different as we like to think?

Foreword

In the dry forests of Madagascar lives an enchanting little creature that would fit neatly into the palm of your hand. It is a pygmy mouse lemur weighing just 1 ounce (30 g) – the world's smallest primate. I went to western Madagascar to film this tiny animal, expecting to have a difficult search since it is solitary and ventures out only at night, but it turned out to be remarkably bold for its size. As I edged towards one sitting on a branch above my head, it stretched down, elongating its soft reddish-brown body to peer inquisitively at me for some moments with its huge, shining eyes, before leaping away into the darkness.

This diminutive primate is of considerable importance because it is very similar to the earliest ancestors of all primates, including, of course, humans. With a slightly pointed face, large round ears, and a thin tail, the pygmy mouse lemur looks rather like a rodent, but it possesses two very important primate features: forward-facing eyes, which enable it to judge distance accurately, and grasping hands, which allow it to leap and climb through the canopy, making it perfectly adapted to life in the trees.

This authoritative and highly readable book traces the evolution of primates and describes how, from such modest beginnings, the same basic primate blueprint has produced the incredibly rich, colorful, and diverse order of mammals to which we belong. From the ancient prosimians to the successful monkeys, the great apes, and ourselves, *Cousins* looks at all aspects of primate life and provides a wonderful insight into our extended family.

Watching primates greeting, bickering, making up, cuddling, assessing strategies, solving problems, and testing their environment, it is apparent that, more than anything, it is our intense sociability and intelligence that make us recognize our close biological relationship with them. It is surprising, therefore, that so little was known about primate behavior until recently. For over a century primates were simply brought back from exotic lands and kept in captivity, where people stared at them with a kind of unsettled awe. Thirty years ago, less than a dozen species had been studied in detail in the wild.

Studying wild animals is never easy, but there are special difficulties associated with primates. They often live in remote and inaccessible places, such as high in the canopy of dense tropical forests. As we have virtually lost that most primate of abilities, to climb trees, much observation involves developing an aching neck from peering up into the canopy in an effort to catch a fleeting glimpse. Thanks to the dedication and determination of primatologists, such as Robin Dunbar and Louise Barrett, who gradually habituate animals, discover their movements and habits, learn to recognize individuals, and painstakingly build up a picture of their social lives, the study of primates has grown rapidly into one of the most dynamic and exciting areas of research.

Face to face: an encounter with a young Bornean orangutan.

Of particular interest has been the study of social relationships and intelligence. This book explores the connection between group life and intelligence in monkeys, and in the final chapter, delves into the minds of the great apes. The apes' capacity for self-awareness, empathy, invention, learning, and even language provide some tantalizing clues about the way in which our own minds have developed. We have evolved both an exceptional intelligence and an avid curiosity about our world, but when we look at our closest relatives we see something very similar reflected in their eyes.

Over the last few decades, we have made great progress in learning about primates, but it's clear that we still have much to learn. The next big challenge that faces us is to protect them. Almost half of all primates are under threat from that most dangerous primate—man. Habitat destruction and hunting have had a dramatic impact on populations, and for many species time is rapidly running out. If we are to reverse this frightening trend, we need to have a better understanding and appreciation of primates. This exceptional book goes a long way towards achieving that goal.

Charlotte Uhlenbroek.

Dr. Charlotte Uhlenbroek, presenter, *Cousins*

1

THE PRIMATE WORLD

WHAT IS A PRIMATE?

An old orangutan swings indolently through the jungle, moving his massive 165 pound (75-kilogram) body from branch to branch with studied care. Hidden in the foliage beneath him, a tiny tarsier weighing barely 3.5 ounces (100 grams) dozes in its nest after a night spent catching insects. Nearby, a group of banded leaf monkeys, chewing meditatively on wads of fig leaves, watch the orang pass by. In the distance, a troop of pigtail macaques crash noisily through the undergrowth on the way to a new feeding site. On the ground, a human leans against a tree trunk, staring through binoculars at the orang and dictating notes into a tape recorder. All are members of the same zoological family: the primates. This is a family steeped in history whose origins go back to the time of the dinosaurs, a family that is both unremarkable for its unchanging and basic body plan, and yet remarkable for its extraordinary range of forms and lifestyles and for the size of its brains.

Previous page: A male gorilla is the largest of the living primates.

WHAT MAKES PRIMATES SPECIAL?

There are around 230 living species of primate. These represent only a tiny fraction of the primate species that have existed since this remarkable group of mammals first appeared on Earth. There will be more to say about that long history later on, but for now there is a a more demanding question to deal with: why do these 230 species belong to the same family? How do they differ from the other 4,000 or so mammal species, such as kangaroos, rabbits, and elephants?

Primates make up one of the "orders" (major subdivisions) of mammals, the group of animals that feed their young on milk. Some mammal orders, rodents, hoofed mammals, and carnivores, for instance, contain many species. Others, such as the flying lemurs, contain just a handful. With 230 species, the primates are one of the most species-rich of the mammal orders.

These 230 species are commonly split into three main groups: apes (the category to which humans belong), monkeys, and prosimians (lemurs, bushbabies, and other small and secretive animals of the night). Apes and monkeys are often lumped together as "anthropoids". All of these primate groups share certain defining features that mark them as having a common ancestry, features that evolved in response to a way of life the primates have shared for many millions of years. A life in the trees. Most primates are animals of the forest, adapted to a life of climbing, swinging, leaping, or crawling

1. An Indian golden langur runs effortlessly to safety in a tree. Primates are well adapted to life in trees.

through the trees. Even those such as gorillas and mandrills that habitually travel along the ground remain largely confined to forested habitats. Only humans, gelada, and patas monkeys provide a true exception to the rule, occupying open habitats where they travel only on the ground. Yet even gelada and patas give a nod to their arboreal ancestry. Their grasping, handlike feet are the feet of primates that evolved in trees. They are competent climbers, even if they are not as skilled as those monkeys that spend their whole lives in trees. Only humans are poor climbers, our feet having lost their prehensile ability to provide a stable platform for the striding walk that is uniquely characteristic of our species.

An ordinary mammal

Anatomically speaking, primates are surprisingly average mammals. They are medium sized and unspecialized in their body form, lacking the obvious defining features of other mammal orders, such as the distinctive feet of the hoofed mammals or the streamlined shape of the whales and dolphins. Primates look like their ancient fossil ancestors and have not changed much since the dawn of the age of mammals 65 million years ago.

Despite this, we can identify a number of key features that most, but not all, primates share: forward facing eyes to allow binocular vision; nails rather than claws; a five digit hand and foot; a thumb that moves the opposite way to the fingers to give a pincerlike grip; a relatively large brain; and a long childhood that extends well beyond weaning. Beyond these features, there is little to distinguish primates from other equally ancient orders of mammals such as the insectivores, like hedgehogs and shrews or the rodents. Primate ears are unspecialized, unlike those of the bats, as are their teeth, unlike the canines of carnivores, and their hands and feet are not too different from the fivedigit hands and feet of the earliest mammals, unlike the hoofed feet of antelope and deer.

Humans fit all these criteria, but not all primates do. Some, such as African colobus monkeys, do not have thumbs, while the gibbons of Southeast Asia have only a vestigial thumb, a bump on the corner of the palm.

1. The sifaka from Madagascar has the hand-like foot typical of all primates, adapted for climbing in trees.

2. The chimpanzee's hand is adapted for climbing as well as for delicate manipulation.

One likely reason for this particular exception is that thumbs get in the way when you travel through trees in the way these two species do – gibbons swinging underarm at high speed from one branch to the next using the hand as a hook, while colobus bound through the treetops. Prosimians have a claw rather than a nail on the second toe of each foot. These "grooming claws" are used for combing the fur.

What all this illustrates is the extraordinary variability that primates as a family exhibit.

In terms of body size, for example, primates vary enormously. The smallest is the western rufous mouse lemur of Madagascar, weighing in at a mere 1 oz (30 g), while the largest, the male gorilla, is 4,000 times larger at 260 lb (120 kg). Some extinct lemur species were larger still, weighing an estimated 440 lb (200 kg). Yet all primates look pretty much the same. They share the same primitive mammalian body plan, the same simple hand, and foot with its five digits.

 Spider monkeys have a prehensile, or grasping, tail that acts like a fifth hand. They can hang by their tail from a branch while using both hands to pluck fruits from the tree.

These short-nosed fruit bats from south India were once considered to be possible members of the primate family. Molecular genetics has now confirmed that, along with the small insect eating bats, the larger fruit bats belong to a different family of mammals.

▷ PRIMATE OR NOT?

Because primates have few specialized body parts, it is difficult to decide where to draw the line between primates and other mammals. Who exactly should be included in the primate family? During the twentieth century plausible claims for primatehood have been made on behalf of many seemingly unlikely candidates.

The primates share certain physical traits (notably their teeth) with fruit bats, for example, and this led some scientists to suggest that these giant bats should be called primates, despite their distinctly unprimate-like 4.5 ft wingspans. Molecular genetics now confirms that the two subfamilies of bats (the fruit bats and the smaller, insect eating bats we are more familiar with outside the tropics) share a common ancestor. Bats, it seems, are bats, and not our cousins.

Other candidates for primatehood were the two species of colugo, or flying lemur, of Indo-China and Indonesia. These catsized mammals have a flap of skin between each arm and leg that stretches into a wing, allowing them to glide up to 150 yards between trees. Although their teeth are in some ways similar to primate teeth, their common name is a misnomer. They are neither lemurs nor are they capable of true flapping flight. However, they may be descendants of the same ancient mammals (the plesiadapids) that lie at the origins of the primates 65 million years ago.

The most successful of the claimants to primatehood have undoubtedly been the tree shrews, a widespread group of shrewlike animals that clamber around in the understory of Southeast Asia's forests. Their primatelike anatomy preserved their claim to family membership until the 1970s, when it was finally concluded on the basis of their reproductive biology that they belong to the insectivore group, along with other shrews, as their name suggests.

DEFINING THE SPECIES

Our modern system of zoological classification owes its origins to the Swedish biologist Carolus Linnaeus (1707–78). Linnaeus tried to organize the animals and plants then known to Western science into a coherent system based on physical similarity. He devised a hierarchical system of classification in which species were grouped first into genera (singular: genus). These were then grouped into families, then orders, and so on up. Of these categories, genus and species are the most important for naming organisms. Following Linnaeus's original system, every species (including our own) is identified by a two word Latin name that specifies first the genus and then the species. So when Linnaeus considered the human species, he gave us the name *Homo sapiens*, or 'wise man'. We are the "wise" (*sapiens*) member (or species) belonging to the "man-like" (*Homo*) genus.

1. Mules are a cross between a male horse and a female donkey. Though stronger and more hardworking than either of its parents, the mule is infertile.

2. Carolus Linnaeus, the Swedish biologist, is the father of modern biological classification.

Classifying differences

In the early nineteenth century, Linnaeus's classification system was interpreted as reflecting common ancestry. Species that had descended from the same, now-extinct ancestor looked similar, it was assumed, because they inherited some of the same characteristics from the common ancestor, even though they might each have evolved some unique traits of their own in the meantime. Physical similarity therefore continued to play an important part in the way zoologists classified different species of animals, including primates. This system, however, was not without its problems. For one thing, how different do two populations of animals have to be in order to be classified as belonging to different species?

It eventually became apparent that taxonomists working with different animal groups did not always use the same yardstick. It seemed that the nearer they got to humans, the more fine-grained the classifications became. The differences used to define two species of monkey, for example, would not differentiate between two subspecies (or biological races) of birds, and would probably not even be noticed by those who specialized in slugs and snails.

Perfect examples

Part of the problem was that early biologists had borrowed their notion of species from the ancient Greek philosophers who adopted the term from everyday usage. They regarded a species as a group of things that were classified together because they shared a set of characteristics. Linnaeus and the biologists of his day thought of a species as a group of individuals striving to achieve a perfect form, and each species became identified by its "type

specimen," the individual regarded as providing the perfect example for the species. Linnaeus in fact used himself as the type specimen for our species, and he remains so to this day!

Natural variation

This typological way of thinking, however, clashed with the new evolutionary view that biologists adopted after Charles Darwin published his landmark book *On the Origin of Species* in 1859. Darwin's view was that the natural world was variable: without variation, there could be no evolution. Therefore, far from the organisms striving to imitate their type, they were, if anything, trying to do the opposite, to be as variable as possible as a basis for new evolutionary developments. The Darwinian view eventually gave rise to the now generally accepted definition of a species: two animals belong to the same

species if they can breed and produce fertile offspring. This reproductive definition provided a natural mechanism for interpreting the gradual (or sometimes very rapid) divergences that occur between two populations of the same species as they evolve into two new species.

The genetic continuum

Zoological classification, however, continues to carry the intellectual baggage of its pre-Darwinian past. We classify what is really a continuum of genetic similarity into discrete categories. Where we ought to specify degrees of relatedness or of genetic similarity, we impose boundaries. We continue to classify humans as belonging to a separate genus from the two species of chimpanzees, even though the actual differences between us barely warrant it.

3. Two closely related species stare inquisitively at each other.

⊕ TOPIC LINKS

1.1 What is a Primate?
p. 15 Primate or not?

1.3 Primates Today
p. 38 Primate classification
p. 40 The molecular clock

3.1 Monkey Lifestyles
p. 114 Guenons: naturally different

4.1 Planet of the Apes
p. 178 Recent history

A TROPICAL LIFESTYLE

In addition to their physical features, primates share another important characteristic, they are all tropical animals. Only tropical forests offer the year-round supply of fruits and leaves that primates require to survive. Forests of temperate latitudes, such as those in the northern half of Europe and North America, are either coniferous (and so unsuitable for fruit- and leaf-eaters) or too seasonal (and so unable to support primates through the winter months). All living species of primate, except humans, are confined to the tropics, with just a handful of species poking up their geographical noses into the subtropical zones of Europe and Asia. Barbary macaques, for example, retain a toehold on Gibraltar at the southern tip of the European continent, and Japanese macaques edge up into the snow-bound winter landscapes of northern Japan.

Humans are the exception in having a geographical range that now encompasses every continent and every kind of habitat. However it was not always so. Since we are recent arrivals on the planet's landscape. Like our primate cousins, we spent most of our evolutionary history within Africa, with limited excursions into the mainly tropical regions of Southeast Asia. Only with the appearance of anatomically modern humans barely 100,000 years ago did we spill out of the tropics and spread across the globe in a surging tide that engulfed everything in its path ($\triangleright$p.210). Aside from the telltale story locked into our fossil record, our body gives our tropical origins away. Our tall, slim, long-legged build is the build of a tropical species rather than one adapted to the cold climates of high latitudes, where shorter limbs help prevent heat loss. Our lack of hair is an adaptation to keep the body cool, forcing our ancestors to wrap

1. A female Barbary macaque surveys the Rock of Gibraltar, the last toehold that primates now have in Europe.

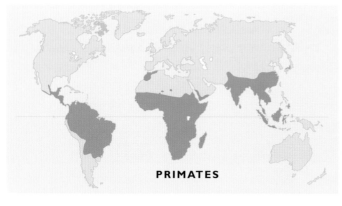

PRIMATES

PROSIMIANS

MONKEYS

APES

2. Although once more widespread, primates other than humans are today confined to the tropics, where they occur mainly in forests.

themselves in skins and sleep beside fires to cope with the night time chill and winter snows of Europe and northern Asia.

Primate habitats

Their restricted ecological adaptations mean that primates, in general, are found only on major continents and not on islands unless these islands have recently been joined to the mainland. This is the most obvious in Southeast Asia, where primates are found on the islands of the Indonesian archipelago (including Sumatra, Java, Borneo, and the Celebes), which were connected to the mainland until around 10,000 years ago, but not on islands such as New Guinea that have been isolated for much longer. The primates on the Indonesian islands were trapped by a sudden

rise in sea level at the end of the last ice age.

It is not impossible for primates to find their way to islands. Some of the Caribbean islands were home to fossil species, the last of which went extinct soon after humans arrived on the islands around 4,500 years ago. These species seem to have invaded the Caribbean islands from the South American mainland only within the last few million years. Once there, however, island species adapt to the conditions where there are few ecological competitors. As a result, they often face problems when aggressive ecological competitors like humans, arrive later.

Primates have done well on islands only in a few places, such as the island chains of Southeast Asia (Indonesia, the Philippines, and Japan) and on Madagascar. Madagascar seems to be a unique case, where colonizing

 Only one species of primate — the gelada — is a true grazer like horses and cows.

Japanese macaques use hot springs to warm up against the winter cold.

TAKING A BATH

The Japanese macaques living on the northern part of Japan's Honshu island are the most northerly populations of any non-human primate. Although the summers are warm and temperate here, the winters are cold and snowbound, and the animals are forced to eke out an existence in some of the harshest conditions.

This region is also quite volcanic, and hot springs bubble to the surface from deep within the Earth's mantle, bringing steaming water into the cold landscape. Some of the monkey troops in this area have taken to sitting in the hot springs during the winter when the outside temperatures are below freezing. They seem to have adopted this habit in the 1960s, probably copying the behavior of human visitors to the area, who enjoyed the opportunity of relaxing in a steaming natural bath. However, the monkeys might have realized the benefits of hot water themselves by sitting on the warm stones above the spring.

How the macaques survive the sub-zero temperatures they face when emerging from hot springs remains a puzzle. Monkeys' coats are relatively waterproof, but a prolonged soak in warm water must reduce their heat-retaining properties and leave the monkeys susceptible to catching chills.

animals from Africa found no competitors and were able to evolve into an amazing diversity of different species. However, they too have succumbed to the consequences of island specialization.

One of the reasons why island populations are so vulnerable is that small areas can support fewer species than large areas. This is known as the "species–area relationship". It applies not only to oceanic islands, but also to isolated forest patches and national parks, which are effectively islands of habitat separated by tracts of inhospitable land. Because small areas also support smaller populations, species on small islands tend to be more at risk of dying out than those on the mainland.

SIZE AND DIET

Primates' dependence on forests colors their diets. Most species are either insectivores or insect-eaters, folivores or leaf-eaters, or frugivores or fruit-eaters, or some combination of these. There are no true carnivores, other than humans perhaps, and no grazers, except the gelada. Even humans are not true carnivores. We would die of protein poisoning on a diet of pure meat. We have to mix meat with vegetables to obtain a balanced diet.

Although insect eating was probably the ancestral diet for the earliest primates, it is not a lifestyle that any species can pursue. Because insects are small and have to be eaten one at a time, a large species cannot survive on a purely insect diet. The key threshold appears to be at about 2 lb (1 kg) body weight. Species larger than this are unable to harvest enough insects every day to maintain life.

Medium sized species up to about 22 lb (10 kg) in body weight, such as spider monkeys, tend to be fruit eaters, whereas larger species, such as colobus monkeys, tend to be leaf eaters. This size difference is mainly a consequence of the fact that smaller animals have to consume disproportionately more food for their size each day to stay alive. Therefore they prefer highly nutritious foods from which they can extract nutrients easily. Large species can cope with a less nutritious diet of leaves, which are harder to digest than fruit and contain fewer nutrients.

Not surprisingly, diet has important implications for both guts and teeth. Because the different sections of the gut, the stomach, small intestine, and large intestine, do different jobs, the size of these components depends on a species' diet. Leaf eaters typically have to ferment leaves, like cattle and sheep do, in order to extract any nutrients from them. This is because the walls of the microscopic cells in a leaf are made of a

1. The crested black macaques of the Sulawesi Islands, Indonesia, are the descendants of populations cut off from mainland Indo-China by rising sea levels after the last ice age.

Primates have brains that are much larger for their body size than any other animal species.

2.(opposite) A vervet monkey from Kenya opens up a fig. The primates' hands allow them to manipulate food items with skill and dexterity.

substance called cellulose, which is difficult to digest. Only bacteria can break down cellulose, so leaf-eating monkeys have special enlarged stomachs that are full of bacteria and act like fermenting vats (▷p. 110). The bacteria are digested as they pass through the small intestine, releasing the nutrients they have garnered from the leaves. In contrast, fruit eaters typically have small stomachs and longer small intestines where nutrients can be absorbed efficiently from the fruit pulp.

Diet and distribution

Diet and body size effect several other important aspects of primates' lives. Large species, such as chimpanzees, need a greater area of forest to satisfy their daily food requirements than small species, so a given area of forest will support a smaller population. Diet adds a further dimension. Fruit eaters need larger ranges than leaf eaters because fruits are a patchy, ephemeral food source, whereas leaves are more evenly distributed in both space and time. Fruit-eaters need a large enough range to ensure there will always be at least one tree in fruit in their territory. Leaf eaters, on the other hand, can simply move into the tree next door when they have eaten all the edible leaves close to hand.

The number of primate species in a given area declines the further away from the equator you go, and only large species tend to be found furthest from the equator. This is because habitats outside the tropics are more seasonal, and large species are better able to survive starvation during the hungry season. Mouse-sized animals have to eat their own body weight in food every day to stay alive, whereas an animal as large as a human can starve for 70 days and survive.

A surprising observation is that, even when there are as many as 12–15 species in a primate community, there will seldom be

1. The rare Zanzibar red colobus is a leaf eater and is one of the most endangered species of monkey.

2. The pygmy mouse lemur of Madagascar is one of the smallest of the primates. To reduce the energy required for survival when food is scarce, it goes into torpor hidden in a nest.

more than one species of leaf-eater. A typical African forest habitat might have seven or eight species of fruit-eating guenons, baboons, and chimpanzees, and perhaps an insectivorous bushbaby or two, but it will have only one species of leaf-eating colobus monkey. Despite this, the colobus monkey might be the most abundant, accounting for as much as half the total mass of primates present. It is not entirely clear why this should be. One explanation is that leaf-eaters can pack themselves in more densely simply because leaves are more abundant than fruit.

Another explanation is that leaf-eaters do not need to compete so much for their food. Fruit-eaters, by contrast, have to compete for a limited supply of food. This forces them to adopt different 'ecological niches' – in other words, each species specializes in its own way of making a living – and this inevitably means being different species. Ecological separation of this kind may involve foraging at different heights in the canopy or specializing on different types of fruit.

Chimpanzees are important seed dispersers, carrying the seeds of the fruits they have eaten for many miles before depositing them in their faeces. This helps forests to regenerate.

 PRIMATES AS SEED DISPERSERS

Primates, it seems, play an unexpectedly important role in the ecology of tropical forests. Without the help of their primate inhabitants, many tropical trees might die out altogether.

The mongoose lemur spends as much as 84 per cent of its feeding time sipping the nectar from the flowers of the kapok tree and may be the main species responsible for ensuring pollination. The greater dwarf lemur is just the right weight to trigger the mechanical lever that releases pollen when it feeds on the nectar of the liana creeper, suggesting that the plant and the lemur have arrived at an arrangement of mutual benefit during the course of evolution.

Primates also play an important role in dispersing seeds. Many trees suppress the growth of their own seedlings when these sprout too close to the parent, so they rely on birds and mammals to carry their seeds far enough to germinate successfully. Monkeys are particularly well adapted to play this role.

Some monkeys have special cheek pouches for storing fruits until they can find a safe place to eat. When seeds are accidentally dropped during feeding, they germinate well away from the parent tree. Many monkeys and apes carry seeds long distances while they are in transit through the gut after being eaten. Although many seeds are destroyed by chewing, some are not. When these are passed during defecation up to a day later, they may be miles from the parent tree. Indeed, the seeds of some trees have to be primed by the acid in a fruit-eater's stomach – unless these seeds pass through an animal's gut, they will never germinate.

Sixty-five million years ago, the age of the dinosaurs was brought to a cataclysmic end when a giant comet smashed into Earth somewhere near Mexico's Yucatán Peninsula. The dust and ash thrown up by the impact obscured the sun and precipitated a "nuclear winter". Unable to cope with the colder climate and consequent change in vegetation, the dinosaurs perished. Freed from competition with the reptiles that had ruled the Earth for 250 million years, the small mammals that scurried through the undergrowth beneath the dinosaurs' feet or scuttered through the tree-tops suddenly found themselves in ecological paradise. Among these species were the plesi-adapids, squirrel-like animals related to present-day shrews and hedgehogs. Free to diversify into new ecological niches, the plesiadapids gave rise to the first primates. From these humble beginnings, by a long and tortuous path through time, eventually humans arrived on the scene.

DAWN OF THE PRIMATES

Primates are one of the most ancient lineages of mammals alive today. Their origins go back more than 65 million years to the age of the dinosaurs, when the small, squirrel-like ancestors of the primates scurried around in the trees. Largely nocturnal, these animals preyed on insects, probably foraging alone and nesting in tree holes, like modern day prosimians such as bushbabies and mouse lemurs.

The plesiadapids

The squirrel-like ancestors of the primates are not considered primates. Instead, they are placed in their own separate order of mammals, the plesiadapids. These tree dwelling mammals had some decidedly unprimate-like characteristics, including long, rat-like central incisors, the biting teeth at the front of the jaw, and small brains for their body size. Some fossils show signs of flaps of skin between the arms and legs,

perhaps used to glide between trees. The plesiadapids varied considerably in size, the smallest weighing a mere 1/3 oz (10 g) (barely the weight of a cigarette), the largest a massive 7 lb (3 kg) (the size of a cat). Typically squirrel sized, they probably behaved and looked like squirrels, except that most, if not all, were nocturnal. They probably fed mainly on insects, though some show adaptations for fruit eating, and yet others may have been leaf eaters.

Plesiadapids were contemporaries of the dinosaurs but they survived the mass extinction that killed the giant reptiles. These small mammals flourished from 70 to 55 million years ago, when they too disappear from the fossil record. Despite their relatively short presence in Earth's history, they were an especially successful group. More than 100 fossil species have been found, many known only from fragments of delicate jawbone with tiny embedded teeth. It is mainly because their teeth resemble modern primates that plesiadapids are classified as being close relatives.

The plesiadapids diversified into many different species, occupying woodland and

1

1. The tiny lower jaw (barely 1/2 in (1 cm) in length) of an extinct plesiadapid from Wyoming, USA. Most plesiadapids are known only from their teeth, which fossilize better than softer bones.

2. The dinosaurs ruled the Earth for 250 million years. Their extinction 65 million years ago allowed primitive mammals, such as plesiadapids, to diversify.

2

1

2

1. Plesiadapids, the very earliest members of the primate family, co-existed with the last of the dinosaurs. *Plesiadapis*, a typical species, probably looked much like this.

2. Extinct as recently as 1000 years ago, *Megaladapis* was a giant 154 lb (70-kg) leaf-eating lemur.

forest habitats throughout the northern hemisphere. During their heyday, the Earth was 50-60 °F (10–15 °C) warmer than it is now. What had once been, and are now again, the temperate northern parts of the Earth were then tropical. Paris and New York boasted climates like those of Bombay and Havana today.

The adapids

A dramatic rise in Earth's temperature 55 million years ago resulted in a wave of extinctions, although this was not as dramatic as the mass extinction that killed the dinosaurs 10 million years before. The plesiadapids succumbed in this new wave of extinctions, but one group of primate ancestors survived. These were the adapids, cat-sized animals that first appear in the fossil record 55 million years ago.

The adapids were the first true primates. They were larger than plesiadapids and had the distinctive anatomical features seen in primates today, such as nails instead of claws,

relatively large brains, and opposable big toes, which allowed them to grip branches and tree trunks rather than run along them. And unlike plesiadapids, they had forward-facing eyes, giving them 3D vision. In most respects, they resembled modern prosimians, like lemurs, bushbabies, and similar primates rather than the monkeys and apes. They were mainly tree living, had a mixture of daytime and nocturnal activity patterns, and fed predominantly on insects and fruit.

The adapids were a successful group. More than 180 species have been found among the fossil beds that date from between 55 and 40 million years ago. They are among the most abundant of the fossil mammals from this period, and some survived as late as 5 million years ago. Like the plesiadapids before them, but unlike the modern primates that evolved after them, these early members of the prosimian family continued to be found only in the then tropical northern hemisphere, in the southern US, southern Europe, North Africa, northern India, and southern China.

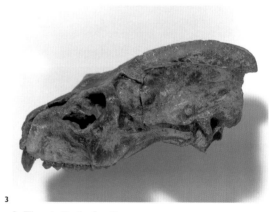

3

3. The skull of a fossil adapid from France. Adapids were widespread in Europe between 55 and 40 million years ago, and were the first true primates.

Primates are one of the oldest families of mammals alive today. Their direct ancestors shared the ancient forests with the last of the dinosaurs.

NEW NICHES, NEW SPECIES

Around 40 million years ago, the fossil record falls silent. For the next 5 million years, there are few fossils of any kind. We know little of what happened during this mysterious gap, other than that by the time it ended, the world had changed dramatically. Temperatures plummeted by more than 50°F (10°C) and sea levels fell by as much as 400 yards, reaching the lowest they have been in the past 65 million years. As the planet cooled, the tropical forests that primates occupied moved toward the equator to take their present position. Now primates were truly equatorial species, confined mainly within the tropics.

Something else had changed too. By the end of the fossil gap, a completely new group of primates had appeared on the scene. They were the anthropoids, the group to which monkeys and apes belong.

First anthropoids

The earliest anthropoid fossils were found in eroded river beds at Wadi Fayum, on the edge of the Sahara Desert in northern Egypt. The sand-blasted cliffs of Fayum have not always been so inhospitable. Around 30 to 35 million years ago, the climate here was lush and wet. Sluggish rivers meandered through luxurious riverbank forests. Oxbow lakes grew stagnant and gave way to swamps and marshes. Crocodiles patrolled the river channels, water birds stepped gingerly across mud flats, and strange, prehistoric relatives of hippos and

4. World temperatures are now much cooler than when primates first appeared. Successive periods of dramatic climate change have often coincided with the evolution of new families of primates.

4

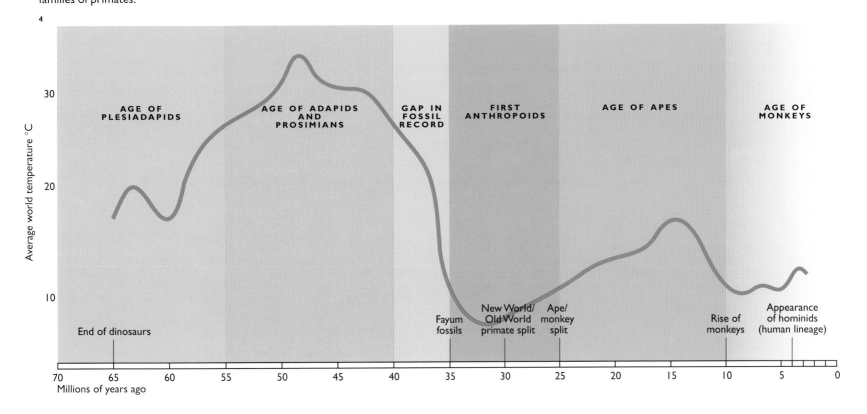

AGE OF PLESIADAPIDS · AGE OF ADAPIDS AND PROSIMIANS · GAP IN FOSSIL RECORD · FIRST ANTHROPOIDS · AGE OF APES · AGE OF MONKEYS

End of dinosaurs · Fayum fossils · New World/Old World primate split · Ape/monkey split · Rise of monkeys · Appearance of hominids (human lineage)

Average world temperature °C

Millions of years ago

elephants grazed the banks.

Above them in the trees, safe from the dangers of the forest floor, a new kind of primate surveyed the landscape, the early anthropoids. They differed strikingly from the adapid prosimians of the previous 20 to 25 million years. The grooming claws on the hind feet had disappeared, and the eye sockets were smaller, indicating a change from a nocturnal lifestyle to activity during the day.

These important changes seem to be related to a shift in diet from insects to fruit. Insect eaters, such as prosimians, typically find their prey by smell and hearing, hence the enlarged smell centers in the brain and their large ears. This makes ecological sense because insects tend to be most active at night when predators that hunt by their vision are at a disadvantage. The shift to a fruit-based diet coincided with a shift to daytime activity, reduced dependence on their sense of smell, and an enlargement of the parts of the brain that process vision.

A transatlantic puzzle

The primates of Fayum and other fossils of the same period show many similarities with

Teeth can reveal much about the behavior of extinct and living primate species. A male olive baboon from Kenya displays the fearsome canine teeth that he will use effectively if an opponent fails to take his threat seriously.

 WHAT'S IN A TOOTH?

Teeth are among the most common fossil remnants, in fact, some extinct primate species are known only from a few surviving teeth. This is because teeth are made of a hard material called enamel, which is resistant to destruction after death. By comparing fossil teeth with those of living primates, scientists are able to glean a surprising amount of information about the habits of extinct mammals.

The size of a tooth, especially a chewing tooth, is a good clue to an animal's size. Large animals need more food to stay alive, so they have bigger teeth to help them process food quickly. The relative size of the different teeth in a jaw tell us about an animal's diet. Fruit-eaters have large incisors, the biting teeth at the front of the jaw, and small molars, the chewing teeth right at the back. The opposite is true of leaf eaters. This is because fruit needs a lot of biting but little chewing, whereas leaves need a lot of chewing and little biting. When examined under a microscope, the patterns of wear on teeth can also tell us a great deal. Ground-living animals that take in a lot of grit with their food have thicker enamel to protect the teeth from wear. They also have more scratches and fewer pits on their chewing teeth.

The relative size of the canine, or eye, teeth can tell us about a species' mating system. Species, such as baboons, where males have much larger canine teeth than females, live in polygamous groups in which the males compete with each other to monopolize matings with the females. Species, such as gibbons, where the two sexes have canines of similar size, or where females have slightly larger canines than males, live in monogamous pairs.

The three tiny bones in our ears that transmit sound between the eardrum and the brain were adapted from the jawbones of our reptile ancestors.

living monkeys in South and Central America. In many ways, they resemble these more than the monkeys or apes of Africa and Asia, although they also share many anatomical features with the latter.

It seems that these early anthropoids lie at the common origin of two major divisions in the anthropoid family, the monkeys of the New World, and the Old World stock that gave rise to the monkeys and apes of Africa and Asia (▷p. 105). Indeed, studies of primate DNA (▷p. 40) strongly suggest that the

common ancestor of New and Old World anthropoids did live 25 to 30 million years ago. Fossil evidence also supports the theory of a common origin in Africa 30 million years ago. There are only a handful of South American fossil primates older than 20 million years, and the few anthropoid-like fossils that predate Fayum are all found in Africa.

This presents us with a real puzzle. How did the ancestors of New World monkeys cross the Atlantic Ocean from Africa? The

▷ SEEING IN 3D

Like most mammals, our ancient plesiadapid ancestors had eyes on the sides of their heads rather than at the front. This arrangement gives all around vision, allowing an animal to spot enemies easily. But the ability to see all around comes at a price. For an animal to see in true 3D, and hence be able to judge distance, the visual fields of the two eyes must overlap. The sideways-facing eyes of plesiadapids gave little overlap, so these squirrel-like animals had limited 3D vision.

By the time the adapids, the first true primates, had evolved, the eye-sockets had moved to the front of the head, giving more forward-facing vision and overlapping visual fields. These animals could see in 3D and judge distance well, an essential requirement for species that relied more on jumping between trees than running squirrel-like along branches. However, the adapids' eyeballs now needed more support than the cheekbones alone could provide. This problem was solved by the evolution of a special ring of bone that held each eyeball in place, a feature seen in prosimians to this day.

Monkeys and apes took the process one stage further, as their fossils demonstrate. Their forward-facing eyes and short muzzles gave a wider field of 3D vision than adapids had. Instead of a bony ring, these animals evolved a solid cup of bone that surrounded and supported each eyeball. This prevented cheek muscles from nudging the eyes during chewing, a problem that continues to bedevil prosimians. Highly mobile eyeballs helped make up for the lack of all around vision.

An interesting exception to this last adaptation is the tarsier, a curious primate that straddles the dividing line between prosimians and anthropoids. Its forward-facing eyes can hardly move. To compensate, it can turn its head 180 degrees to see behind it, like an owl.

A black-and-white colobus monkey from Uganda displays typical agility when leaping between trees. Forward-facing eyes give them the 3D vision necessary to land safely.

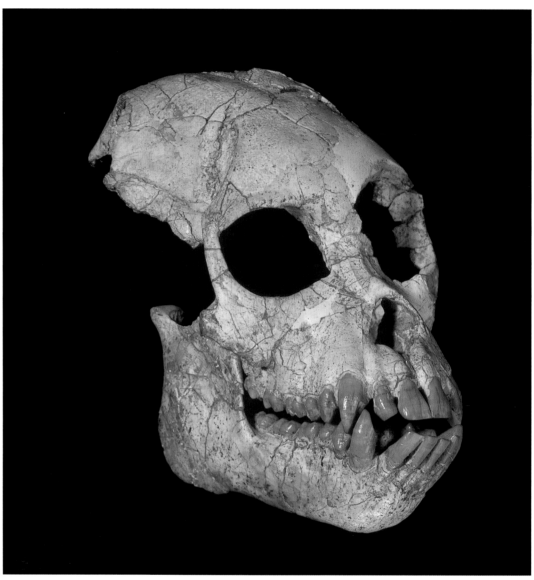

1. *Aegyptopithecus zeuxis* was typical of the new primate species that appeared around 30 million years ago. These first anthropoids were the ancestors of the apes and monkeys of today.

2. Living around 20 million years ago, *Proconsul* was one of the most successful and widespread of the early African apes.

question has baffled scientists for decades.

One thing is sure. The South American primates could not have evolved from the adapid prosimians of North America. The molecular evidence confirms that they evolved from the same stock as the Old World monkeys and apes and not from the prosimian branch of the primate family. In addition, South America and North America were two separate continents until 20 million years ago, with South America much further south than its present position.

The most likely possibility would be migration from Africa either directly across the Atlantic or via Antarctica. Crossing the Atlantic is not implausible. Thirty million years ago the Atlantic Ocean was only about 310 mi (500 km) wide at its narrowest point. The New and Old Worlds have been drifting apart steadily since the age of the dinosaurs and are still drifting today. More importantly, there was a chain of islands down the middle of the southern Atlantic that could have acted as stepping stones for migrants. Today these islands are submerged and form part of the mid-Atlantic ridge, a huge mountain range on the ocean floor where the American and Afro-European continental plates are being pushed apart. The low sea levels at the time would have exposed large areas of continental shelf around Africa and America, making the ocean even narrower.

So the distance the animals had to travel across open water was not enormous. All that was needed was for a group of individuals to be washed out to sea on a floating tree or a raft of vegetation, perhaps during a particularly torrential storm. Westward ocean currents would have carried the raft to the vicinity of Brazil. Even today, leatherback turtles follow this route every year from their feeding grounds around Ascension Island to their breeding grounds in the Caribbean.

An Antarctic route is also more plausible than it might seem at first sight. Until about 20 million years ago, South America and Antarctica were joined by the spur of land that still reaches out towards Cape Horn across the Antarctic Ocean. Although Antarctica is icebound now, it has not always been so. Indeed, the young botanist John Wilson's lasting gift to us – before he died with Captain Scott on their ill-fated expedition to the South Pole – was to demonstrate that Antarctica had once been forested. The Antarctic route acquires some further plausibility from the fact that many of the earliest fossil sites in South America are located in southern Argentina and Chile, the part of the continent closest to Antarctica.

⭐ Until about 5 million years ago, apes were much more common than monkeys.

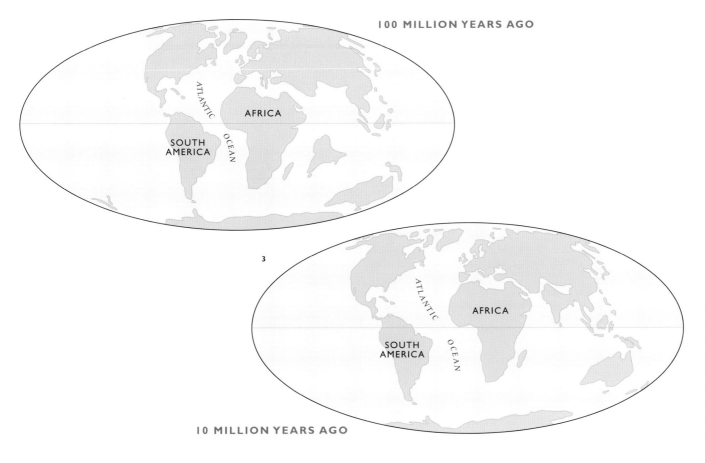

100 MILLION YEARS AGO

3

10 MILLION YEARS AGO

3. How primates reached South America from Africa 30 million years ago remains a mystery. However, Africa and South America were then much closer than they are today.

ANCIENT TO MODERN

Humans belong to the family of anthropoids known as apes, along with chimpanzees, gorillas, gibbons and the orangutan. We tend to think of apes as belonging to a newer lineage than the monkeys. But if anything, the apes represent the older, more established, lineage, and it is the monkeys – and in particular the baboon/macaque/guenon group of monkeys – that are the new kids on the evolutionary block.

Ancient apes

The history of primate evolution in the Old World becomes a little hazy after the rich early fossil deposits of Fayum and elsewhere. But as the fossil record improves, again from around 20 million years ago, it soon becomes clear that the Fayum primates had by this time split into two main groups, apes and monkeys. The monkeys, however, are a minor sideshow on the stage of history, for the dominant primates of the Old World at this time are undoubtedly the apes. They are everywhere, with some 60 known species spanning the whole of Africa and stretching across southern Eurasia from Spain in the west to China in the east. Although none appears to be a direct ancestor of the living apes, they are nonetheless apes: they share the characteristic molar teeth of living apes and the lack of a tail.

The ancient apes were highly successful, occupying many of the forest and ground niches filled today by monkeys. Some reached incredible sizes. The aptly named *Gigantopithecus*, whose two species roamed the woodlands of India and China 5 to 10 million years ago, weighed an estimated 440-660 lb (200–300 kg). These monsters are known only from their jaws and teeth, many of which originally turned up in Chinese herbalists' shops where they were ground down to be

1

added to traditional medicines. At four times the weight of a man, *Gigantopithecus* was the largest primate that ever lived. It was so big that it could not have been anything other than a ground-living herbivore.

Twenty million years ago, apes accounted for 80 percent of all the anthropoid primate species in Africa. Then, around 10 million years ago, disaster struck and numbers fell to the current low of just 20 percent of African primate species. The apes were being replaced by the monkeys.

It seems that the apes were shortchanged by the drying and cooling of Earth's climate 10 to 15 million years ago. The result was a major contraction of the forests that had clothed

1. *Gigantopithecus* weighed in at over 440 lb (200 kg) and was the largest primate that ever lived. Common in China about 5–10 million years ago, it is known only from fossilized teeth.

2. Ancient Chinese herbalists' manuscripts prescribed the ground-down teeth of 'dragons' (such as the massive *Gigantopithecus* tooth on the right, below) for certain ailments.

2

Africa in particular. The change of habitat from forest to more open woodland favored the monkeys for several reasons. One was the fact that monkeys had evolved the ability to eat fruits before they were ripe. All apes, including humans, are unable to digest unripe fruits. We lack an enzyme that can detoxify chemicals called tannins that trees use to protect fruits before the seeds are ready to germinate. Tannins give us a dry sensation in the mouth as well as a stomach ache and worse. However, once the seed is ready, these toxins break down naturally and the fruit becomes sweet and palatable.

While the apes are ripe-fruit specialists, their monkey cousins evolved the ability to detoxify tannins and eat unripe fruits. As Africa's drying forests began to break up, the monkeys came into their own. Not only could they could exploit the dwindling supply of fruit before the apes could cope with them, the monkeys branched out into the savanna and forest edges to eat the nut-like seeds in these new grassland habitats. The apes were simply out-competed and paid the price.

Only one lineage of apes survived and flourished – but barely by the skin of its teeth. That lineage also stepped out from its forest home and began to exploit the woodlands and grasslands around the forest edges. It was touch and go for animals that were less than perfectly adapted to their new habitats. But in the end they survived, and we are the product.

3. Vervet monkeys successfully invaded the woodland habitats of Africa from their ancestral forest home. This one feeds on the flowers of the spiny accra tree.

The rise of the monkeys

The Old World monkeys, of course, have an ancient history too. Studies of their DNA confirm that their common ancestor with the ape lineage dates back to about 25 million years ago. Nonetheless, the monkeys remained a small and insignificant part of the African and Asian landscape until much later. Then they exploded out of the forests and their numbers took off.

The ancient monkeys of Africa were similar in appearance to the leaf-eating colobus monkeys that still live throughout the forests of sub-Saharan Africa. Whether the ancient monkeys were also leaf-eaters is unclear, but an early adaptation to leaf-eating within the monkey lineage seems plausible. When the climate changed around 12 million years ago, a new monkey lineage appeared. These were the fruit- and seed-eating cercopithecines – the baboons, macaques, guenons and their relatives.

This new lineage was soon represented in Asia by the macaques, who spread rapidly from their ancestral home in Africa – first into southern Europe and then across Asia as far east as the Japanese archipelago. Within Africa, baboons – Africa's largest and most widespread monkey species – appear in the fossil record around 5 million years ago, pass through an evolutionary phase, and then radiate into the five subspecies that we find today.

Some of the ancient baboons were decidedly exotic. The giant grazing baboon *Theropithecus oswaldi* was the size of a small gorilla. It roamed the savanna grasslands of eastern Africa until as recently as 50,000–100,000 years ago, but its massive size and ponderous bulk made it easy prey for the fleet-foot hunters of the newly emerging human species. *Theropithecus* bones abound at fossil campsites in Africa where our ancestors regularly dismembered their kills. Its close relative from northern Kenya and southern Ethiopia,

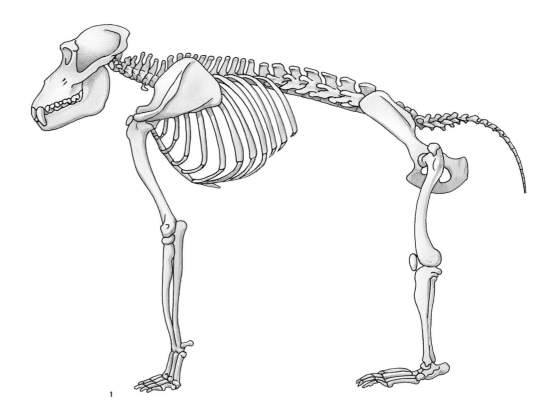

Theropithecus brumpti, may have been only half the size of *Theropithecus oswaldi*, but what it lacked in size it made up for with its spectacular face. Massive flanges on its cheekbones protruded sideways and forwards in a manner quite unlike that seen in any other species of living or extinct primate. It is difficult to see any obvious function for these flanges. Perhaps the most plausible suggestion is that they supported colorful surfaces that males used in competing for females, rather like the multicolored snouts of mandrills.

In the forests of central and West Africa, the 'forest baboons' – the drill and mandrill – and the more monkey-like mangabeys evolved into their present forms. And, finally, as the ice sheets were expanding and contracting in Eurasia to the north, the small guenon monkeys diversified and radiated in the forests of central Africa (▷p. 114).

1. Skeleton of the extinct giant baboon *Theropithecus oswaldi*. The gelada is the closest living relative of this species.

2. (opposite) The mandrill is a large terrestrial forest monkey from West Africa. Males like this one sport blue and red facial markings that probably evolved as a result of competition between males.

PRIMATES TODAY

Ever since their first appearance in the fossil record, primates have been successful colonizers of the world's tropical habitats, but they have remained tropical animals. Only one lineage of primates has broken loose from that ancestral constraint, and this was the lineage that gave rise to modern humans. Our ability to survive in temperate and subarctic climates, to invent agriculture and build canoes, has opened up possibilities beyond any available to our primate cousins. However the success of the human species has caused a population explosion that now threatens the survival of many of the world's other species. Currently we are witnessing the sixth major extinction event in the history of the planet. The first to have occurred since the disappearance of the dinosaurs. Our primate cousins have not been spared. All over the world, they are in decline. Most will not be celebrating the next millennium with us in 1,000 years' time.

PRIMATE CLASSIFICATION

Primate species of today are divided into two main groups: prosimians, "before apes", and anthropoids, "man-like" primates. The prosimians are the direct descendants of the adapid primates of 40 million years ago, and resemble them in a number of important respects, including their typically nocturnal lifestyle, although some are active by day, and aspects of their reproductive biology. In contrast, the anthropoids, ape and monkey species of the Old and New Worlds, are the result of a new evolutionary development from that same ancient prosimian stock. This development led toward a diurnal, herbivorous lifestyle associated with a more intense social life, often played out in large, permanent groups.

Prosimians

The prosimians are a diverse group of primates whose physical forms vary. However, all prosimians share a number of primitive characteristics that set them apart from the anthropoids. They are more reliant on scent and have larger smell areas in their brains than the anthropoids. They also have smaller brains in relation to body weight than monkeys or apes, and in this respect they more closely resemble the insectivores like shrews, hedgehogs, and their relatives, whose origins date back to the dying days of the dinosaurs.

Among the prosimians, we can distinguish several different groups. Conventionally, the tarsiers are separated into a group of their own because genetic studies have revealed they are more closely related to monkeys and apes than to other prosimians. Tarsiers resemble other prosimians because of common adaptations to a similar ecological niche, that

1. The white-footed sportive lemur is typical of Madagascar's unique prosimian primates. This one displays the "tooth comb", formed by the lower incisors and used in grooming, that is found only among prosimians.

of the tree-dwelling, nocturnal insect hunter.

The rest of the prosimians are split into two major groups, the lorisids and the lemurs. The lorisids include two major groups: the bushbabies of Africa, of which 11 species are currently recognized, and the lorises and pottos, made up of three species of loris in Southeast Asia and four species of potto in Africa. The other group, the lemurs, are unique in many ways. They are found only on the island of Madagascar off the southeast

A total of 234 different species of primate are known, although more are still being discovered.

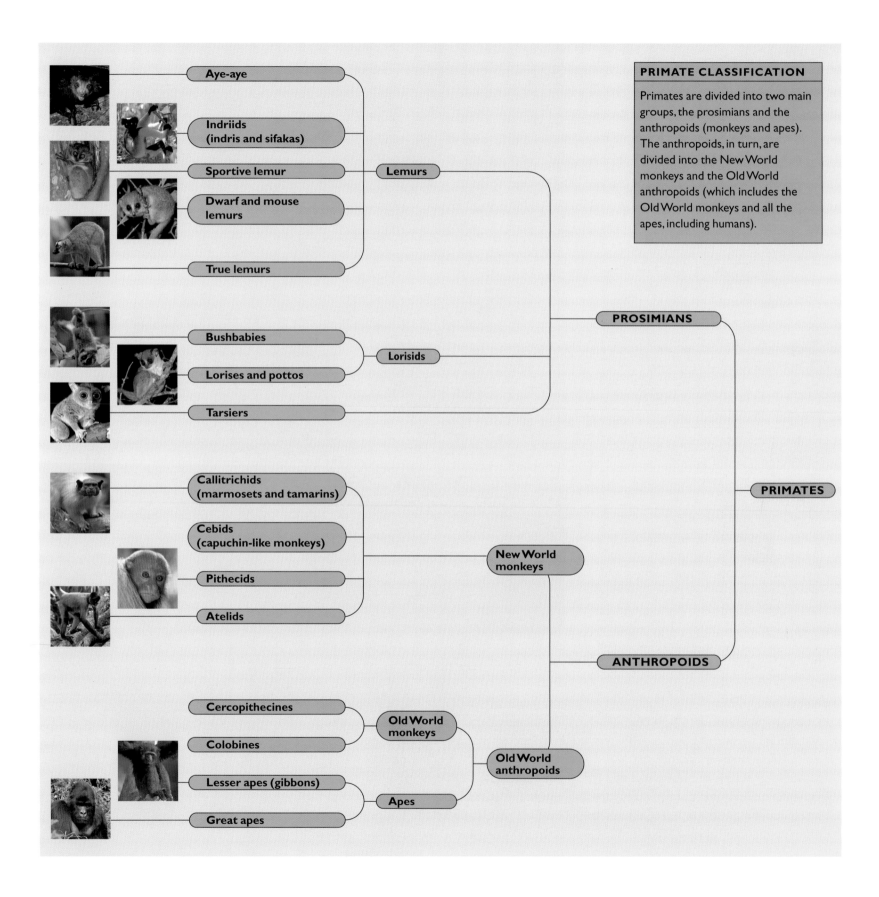

PRIMATE CLASSIFICATION

Primates are divided into two main groups, the prosimians and the anthropoids (monkeys and apes). The anthropoids, in turn, are divided into the New World monkeys and the Old World anthropoids (which includes the Old World monkeys and all the apes, including humans).

Aye-aye

Indriids (indris and sifakas)

Sportive lemur

Dwarf and mouse lemurs

True lemurs

Lemurs

Bushbabies

Lorises and pottos

Lorisids

Tarsiers

PROSIMIANS

Callitrichids (marmosets and tamarins)

Cebids (capuchin-like monkeys)

Pithecids

Atelids

New World monkeys

PRIMATES

Cercopithecines

Colobines

Old World monkeys

Lesser apes (gibbons)

Great apes

Apes

Old World anthropoids

ANTHROPOIDS

coast of Africa. Here, they are represented by an unusually rich array of species that are remarkably variable in physical appearance and lifestyle, and occupy a wide variety of ecological niches. There are 33 living species of lemur, and at least 15 more that became extinct as recently as 1,000 years ago. It is likely that more extinct species remain undiscovered, since all the fossil specimens are large-bodied species. Smaller animals fossilize less easily because of their more delicate bones.

Anthropoids

Monkeys and apes, collectively known as anthropoids, form the other main branch of the primate family tree. In contrast to prosimians, anthropoids are large-bodied and, with only one exception, active by day, diurnal. They are also characterized by larger brains, by color vision, associated in many cases with a fruit-based diet, by considerable intelligence, and by an intensely sociable lifestyle.

We normally group the species that make up the anthropoids into two main categories, monkeys and apes. Scientifically, however, the anthropoids are normally categorized into two different groups, the New World monkeys, and the Old World anthropoids, with the latter including both monkeys and apes. Both of these grouping systems can be justified, on different grounds. On one hand, the monkeys of the New and Old Worlds have many features in common that distinguish them from the apes. Some of these features are trivial, for example, all monkeys have tails, but no apes do. Others are more important. Apes and humans have larger brains and are more intelligent than any of the monkeys. In these respects, monkeys and apes represent different "grades" of evolution, the apes being more intellectually advanced than the monkeys.

On the other hand, placing the division between New World and Old World primates accurately reflects the evolutionary history of primates and genetic relationships between them. The apes, including humans, are more closely related to the Old World monkeys than either group is to any New World species. This grouping is echoed in several distinct differences in anatomy. New World monkeys have wide nostrils that point sideways, and Old World anthropoids, including humans, have narrow nostrils that point down. Old and New World species also differ in the way the skull bones fit together, and in their teeth. Humans and all other Old World species have eight premolars, or chewing teeth, while the New World monkeys have 12, a pattern more like that of the prosimians and the ancestral fossil primates of 40 million years ago.

These differences suggest that the New World monkeys are similar to the common ancestors of the New and Old World anthropoids. In fact, in many ways, New World monkeys look like the ancient anthropoid fossils found in the riverbeds of Fayum in Egypt(▷p. 27). Far more than Old World species do. This is because the Old World monkeys have undergone further changes since the two sets of species became isolated from each other, probably around 30 million years ago.

New World monkeys

The monkeys of the New World live only in the tropical regions of South and Central America. They are divided into four (sometimes three) major groups. One, the callitrichids, consists of marmosets and tamarins, and is a particularly species-rich group of small monkeys, typically weighing 7-17 oz (200–500 g), about 30 species in all.

Over 8 million monkeys are consumed each year by people in the Amazonia region of Brazil.

The callitrichids are birlike in the way they scamper through the low forest vegetation of the Amazon basin, maintaining a constant twittering chorus as they go. In many ways, they occupy the fruit-eating niche usually filled by birds, since South American forests have surprisingly few birds of this kind. A second group, the pithecids, consists of around 30 species of slightly larger monkeys, such as the titi, the saki, and the night monkey who is the only nocturnal anthropoid. The other two groups, the cebids and atelids, include the remaining 20 monkey species of South and Central America. These groups contain the largest of the New World monkeys, weighing up to 22 lb (10 kg) as adults, and include spider monkeys and howler monkeys among the atelids, and capuchins and squirrel monkeys among the cebids.

Old World anthropoids

The Old World anthropoids are divided into two major groups: the Old World monkeys and the apes, the group to which humans belong. The apes are defined by their lack of a tail and features of their molar teeth. They also tend to be larger and bigger brained than monkeys. There are four kinds of ape alive today, besides ourselves. The smallest are the gibbons or lesser apes, whose eight or nine species (depending on how you count them)

The DNA molecule provides the recipe from which every part of the body is made. Relationships between species can be determined from the similarities in their DNA.

 THE MOLECULAR CLOCK

After the discovery of DNA by Francis Crick and James Watson in 1958, it became possible for scientists to work out how closely related different species are by comparing their DNA and counting the number of differences. Over thousands of years, the DNA in any species gradually alters due to random changes called mutations. If scientists know the rate at which these mutations happen, they can also work out how long it has been since two species last shared a common ancestor. The technique is known as the molecular clock.

The molecular clock has, in some cases, turned our understanding of primate evolution on its head. One of the most startling examples of its use concerns our own relationship with our closest living relatives, the great apes.

The traditional classification, based on physical similarities, divided the hominoids or human-like primates, into two groups: the great ape family, which included chimpanzees, gorillas, and orangutans; and humans and, our fossil ancestors. Our group formed a separate family that was assumed to have branched off from the great ape tree about 15 million years ago. However, the molecular clock revealed that humans and the two chimpanzee species share a common ancestor at most 5 million years ago (▷p. 179). The common ancestor of these three species and the gorilla lived perhaps a million years earlier. It is only the orangutan that having branched off from the other great apes and ancestral humans around 15 million years ago.

Therefore, far from being set aside on a pinnacle of evolution, we turn out to be an ordinary member of the African great ape family. In the words of biologist Jared Diamond, we are really just the third species of chimpanzee.

1. (opposite) A five-year-old male orangutan displays the long arms and short legs characteristic of all the apes, aside from our own species.

are found exclusively in the Indo-China peninsula and the islands of the Sunda Shelf in Indonesia and Borneo. The other three are the orangutan, gorilla, and the two species of chimpanzee. Collectively these are known as the great apes. All are largebodied and typically weigh 75-220 lb (35–100 kg). The orang lives only in the islands of Southeast Asia, and the others are only found in Africa.

The Old World monkeys, by contrast, number about 90 species and are found throughout Africa and Asia, and even have a toehold in Europe at Gibraltar. Once again, there are two main groups, the colobines and the cercopithecines, both widely distributed throughout the Old World. The colobines are the more ancient lineage and are typically leaf eaters. The Asian and African species belong to two different groups, the langurs and colobus monkeys respectively. Some of the latter boast spectacular white shoulder capes set against black body fur. In contrast, the cercopithecines are fruit eaters, of recent evolutionary origin and, perhaps because of this, very species rich. Two subgroups, the macaques and the guenons, each number more than 20 species. The cerco pithecines, which also include the baboons and the mangabeys, are highly adaptable, intelligent and very social. Unlike most primate species, they often survive well in the close company of humans.

The rhesus monkey population in India fell by 90 percent between 1959 and 1980 due to live exports to research laboratories in the West.

A young rhesus macaque on Cayo Santrago, a Caribbean island. This species was released on to the island during the 1930s.

PRIMATE PESTS

While most primate species face the future threat of extinction due to human activities, in a few places it is the primates themselves that threaten to drive other species extinct. In several cases, primates have been deliberately or accidentally released onto tropical islands by people, and have proceeded to survive and prosper in their new environment, like the ancestral lemurs did on Madagascar.

There are now substantial macaque populations on the island of Mauritius in the Indian Ocean and Puerto Rico in the Caribbean. African vervet monkeys have established themselves very successfully on the Caribbean islands of Barbados and St. Kitts. In most of these cases, the monkeys have become a nuisance to local farmers and a serious threat to the original animals and plants of the islands, some of which have been driven to extinction. The scale of the problem is illustrated by what has happened on Mauritius. About six longtail macaques were released on the island in the early 1700s. Three centuries later, there are now more than 30,000 despite the numbers that have been removed by farmers.

These invasions raise ethical dilemmas for us, should we exterminate the populations because they are of exotic origin and damage the islands' native faunas and floras, should we allow them to stay because it was through human action that they came to be there?

LIFE ON THE KNIFE EDGE

During the last 400 years, most of the families within the animal kingdom have lost around 20 percent of their species. By comparison, primates have been relatively lucky. We know of no primate species that has gone extinct during this period. However, we should be wary of jumping to overly optimistic conclusions. Widen the time frame to 1,000 years, and we find at least 15 species of lemur that have gone extinct. They represent a third of all modern lemur species, and about 7 percent of all living primate species. And these are just the ones we know about.

Worse still, we cannot be sure that we have seen the full force of extinctions on primates. Because primates are long lived and relatively adaptable compared to many mammals, it may take longer for them to succumb to the effects of habitat destruction and hunting. A quick glance at the endangered species lists drawn up by organizations such as the International Union for the Conservation of Nature leaves us less sanguine. No fewer than a third of living primate species are considered to be at risk of extinction in the near future.

An evil quartet

The main problems affecting primates' long-term survival are fourfold: habitat destruction, hunting, small population size, and pressure from the human population.

Habitat destruction has been proceeding throughout most of the last two centuries in those countries where primates live. Tropical hardwoods are much in demand for timber, but they are slow growing. Individual trees can take centuries to reach maturity. The rate of deforestation is consequently much faster than the rate of regrowth. This problem is exacerbated by the fact that deforested land is often exploited for farming, removing the land altogether from the pool of potential forest.

Countries such as Uganda and Nigeria have lost as much as 90 percent of their forest cover in the past two centuries. Most timber-exporting countries are denuding their natural resources at rates that they cannot sustain in the future. Part of the problem is that forests are worth more money cut down and sold than they are left standing. Their future monetary value is simply not as much as their current value as logs. Our long term

1. East African colobus monkeys have been hunted for centuries in order to make rugs out of their spectacular black and white fur.

1. The maroon leaf monkey of Southeast Asia will survive only if the forests on which it depends are not cut down for timber.

problem is to find ways of making forests more valuable to the countries that have them.

As well as suffering from loss of their habitat, primates are under threat in many parts of the world because they are a valuable source of meat. In South America, where primates are often the most abundant large mammals, they are a traditional source of food for Indian tribes. In West Africa, the so-called bush meat trade is a long-standing economic activity, and primates, including chimpanzees, are a conspicuous component. Some species, such as drills, have been hunted to near extinction in certain areas. In the Far East, primates are a delicacy.

Other species have been hunted for different reasons. In Ethiopia and East Africa, hundreds of thousands of black-and-white colobus monkeys were harvested for their attractive pelts. Between 1871 and 1891, some 1.75 million skins passed through the London fur markets. Until recently, the skins were used to make rugs for the local tourist trade, with up to 25 monkeys needed for a single small rug.

These effects are made worse by the continuing human population explosion. This is especially true of those species that are rare, because small numbers make species more susceptible to extinction. Primates are not alone in this situation. We are currently witnessing species extinctions on a scale that the planet has seen only five times previously in its history. The last of which involved the demise of the dinosaurs.

These rare cases of sudden mass extinction are known as "mega-extinctions." The present mega-extinction differs from the five previous ones in one important respect. Where past major extinction events were the result of climatic changes affecting the planet, this time it is humans that are the cause. Human populations have exploded out of control over the past few centuries. Land has been converted to farmland to sustain these populations, and we have begun to make serious and disastrous inroads into the planet's natural habitats. Vast tracts of forest are cut down every year to feed our appetites for building materials, paper and fuel. An area of forest the size of Wales is removed from the Amazon forests in Brazil every year.

Preservation versus conservation

The traditional solution to the problems of conservation has been to demarcate areas of wilderness for national parks or reserves. The local human population has often been excluded from such parks, and the wildlife given maximum protection. The problem with this approach is that it often fails to work. Excluding people from their traditional pastoral or farming areas causes resentment. Meanwhile, population growth has led to land shortages, with consequent encroachment into the reserves. Local governments are often powerless or reluctant to act against those who infringe their wildlife laws. Fear of political instability and the often legitimate demands of impoverished indigenous peoples have made it difficult to balance the demands of conservation against the demands of the human population. This, in turn, has often meant that new national parks were established in areas where few people lived. This minimized conflict with the local population but did not always protect the best habitats for the animals.

The 1970s saw the beginning of a new movement that placed more emphasis on conservation than preservation by exclusion. Conservation implied working more closely with the interests of local people, and giving them a stake in the business by providing them with a share of income from tourism. The idea was that, if you made conservation worth people's while, they would act to promote it themselves. Unfortunately, this more enlightened approach has also not always proved as successful. Farmers' interests do not always coincide with those of conservation. For example, crop-raiding primates remain a frustrating nuisance for farmers would rather be rid of them.

Try as we might to avoid it, the conflict between conservation and human economic and social development threatens to overwhelm us. Ultimately, it is the rate at which the human population is growing that lies at the root of the problem. As much as anything, it has been our inability to act on sensible suggestions about how to solve the problems facing us that has been the cause of our failures to date. We will no doubt survive so long as technology allows us to reap greater rewards from the planet. However, unless drastic action is taken now, it is doubtful whether we will have the privilege of entering the fourth millennium in 1,000 years in the company of many of our primate cousins.

2. Every year in the Amazon forest a huge area is cleared for timber or farmland. Here, in northern Brazil, plantations with crops (yellow- green and brown) show up as a patchwork within the remnants of the original rainforest (bright green).

3. The ever-rising human population is the most serious threat to the survival of primates. The resource demands of expanding cities cause huge environmental stresses, like here in La Paz, Bolivia.

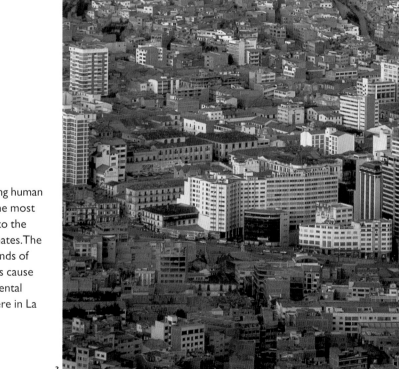

THE BUSHMEAT TRADE

Hunting currently poses a serious threat to the survival of many of the world's primate populations. The problem is not a new one, however. In the last 1,000 years, human hunting pressure has caused the extinction of the orang-utan in Java and 15 species of giant lemur in Madagascar. The most serious threat comes not from subsistence hunters, who kill to feed their families, but from the growing market for primate meat among urban populations. Primates are widely hunted for food in Africa and Latin America, but less so in Asia because three of the main religions (Islam, Hinduism, and Buddhism) do not permit monkey flesh to be eaten. However, Asian primates are still under threat because they are highly prized ingredients in many traditional medicines.

Hunting methods

Primates are usually trapped or shot. Traps range from simple snares to elaborate cage traps, but given the difficulty of trapping intelligent, tree-living animals, shooting is generally the preferred option. Some primates, however, require more specialized hunting techniques. Groups of drill monkeys, for example, are tracked by dogs as they run away from hunters and are eventually chased up into trees. Once the group is trapped, the hunters pick off individuals with guns. A less sophisticated method is employed by the Hadza people of Tanzania to hunt baboons. The hunters surround a sleeping site, dislodge

1. A hunter returns home with the day's catch of monkeys slung over his shoulder.

the baboons by making a lot of noise and firing arrows at them, and finally club them as they attempt to escape the circle of hunters.

Professional hunting takes its toll

Among subsistence hunters, a proportion of the captured primates are sent for sale at markets, but most are used to feed the hunters' families. Low-level subsistence hunting of this kind does not represent much of a threat since single hunters do not kill enough to have an impact on primate populations. However, professional hunting operations kill very large numbers of primates solely for sale at markets. This can have a devastating effect on primate populations, since the loss of many individuals at once does not allow the population sufficient time to recover.

From hunter to customer

The primate meat trade revolves around roadside stalls and local markets that supply villages, towns, or cities with wild meat. The animals may be sold alive or as fresh carcasses, but in most cases they are smoked because this prevents the meat rotting before it reaches its destination. The way that wild primate meat makes its way from the hunter to the customer depends on whether it was hunted by a farmer or a professional hunter, and also on whether it is destined for a small village or a large town or city. Generally speaking, it tends to involve a whole chain of middlemen, such as taxi drivers and stall owners, who transport and sell the meat to the final buyer. Although most wild meat trade is local, it does cross international borders, such as that between Nigeria and Cameroon.

A growing business

The so-called 'bushmeat' trade might well pose the biggest threat to the survival of many primate populations in West Africa, where primate meat is extremely popular.

2

3

2. The bushmeat trade is a major incentive to small-scale hunters, especially in West Africa and South America.

3. Fresh heads join a benchful of trophies. Even now, rare gorillas (on left) do not escape.

The annual value of the trade in Nigeria alone was estimated at $25 million (£15 million) in the late 1960s, but could be as much as $250 milliom (£150 million) in recent years. In other regions of the world, the commercial hunting of monkeys occurs on a much smaller scale; indeed, in some areas of West Kalimantan in Borneo, for example, primate meat is not considered worth buying or selling. Even so, commercial hunting of primate meat currently threatens to become a very large danger to populations in many areas where primates were previously hunted for subsistence alone.

◈ TOPIC LINKS

1.3 Primates Today
p. 43 Life on the knife edge

2.4 The Last Refuge of the Lemurs
p. 90 Living under threat

3.4 A Unique Intelligence
p. 152 Crop raiders and harvest helpers

4.1 Planet of the Apes
p. 180 Disappearing forests

4.5 Family Portraits: Apes
p. 228 Gorilla

THE PROSIMIANS

CREATURES OF THE NIGHT

The word "prosimian" means "before apes." As befits the name, these primates are not in the least ape-like, or even monkey-like, in their appearance or behavior. Some actually resemble mice rather than monkeys, although their human-like grasping hands give away their primate heritage. Others, now sadly extinct, were giant, sloth-like creatures specialized for a life consisting of little more than hanging upside down from the trees. Still others, such as the aye-aye, are unlike any other creature on Earth, either living or extinct, and seem to have come from another world entirely.

In a sense they have, of course, since the world of prosimians is not the daylight, vision-dominated world that we and most other primates inhabit. Instead, most prosimians are creatures of the night, using their keen senses of smell and hearing to explore a secret nocturnal world full of scents and sounds.

Previous page: Sifakas are large Madagascan lemurs. They live in small family groups and are active by day.

SURVIVORS OF THE PAST

The prosimians are often considered to be the poor relations of monkeys and apes. Biologists describe them as primitive because, anatomically speaking, they are similar to the adapids, ancient fossil primates who lived in Earth's forests 40 million years ago, long before the appearance of the more "advanced" monkeys and apes. In fact, in some respects the prosimians resemble their distant relatives, the insectivores and rodents, more than their close primate cousins. When monkeys and apes finally arrived on the evolutionary scene, the ancestors of the prosimians fared badly. Many retreated into the darkness of the forest and became active only at night.

Their nocturnal lifestyle is partly why prosimians look so different from what we think of as a typical primate. The need for a well-developed sense of smell means that, like dogs, they have sensitive, wet noses and an upper lip that is split in the middle and attached to the nose, all of which increase their ability to detect scent with a special organ inside the nasal cavity called Jacobson's organ. The lack of a mobile upper lip limits the facial expressions they can display, again making them look less like typical primates,

The name "indri" actually means "there it is" in the language of Madagascar. The first European explorers on the island mistook their native guide's exclamation for the animal's name.

1. Like most prosimians, this slender loris from Southeast Asia has large eyes to help it see in the dark, and a sensitive, wet nose that can detect even the faintest trace of scent.

and restricts their ability to communicate visually. Other hallmarks of a life spent in the dark include large, independently mobile ears to help hear prey, sensitive whiskers, and large eyes. Like cats' eyes, the eyes of most prosimians have a reflective layer in the back to improve vision in dim light. And unlike typical primates, some prosimians have more than one pair of nipples, reflecting the fact that they can give birth to litters.

Some of these characteristics are shared with other nocturnal mammals, but forward-facing eyes, grasping hands and feet, and flat nails instead of claws make it clear that prosimians are primates. These defining features are found in the earliest primate fossils and, anatomically at least, the prosimians give us our best idea of what those prehistoric animals were like. However, it is likely that prosimians have changed over the past 40 million years, therefore it would be wrong to think of them as living fossils.

Our interest in the prosimians far exceeds their role as a link between the first primates and the monkeys and apes of today. They are a fascinating group in their own right and possess features seen nowhere else in the animal kingdom. And although they may be primitive in evolutionary terms, their behavior is anything but. The ways they communicate, mate, rear offspring, and guard against danger reveal an intriguing and often complex world.

 A tarsier's eyeball is larger and weighs more than its brain. The eyeballs move very little in their sockets, so the tarsier turns its head like an owl to see things on either side.

1. (opposite) As well as eating insects, the tarsiers of Southeast Asia also eat lizards, bats, and even birds.

The eyes of a slender loris shine in the dark.

▷ HOW TO SEE IN THE DARK

A very effective way to find prosimians is to venture out at night armed with a flashlight. If you're lucky, the flashlight's beam will soon pick up two tiny circles of light that shine brightly in the ghostly blackness of the forest canopy. These are the eyes of a prosimian. They shine in the dark not for the benefit of prosimian watchers, but to improve the animal's night vision.

Prosimian eyes glow in a flashlight's beam because of a shiny surface, called the tapetum, inside the back of each eye. The tapetum consists of a film of plate-like crystals and forms an extra layer of the retina, the light-sensitive cells that line the inside of the eye. These crystals increase the eye's ability to detect incoming light rays by causing a shift in the wavelength of the light as it hits the tapetum. The light receptors in the retina are most sensitive to yellow light, so by forcing the wavelength of light that reaches the retina into this range, the tapetum causes the retina to be more stimulated than it would be otherwise. The tapetum also reflects light back through the retina, giving the retinal receptors a second chance to detect dim light. It is this reflection that creates the eye-shine effect.

LIVING IN THE DARK

Generally speaking, prosimians are small, secretive tree dwellers that emerge only at night when they forage alone for insects and other foods. They are found only in the Old World of Asia and Africa, there are no prosimians in the Americas. In Africa there are bushbabies, or galagos, and pottos, in Madagascar there are lemurs, and in Asia there are lorises. Asia is also home to a intriguing prosimian known as the tarsier. This tiny animal has a mixture of primitive and modern characteristics, and some scientists see it as a missing link between prosimians and monkeys.

Bushbabies and lorises often share their habitat with monkeys or apes but, being strictly nocturnal, they do not compete with their larger cousins, who are diurnal, or active only by day. Avoiding competition with diurnal species is one of the advantages of working the night shift. It also means that more animals can coexist in a habitat and fill all the available "ecological niches", a way of making a living in a habitat. Prosimians usually fill the nocturnal, insect-eating niche, while monkeys generally occupy a daytime, fruit-eating niche.

As we see later, the lemurs are an exception to this rule. The lack of other primates on the island of Madagascar has allowed many lemurs to exploit the daytime, fruit-eating niche that would otherwise be filled by monkeys. The traditional prosimian niche is taken here by the tiny dwarf lemurs and mouse lemurs, who come out after dark to hunt for their insect prey.

Getting around

Although they share the same twilight world, prosimians have different methods of making their way around the forest canopy. Mouse and dwarf lemurs scurry along branches like small rodents. Pottos and lorises creep slowly on all fours, often moving so slowly that they appear to be in slow motion. Bushbabies are highly active, fast-moving clingers and leapers. Propelled by long hind legs, they make spectacular jumps through the canopy, holding their bodies upright as they fly through the air. While dwarf and mouse lemurs have no special adaptations for movement, both bushbabies and lorises have distinct features that help in their unique style of movement.

In order to make their impressive leaps, bushbabies have long hind legs, with particu-

A dwarf lemur feeds on gum.

 GOING IT ALONE

Most nocturnal prosimians are solitary foragers. They spend most of their waking hours alone, although females may be accompanied by their young offspring. Why these nocturnal animals tend to be solitary is not fully understood, but it may be linked to their choice of food. Prosimians feed largely on insects and gum, a sweetish, sticky substance produced under the bark of some trees. Both these types of food are difficult to share, unlike the leaves and fruit that monkeys and apes eat, and insects are best hunted alone.

Another explanation is that foraging alone makes it easier to hide from predators. While primates that are active by day gain protection from living in groups, more eyes and ears on the alert make it easier to spot attackers, the same does not hold true for nocturnal animals. Extra pairs of eyes and ears would be no help in the dark because nocturnal predators, such as leopards, often wait in silent ambush for an unsuspecting victim to pass. Under these circumstances, the best way for an animal to avoid being eaten is to try to ensure that a potential attacker does not realize it is there. Blending into the background using camouflage is one way of doing this. Another way is to move around alone, since a single animal is much less noisy and conspicuous than a group.

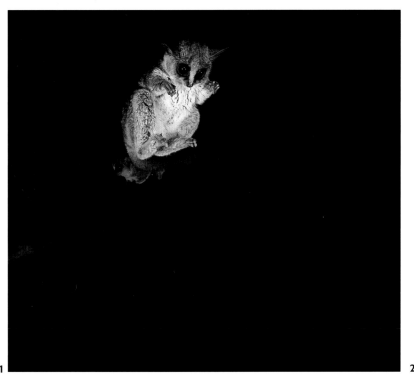

1. The well-developed legs of the lesser bushbaby allow it to make spectacular leaps through the air.

2. A young pygmy loris creeps slowly through the canopy in order to avoid detection by predators.

larly long ankle bones, and a long tail for keeping balance. Their habitats range from dense forest to scrubby savanna, and their distinctive form of movement serves them equally well throughout. They have large eyes for good night vision, essential for spotting insect prey, and they can move their large, membranous ears independently, like a bat, to pinpoint where a sound is coming from. They are so skilled at this that they can snatch insects from the air as they fly past. Most bushbabies also eat fruit and some eat gum. Quick reflexes combined with great agility mean that evading predators is no problem at all. With a succession of quick-fire leaps, a bushbaby can cover 10 yards in a mere five seconds.

In stark contrast, pottos and lorises have become so well adapted to life in the slow lane that they have lost the ability to leap. Unlike bushbabies, lorises have very small, stubby tails, and their arms and legs are roughly the same length. Their ears are much smaller than those of bushbabies, with the result that, as primatologist Pierre Charles-Dominique puts it, they look like "slow and cautiously moving bear cubs." Lorises move in such a slow, smooth, and coordinated way that they are difficult to spot and can pass through even the thickest vegetation without making a sound. Their slow and secretive movement has two advantages: it makes them almost invisible to predators, and it allows them to sneak up on prey. They hunt by smell, keeping their nose to the branch as they move and sniff out slow-moving items, often things that others would avoid, such as caterpillars bearing irritant hairs, foul-smelling beetles, or poisonous millipedes. Unlike bushbabies, lorises live only in forests since their style of movement works best in thick vegetation. The more open conditions of the savanna would leave them too exposed to predators.

Keeping out of danger

Moving slowly reduces the chance of being seen, but it puts the animals in danger when they accidentally bump into enemies. On these occasions, lorises do not try to escape. Instead they freeze, becoming completely immobile and silent. They can keep still like this for hours, thanks to a special network of blood vessels in the hands and wrists that prevents them from succumbing to pins and needles and having to release their grip.

Many species also have special defenses to deter predators. The potto, for example, has a shield of thickened skin overlying bony bumps on its back. The shield is covered with long, sensitive hairs that can detect a potential attacker. If threatened, the potto tucks in its head and lunges at the aggressor, either striking it with its shield or biting it. If successful, the attacker will fall off the branch and be unable to find its way back to its victim.

TARSIERS: THE MISSING LINK?

From an evolutionary point of view, tarsiers are the most intriguing of all the primates. Anatomically, tarsiers show a mixture of primitive prosimian characteristics along with some of the more sophisticated characteristics of the monkeys and apes. This combination means that tarsiers are good candidates for being the common ancestor linking the prosimians to all the other higher primates. The physical traits they display might give us some valuable clues to how monkeys could have evolved from a nocturnal prosimian ancestor. The idea of a "missing link" between the prosimians and the monkeys and apes is attractive, since it helps tie together these two disparate primate families and make sense of the primate family tree.

1. Unlike most other prosimians, tarsiers do not eat any vegetable matter. They live on a diet of invertebrates and other small animals, such as lizards.

2. Tarsiers give birth to a single young. This is a monkey-like pattern. Most small prosimians give birth to more than one offspring at a time.

Living the high life

Tarsiers are tiny, bug-eyed creatures that live deep in the forests of Southeast Asia. There are three species: the Philippine tarsier from the Philippine Islands, the western tarsier from Borneo, and the spectral tarsier from Sulawesi. They are all similar in size and color, have soft, velvety coats, and extremely long hind legs. Like the bushbabies of Africa, they are vertical clingers and leapers, who jump from tree to tree with their bodies held upright. All three species have a diet consisting mainly of insects and small vertebrates, such as lizards and bats, although the western tarsier is also capable of catching and killing birds larger than itself. Since they are nocturnal creatures, tarsiers have enormous eyes, but their eyeballs have restricted movement. To compensate, they turn their heads almost 180 degrees, like owls.

Similar, yet different

From the above description, tarsiers might sound like average nocturnal primates, but closer inspection reveals their transitional makeup. Like other prosimians, tarsiers have a jawbone that is made up of two separate halves, grooming claws on their toes, multiple nipples and a womb that is split into two separate chambers. However, unlike their nocturnal cousins, they do not have a reflective layer (the tapetum) in the back of their eyes. Nor do they have a wet nose. Instead, like the monkeys and apes, they have a warm, dry nose, plus a mobile, furry upper lip. Their teeth are also much more similar to those of monkeys, with large, upper central incisors, small lower incisors, and large canines. They also show no sign of the tooth comb, a special tooth used for grooming, which is such a distinctive feature of the prosimians. Another characteristic that tarsiers share with monkeys is monthly sexual swellings and a menstrual cycle. They do not have the prosimians' highly restricted estrus cycles.

Backwards evolution?

Despite this mixture of characteristics, it is possible that tarsiers are not any kind of missing link at all. It is just as likely that they are a small monkey species that went back to a nocturnal, prosimian-like life some time after the monkeys first evolved. This return to a nocturnal lifestyle would have been made possible by the fact that the bushbabies never reached Asia, so the niche they would otherwise have occupied was left free. The prosimian traits that tarsiers display today might occur not as a consequence of their being more closely related to the prosimians than the monkeys, but because these are the traits that are needed for a successful nocturnal lifestyle. Tarsiers might therefore represent not a step forward along the prosimian line, but a step back from the monkey line.

Both the "missing link" and the "dwarfed monkey" theories applied to tarsiers are controversial and hotly debated. It's unlikely that we will ever know for certain which evolutionary pathway the tarsiers took. Nevertheless, a greater understanding of the behavior and ecology of these strange and intriguing animals will undoubtedly provide us with some useful pointers.

PROSIMIAN FEATURES

MONKEY/APE FEATURES

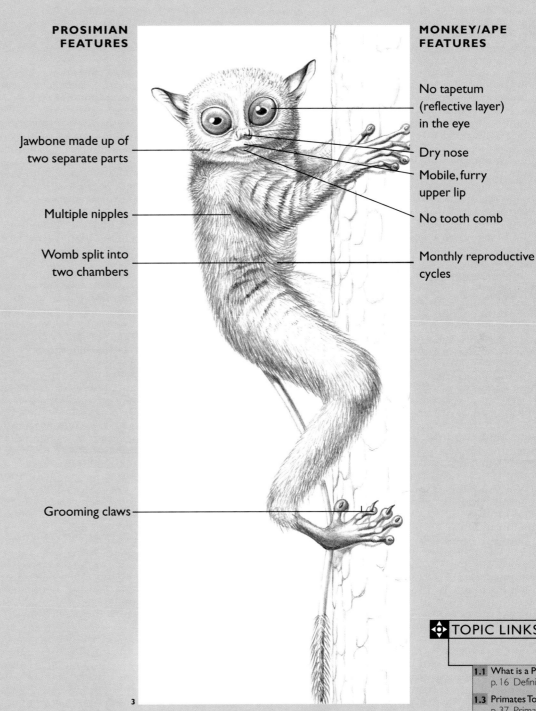

Jawbone made up of two separate parts

Multiple nipples

Womb split into two chambers

Grooming claws

No tapetum (reflective layer) in the eye

Dry nose

Mobile, furry upper lip

No tooth comb

Monthly reproductive cycles

3

3. The anatomy of tarsiers has some distinctively prosimian features, while other features are characteristic of monkeys and apes.

SOCIAL LIFE

Because they need to forage alone and stay hidden from predators, prosimians cannot mingle together as easily as other primates. However, they are far from hermits. Although their social behavior is not as intense as that of monkeys and apes, prosimians can nevertheless communicate effectively through scent marks or calls (▷ p. 58). This means that animals can forge bonds with each other and maintain quite complex societies, despite the fact that they are rarely in the same place at the same time.

Bushbaby society

Bushbabies have the most complicated social structure of mainland Africa's prosimians. The females live in well-defined territories that they share with their offspring but defend against rival females by leaving scent marks and making special calls. When males reach sexual maturity they leave their mother's territory to set up home elsewhere, but females stay in the mother's territory for life. This gives rise to small groups of related females and their offspring, although each female tends to stick to her own patch of the territory and forages alone. Occasionally, females will share a sleeping nest during the day, often with an adult male as well, and they sometimes meet up at night to groom each other or play.

The difference in the way that males and females establish their home range might account for the curious, male-biased sex ratio that occurs in some bushbabies. Thick-tailed bushbabies, for example, give birth to 57 males for every 43 females. Perhaps this unequal ratio reduces competition for food among females, who stay in the home territory and share the same resources. Exactly how females manage to give birth to more males than females is a mystery, but it seems likely that levels of certain hormones, particularly testosterone, might effect the chance of males rather than females being conceived.

Male competition

Male bushbabies establish large territories that encompass the homes of more than one group of females, and they generally mate with all the females in their territory. Competition between males to establish a territory is intense since this is the only way to obtain mating opportunities. As a result, dominant males are usually replaced every year, whereas females can stay in the same territory for years on end.

There are two classes of sexually mature male bushbabies: A-males, who are older and heavier and can often be found in sleeping groups with females, and B-males, who are younger, lighter, and non-territorial. A-males hold territories and have a special bond with the females in them, a bond they maintain both by direct contact and by calling and making scent marks. The A-males exclude other A-males from their territories, possibly to prevent them from bonding with the females. B-males, by contrast, hang around on the margins of territories, often in the company of other B-males, waiting for the opportunity to take over should an A-male disappear. If this happens, they become A-males themselves. But A-males do not bother to exclude B-males from their territories. They merely chase them away from their immediate vicinity. A-males seem only to concern themselves with other high-ranking males who threaten their hold over the territory and their mating opportunities.

Lazy loners

Pottos and lorises are more solitary than bushbabies and engage in only low-key forms

1. Thick-tailed bushbabies are found in East and southern Africa. In some populations of this species, females have been found to give birth to many more sons than daughters.

of communication, such as scent marking, rather than calling to each other. This is probably related to their slow metabolism. These animals need 40 percent less energy to fuel themselves than would be expected for animals of their size. The low metabolism reduces the amount of food they need, but it also limits their ability to engage in energetic activities, particularly those of a social nature. It seems likely that it is their slow metabolism, rather than their nocturnal lifestyle, that limits contact with other individuals.

Sleeping it off

Dwarf and mouse lemurs have a social system like that of bushbabies, with large male home ranges overlapping smaller female ones. However, their social structure is simpler than in bush-babies. Females, for instance, do not live in family groups although they sometimes nest together. In addition, and uniquely among prosimians, some mouse and dwarf lemurs hibernate.

Madagascar has a long dry season when food is hard to find. Both the fat-tailed dwarf lemur and the greater dwarf lemur get around this problem by hibernating. During the 6 to 8 months that they are dormant, they survive on fat reserves stored in their tails. When the rains return, the animals wake from their sleep for a brief but intense mating season.

Gray mouse lemurs also store fat and hibernate, but males and females do it differently.

The word "loris" comes from the Dutch meaning "clown," referring to the clownlike expression on these creatures' faces.

2. Active only at night, a potto sleeps through the day in a hole it has found in a tree.

3. Fat-tailed dwarf lemurs hibernate for up to eight months of the year. They store fat in their tails to see them through this period.

Mouse lemurs double their body weight during the wet season. Most of the extra weight is fat stored in their tails.

Like the fat-tailed dwarf lemur, female mouse lemurs put on weight between February and April and then hibernate until September. They can save around 40 percent by of their energy adopting this strategy, but it only works if they store enough fat to see them through the hibernation period. If they are in poor condition and unable to store sufficient fat, they go into hibernation later or do not hibernate at all, in which case they are active sporadically and go into daily torpor, a state in which metabolic processes slow down but to a far lesser extent than during true hibernation.

In contrast, male gray mouse lemurs either do not hibernate at all or they hibernate for about a month. They wake earlier than females from hibernation and prepare for the breeding season by increasing both body and testes size. The fact that they do this during a period of the year when food is scarce and the risk of being killed by predators is high suggests there are mating benefits from advance preparation. Perhaps well-prepared males are able to spend more time searching for females in the breeding season.

Since females mate simultaneously and for only a short period each year, a single male cannot monopolize a group of females in one territory. There are too many females to keep track of and defend against the attentions of other males. The only way that males can achieve high mating success is by searching the area for females and mating with as many as possible. This scramble for mates effects the appearance and behavior of male mouse lemurs. Since they do not fight over females directly, they do not have the same weapons as other male primates, such as enlarged canine teeth. Instead, male mouse lemurs rely on scent marking to intimidate their rivals.

Together for life

Although scientists are not sure, it seems that the fork-marked dwarf lemur may be monogamous, a way of life that is rare among the primates. This species, named for its striking head marks, is a specialist gum feeder. It has special lower teeth for scraping gum from bark, a long and narrow tongue, and sharp nail tips to for cling to broad tree trunks. Males and females travel together, calling to each other constantly to maintain contact. When they stop to feed, they do it separately, and the female having first choice of the available spots. Little is known about this secretive animal, and so the reasons for its unusual behavior remain a mystery.

1. (opposite) A mouse lemur from Madagascar. Weighing only 2 oz (60 g), this is among the smallest of all the primates, .

1. A fork-marked lemur feeding on gum. This species has specially adapted lower teeth to help scrape at bark and allow the gum to flow.

SCENTS AND SOUNDS

As dusk falls in the tropical forests of Africa and Asia, the prosimians emerge from their sleeping nests and claim the forest as their own. Leaping through the canopy, bushbabies begin to feed on the insects that they catch on the fly, while lorises and pottos creep along cautiously, freezing at the slightest hint of danger. The forest comes alive with strange sounds, rustlings in the canopy, and smells. In the pitch dark, scent marks stand out like glowing beacons, guiding animals around their home range and showing where friends and neighbors have passed. Sensitive, wet noses pick up the faintest scents, revealing whether potential mates are ready to breed. Large ears detect the whirr of insect wings and the territorial calls of rivals. In order to reveal the secrets of this nocturnal world, it is necessary to become fluent in the language of sounds and smells. Only then does the world of the prosimians begin to make sense.

MESSAGES IN THE DARK

As creatures who are active by day, monkeys, apes, and humans live in a world dominated by the sense of vision and use a wide range of visual signals to communicate. The same is not true for our nocturnal cousins, the prosimians. Living in the dark means that the senses of smell and hearing are far more useful for keeping in touch with friends and neighbors, especially when most individuals feed alone and rarely encounter others face to face. Large, sensitive eyes enable prosimians to see more in the dark than other primates-can, but night vision requires special modifi-cations to the eyes that reduce their ability to see color or detail. Unlike monkeys and apes, whose superb color vision helps them find food and communicate in many ways, prosimians must rely on other senses to explore their world.

Scent glands

Scent marks are an enormously efficient means of communication for nocturnal animals. They allow them to communicate over distances of time as well as space. Once deposited, a scent mark may linger for as long as a week, enabling animals to detect who has passed that way before them. Most prosimians have at least one set of scent glands that they use to mark their territory as they move around. Even species active by day still use scent to get their message across.

Scent glands are formed from modified sweat glands that may be on the head, chest, abdomen, forearms and, in particular, the region surrounding the anus and sex organs. The glands produce strong-smelling, rapidly evaporating chemicals that can tell other animals all sorts of information, including an individual's age, sex, and whether it is ready for mating. As prosimians move around their

1. Bushbabies mark the boundaries of their territory by scent marking with urine.

1

1. The scent glands are clearly visible on the arms of this male gold bamboo lemur.

2. (opposite) A female ring-tail displays her striking tail as she scent marks on a tree using scent from glands near her genitals.

habitat depositing scent marks on trees and bushes, they provide a continuously updated record not only of their movements, but also of their personal details. Other animals can keep track of their movements and of the events happening in their lives.

Some species have specialized body parts, in addition to their scent glands, to aid in scent marking. Male ring-tailed lemurs, so called because of the distinctive black and white bands on their tails, have scent glands in their armpits and on their wrists. Above each wrist gland is a horny spur, like a claw, that helps embed the scent into the bark of trees. When males leave scent marks, they wipe the wrist gland over the gland in their armpits and then draw their forearm across the tree trunk. This leaves both a scent mark and a comma-shaped scar in the bark. Males can spend as long as 20 minutes at a time marking trees in this way.

Male ring-tails also mark using scent glands near their sex organs, but the amount of genital scent marking an animal performs depends on its rank. Ring-tails live in social groups with a distinct hierarchy. High ranking males do much more genital scent marking than subordinates, although the amount of wristmarking they do is about the same. The reason for this is not clear. It could be that dominant males have larger genital scent glands than other males in order to mark more frequently. Alternatively, subordinate males may be unable to produce scent as speedily as dominant animals.

Urine marking

Pottos and lorises, the slow-moving prosimians of Africa and Asia, do not have proper scent glands. Instead of scent, they use urine. The potto, in particular, is renowned for its habit of carefully urinating on its hands and feet just before embarking on a nightly tour of its range,

where it leaves a trail of smelly footprints in its wake. To another potto, these footprints stand out with all the intensity of fluorescent paint under ultraviolet light. They virtually see with their noses.

Marking and mating

Most prosimian species step up the rate of scent marking during the breeding season. Females do this so that males are aware they are fertile and ready to mate. Male scent marking during the breeding season is mainly to warn rival males to keep away.

Mouse lemurs have elevated the intimidation of rivals to a fine art. Their urine contains a number of chemicals that can actually influence the ability of other animals to reproduce. Male mouse lemurs who are exposed to the smell of a more dominant male's urine become sterile due to a drop in their level of the sex hormone testosterone. Males with low testosterone are not only sterile, they are also unable to make special calls, called trills, that they use to attract females and encourage them to mate.

These effects are particularly strong at the peak of the mouse lemurs' breeding season, when competition for mates is at its most intense. It makes sense for dominant males to put other males out of action in this unusual way because female mouse lemurs all come into season at exactly the same time. This makes it impossible for a male to monopolize a group of females. He can defend only one female at a time from the attentions of other males, and when all the females are fertile at once, there are too many to defend. Therefore the best solution is not to defend females, but to reduce the number of competing males. Producing urine that makes other males sterile ensures that the dominant male will father the maximum number of offspring during the breeding season.

STINK FIGHTS

Ring-tailed lemurs are among the most sociable of all prosimian species. These daylight active animals live in groups ranging in size from five to 30 animals. Because of their sociable lifestyle, ring-tailed lemurs have developed a wide range of signals to communicate with each other. The most individual of these signals are chemical, that is, based on the sense of smell. Like most other prosimian species, ring-tails have specialized scent glands that allow them to leave their smelly signatures all over the habitat. As well as marking territory, scent marking, combined with visual tail signals, is used by male ring-tails to intimidate rival males in "stink fights."

Seeing by nose

As in most prosimian species, scent marking by ring-tails increases dramatically during the mating season. At this time, females deposit scent marks in order to attract mates and also to compete with other females. Male scent marks appear to have very little to do with attracting females, but are used instead to intimidate and confuse rival males. When a male ring-tail encounters the scent mark of a female, he tends to deposit his own scent mark on top of it. This masks the scent of the female and prevents information about her readiness to mate from being picked up by other males. Female ring-tails also overprint scent marks, particularly those of lower ranking rivals, perhaps in an attempt to divert attention back to themselves.

1. Ring-tailed lemurs on the alert for possible danger. If this is in the form of rival males, a stink fight may follow.

2. A male ring-tail scent marks using glands on his upper arms and wrists.

Visual signalling

Ring-tailed lemurs increase the effectiveness of scent marking with visual signalling. The striking black-and-white tail, from which the species gets its name, is frequently used as a signal during aggressive interactions between lemur males. This is especially the case when new males try to enter a group. To signal danger, males hold their tails erect and wave them over their heads.

Smelly showdown

Males combine visual and scent-based modes of communication to their greatest effect in the highly ritualized territorial displays known as "stink fights". During these confrontations, males rub the scent glands on their wrists across glands located in their armpits, then sweep the tail along the fore-arms so that the horny spur located just above the wrist gland combs through the tail fur and impregnates it with the combined scent. The males then arch their tails over their backs and wave them in the direction of their rivals. At the same time, they rub their genital scent glands against low branches. The outcome of these fights is usually the retreat of one or other of the males and the territorial boundaries are redrawn.

Although males engage in these fights with great vim and vigor, they rarely get involved in any real physical combat. They seem to rely on intimidation to fend off their rivals. This is just as well, since male ring-tails are ille-quipped for the kind of armed combat seen in most primate males. They are quite small, often smaller than the females, and they lack the large canine teeth that males of other species use to inflict harm on each other. Harsh environmental conditions also make it too energetically expensive for ring-tail males to engage in true physical combat. It seems that stink fights provide an acceptable compromise.

3. At the height of a stink fight, males mark trees with scent, as well as wafting their scent-impregnated tails toward their rivals.

◆ TOPIC LINKS

2.1 Creatures of the Night
p. 58 Male competition

2.2 Scents and Sounds
p. 63 Messages in the dark
p. 68 Pheromones

3.2 Group Living
p. 125 Dominance in males

4.2 Life in a Dispersed Society
p. 189 The dispersed society

Warning others

As well as helping animals get ahead in the mating game, scent marks also ensure that animals actually live long enough to mate. Bushbabies, for example, show bouts of highly frenzied scent marking when they detect a predator in their midst. This alerts other bushbabies in the area to danger, allowing them to gang up and mob the predator to scare it away. Brown lemurs also scent mark when they detect a potential attacker and sometimes scream and swing their tails to appear intimidating. When faced with a dangerous predator, they too may join forces and mob their enemy.

The angwantibo, one of the African loris species, relies on concealment to avoid predators. When it spots a predator, it makes scent marks as discreetly as possible to warn nearby angwantibos of danger without attracting the predator's attention. When a mother is alarmed, she produces a scent that immediately makes her offspring freeze. This reduces the chance of being seen. This same scent makes babies cling tightly to their mother, allowing them to be carried silently to safety.

Defending their patch

In order to defend their home range against intruders, many prosimians place scent marks around the area's periphery. Animals entering the area can then tell that it is an occupied territory, which means they might face a fight if they bump into the owner. Female bushbabies, for example, defend their territories against other females by scent marking, and territorial males mark the same areas to warn intruding males that the females are spoken for.

Sifaka (pronounced "shifark") females defend their territories by marking trees and branches with scent from glands around the anus and genitals. Males also mark, but they use scent from a gland on the throat, particularly during the mating season. However, actual fights are rare because the detection of scent is usually enough to ward off intruders. Ring-tailed lemurs show far more interest in the scent marks of strangers than those made by other members of their group, and males in particular spend a long time sniffing the marks of animals they do not recognize, especially during the mating season.

 PHEROMONES

The behavior of all primates, humans included, is strongly influenced by hormones. These special chemicals are produced in certain organs and released into the bloodstream, with wide-ranging effects on the body. The hormone adrenalin, for example, is produced by the adrenal glands, which are small glands on top of the kidneys, in response to frightening situations, and prepares the body for sudden action – to fight or flee, for instance.

Many animals also produce chemicals called pheromones. These are similar to hormones in their composition and effect, but different in two important ways. They are released into an animal's environment, not into the bloodstream, and they affect the behavior of the animals that smell them, rather than the animals that produce them.

Pheromones are most often used to attract mates. When an animal detects a pheromone in the air, it knows that somewhere nearby there is a potential mate, and begins to search for it. The nocturnal prosimians, who rely heavily on smell to communicate, often find mates in this way. A number of South American monkeys also seem to produce sexual pheromones, and it has even been suggested that human sweat might contain pheromones that work on an unconscious level to attract partners. More unusually, some species use pheromones to discourage rivals, not to attract mates. In the mouse lemur, the urine of dominant males contains high levels of a pheromone that causes males who smell it to become sterile.

☆ Sportive lemurs get their name from the intensely territorial behavior of the males. They give loud, crow-like calls and often engage in sparring matches with each other.

1. (opposite) In addition to scent marking, ring-tailed lemurs use vocalizations to communicate with each other. Their calls alert other animals to danger and keep rival groups at a distance.

VOCAL SIGNALS

Some prosimian species, such as ring-tailed lemurs, are active during the day as well as the night. As a result, they live in social groups to defend themselves more effectively against daytime predators.

These species use alarm calls rather than scent marks to alert group members to possible danger. Their calls differ according to the type of predator. Ring-tails rasp or shriek when they see a bird of prey, but yap when they see a ground predator. The different calls enable members of the group to take the most appropriate evasive action, either up into the trees to escape from ground predators, or down into the undergrowth to hide from birds of prey.

Ring-tails also respond to the alarm calls of the sifaka, another day-active lemur that shares the same habitat. Like ring-tails, sifakas have different calls for the two types of predator, a rasping sound, like a football rattle, for birds of prey, and a call that sounds like "shifark" for ground predators (hence their unusual name). Sifakas' calls are similar to those of ring-tails so perhaps this is why the ring-tails can understand them.

Territorial songs

Loud calls can also serve to defend a territory, but these are mainly used by day-active prosimians, such as the indri. This is one of the largest of the lemurs and looks somewhat like a startled teddy bear. Unusuale for an animal of its size, it moves by clinging and leaping in much the same way as a bushbaby does, by using large, powerful hind legs to spring from tree to tree. Indris defend their territory by howling in an extraordinary and eerie manner. Their calling bouts, or songs, as they are called, occur up to seven times a day and are highly infectious. Once a group begins singing, other groups in the area join in. As well as defending the territorial boundary, the songs bring separated members of the group back together. This helps the group present a united front against intruders, should the need arise.

The spectral tarsier of Sulawesi, one of the small, nocturnal primates of Southeast Asia, also defends its territory by using a variety of calls. Pairs or family groups congregate

An Allen's bushbaby clings to a researcher's hand.

 WHEN I'M CALLING YOU

Studying prosimians in the wild is hard. They are small, they live in the dark, and they live on their own. It takes a lot of dedication and patience to learn anything about prosimian life, and it is easy to be uncorrect. The bushbabies are a perfect example. When people were first trying to figure out how many species of bushbaby there were, they could not rely on direct observations of the animals and had to work instead on dead, preserved specimens. However some bushbaby species are similar in size and appearance and were mistakenly lumped together as a single species.

The advent of behavioral field studies, aided by radio-collars, nightscopes, and sound recording, allowed people to study these animals in their natural habitats for the first time. It soon became apparent that there were many more bushbaby species than anyone had suspected. The reason this had been missed was because bushbabies can be told apart only by their calls. Each species has a distinctive mating call to which only a member of the same species will respond. For nocturnal animals, calls are a much better way of identifying a species than appearences and ensures that animals do not mate with the wrong species by mistake. Since the different calls provide an almost foolproof way males and females of the same species to identify each other, it does not matter if different species look. Among the bushbabies, love may be blind, but it is certainly not deaf.

near their sleeping site in the center of the home range and call to warn other tarsier groups to keep their distance. During these calling bouts, male and female tarsiers perform duets. Combining their different voices, they produce a song that is delightful to the human ear, but not to the neighboring tarsiers, who are being told to keep away.

As these examples illustrate, scents and sounds are as efficient as visual signals for getting a message across. Prosimians may use forms of communication that differ enormously from those of daylight-living primates, but the reasons for communicating are familiar to all primates, to protect food resources, find mates and warn of danger.

1. Ring-tailed lemurs defend their territories using loud calls to keep rival groups at bay. Softer calls are used to allow the members of a group to stay in contact with each other.

All mammals invest time and effort in procreating and rearing offspring, but primates spend more effort than most. Since they have large brains, primate offspring have more to learn than other mammals, and, therefore, they depend on their parents for a longer amount of time. However the amount of parental care they receive varies across the primate world.

Compared to monkeys and apes, prosimian babies require less care and attention, and they develop quicker. However, reproduction is difficult on prosimian mothers. This is especially true of Madagascar's lemurs. Food is often scarce on the island of Madagascar, and finding enough to survive and feed a growing baby is a full-time job. Mothers ease the burden by making sure that they are always first in line for food. In the lemur world, males are second-class citizens.

FAST AND FURIOUS REPRODUCTION

Reproduction is arguably the most important part of any animal's life, and the different ways that animals choose mates and rear offspring highlights the fascinating diversity of lifestyles found in the animal kingdom. Among the monkeys and apes, raising offspring successfully is the most time-consuming part of the reproductive process. Having large brains infants take a long time to grow and develop into adults, and they depend on their mothers for food and safety for much longer than other young mammals. For prosimians, who have relatively small brains, it is different. Their patterns of reproduction are more like other nocturnal mammals than their primate relatives.

Prosimian babies develop much more swiftly than the higher primates. For example a female bushbaby is ready to mate and reproduce only nine months after birth. Many species also produce more than one offspring at a time. Both these factors mean that the number of babies produced in a given period of time is much higher for prosimians than for monkeys, apes or humans.

This fast breeding reflects an important difference between the reproductive strategy of prosimians and that of other primates. Prosimians go for a fast and furious strategy – they produce a relatively large number of offspring and provide them with less care than do monkeys and apes. Less care means that their offspring are more likely to come to a sticky end, but the increased numbers produced compensate for this, ensuring that at least some make it to adulthood and produce babies themselves. Monkeys and apes have a slow but sure strategy. They have fewer offspring but provide a lot more care, giving each infant a good chance of survival.

1

However, the larger, diurnal species of prosimians, such as the sifaka and indri, are rather monkey-like in their reproductive strategy, giving birth only once every 2–3 years and investing much more time and effort in their offspring compared to the smaller prosimians.

2

1. Sifakas are large lemurs and have relatively few offspring compared to other lemur species. Here a sifaka infant hitches a ride on its mother's back.

2. This young potto, like most prosimians, will develop rapidly. The youngster will have already reached puberty by the time it is a year old.

Reproductive biology

The reproductive biology of prosimians is something of a halfway house between that of monkeys and apes and that of most other mammals. Like many mammals, prosimians have a uterus that is split into two, and one or more eggs are shed into each half of the uterus from the ovary on that side of the body. In monkeys and apes, however, the uterus is unified and the two ovaries take it in turns each month to shed (usually) one egg into the uterus. Monkeys and apes also have a special placenta that burrows into the wall of the uterus and taps directly into the mother's blood supply, whereas prosimians – like most non-primate mammals – have a placenta that simply sits on the surface of the uterus and absorbs nutrients across its wall.

Prosimian reproductive system

Ovaries

Uterus

Monkey/ape reproductive system

Ovaries

Uterus

1. The prosimian uterus (womb) is divided into two separate parts, whereas monkeys have a unified uterus like that of humans and other apes.

A young slender loris "parked" for the evening.

▷ BABY PARKING

The babies of nocturnal prosimians are less developed at birth than baby monkeys or apes. Bushbaby infants, for example, are born with little fur and cannot open their eyes. They are unable to move around alone or even cling to their mother's fur. As a result, the mother builds a nest where she can leave them in safety while she forages. If she needs to move them, she has to carry them in her mouth, like a cat with her kittens. Bushbaby infants must be at least one month old before they can cling to their mother's back and accompany her on nightly foraging trips.

In contrast, the other major groups of nocturnal prosimians, the lorises, have much longer pregnancies than bushbabies of the same weight, and their young are born at a more advanced stage. Loris mothers do not need nests because their offspring can cling to the fur of the mother's belly as soon as they are born. However, mothers do not carry their offspring for long, preferring instead to "park" them on a convenient branch for the evening while they feed, and then returning to pick up them up later before going to sleep. While the mother is away, the baby remains immobile so that it does not attract the attention of passing predators.

Mothers who leave their infants in nests or parked on branches cannot feed them as often as mothers whose infants remain with them. Consequently, the milk of prosimian species, such as lorises, tends to be richer than the milk of primate species, who carry their offspring.

Prosimians also resemble non-primates in the way their mating behavior is controlled. Most mammals, prosimians included, have what is known as an oestrus cycle: a female's hormones control both the inner workings of her reproductive system (such as when eggs are shed from the ovaries) as well as her willingness to mate. Females come into estrus (are 'on heat') and are willing to mate only during the fertile period when eggs are released. By contrast, monkeys and apes have menstrual cycles, and mating can occur at all times.

Short breeding seasons

In many prosimian species, all the females come into oestrus together during a short breeding season. This occurs just once a year. In some species, females are fertile for only a single day each year and never mate at any other time.

This limited mating period creates intense competition between males for mating access to females. Males roam around trying to mate with as many females as they possibly can in order to make the most of their one shot at fatherhood for the year. They put enormous efforts into both searching for females and trying to outdo other males. Although the breeding season may last just a single day, it is physically exhausting. To get through it successfully, males have to build up large stores of fat and be in peak physical condition.

Even in species where the breeding season lasts for a few days or weeks, there is still a great deal of competition among males since all females come into season at exactly the same time. A single male cannot keep all the

⭐ The breeding season of some lemurs lasts one or two days a whole year.

fertile females to himself under these circumstances as it is impossible for him to be in two places at once. While he is busy mating with one female, he is unable to keep a watchful eye on the others. It is a case of "you snooze, you lose" – a male who is not quick off the mark will find his mate has been taken by somebody else. And any male who fails to find a mate will have to wait a whole year for another chance to become a father.

1. During the brief mating period of the ring-tailed lemur, the male dominant hierarchy breaks down and there is a free-for-all, as males attempt to mate with as many females as possible.

SPECIAL RELATIONSHIPS

Although most lemur species show female dominance, some of them have hit upon a more equitable way of co-existing. Red-fronted lemurs live in groups containing an equal number of males and females. No dominance relationships are observed in these groups, especially not between males and females. In fact, very high levels of friendly behavior are the norm. For example, males and females form pairs that huddle together while resting, and males often scent mark and rub the top of their partner's head. In this way, red-fronted lemur males and females show a particular preference for each other and form 'special relationships'.

2

1

1. Red-fronted lemurs live in small social groups containing an equal number of males and females.

2. A male–female pair of red-fronted lemurs rest together in a tree.

Close bonds

The partners in red-fronted lemur relationships tend to associate more frequently with each other than they do with other animals: they groom each other more frequently and support each other during aggressive incidents. Males who are bonded to a female in this way always attempt to mate with their female partners, and often seem to ignore other fertile females. Similarly, females seem to prefer their special partners as mates over other males in the group. However, not all red-fronted lemur groups have special relationships between males and females. In some, there is a central male who monopolizes all the females.

Strictly seasonal

The Madagascan climate has resulted in very strict seasonal breeding among lemur females; this ensures that their offspring are born at a time when food is most available to fuel milk production, but it does pose difficulties for the males. With all females becoming fertile within a very short space of time, males are hard-pressed to guard more than one effectively and thus prevent other males from mating with them. As a result, it probably pays males to concentrate on forming a strong bond with only one female, rather than attempting, and failing, to mate with many. The bond also ensures that the female mates with her male "friend" in preference to any other male on offer.

Hidden ovulation

Forming a relationship with just one female may also be advantageous because females have concealed ovulation. This means that there are no physical clues that males can use

to identify when a female is ready to mate. In a number of monkey and ape species, females develop large swellings on their rear ends to indicate the females' most fertile period. Red-fronted lemur females do not produce such obvious signs, so males are left in the dark and cannot pinpoint a female's most fertile period. Although males can tell that the breeding season has arrived by the females' increased willingness to mate, they cannot tell when a female is ovulating. Conception is most likely to occur if mating takes place around ovulation. If males cannot detect the time of ovulations with any accuracy, then they might do better reproductively by sticking with one female throughout the entire time that she

willing to mate. That way, a male can make absolutely sure that he has mated with a female at the optimum point in her cycle.

Friends and protectors
The male-female partnerships in red-fronted lemur society reduce the need for dominance behavior of any kind within troops. Males support their female friends in fights with other females, and males are also directly aggressive towards females who are not their "friends." The result is that females save a lot of energy that would otherwise be used up in fights, and can therefore devote more time to feeding, safe in the knowledge that their male friends will protect them.

3. Aggression is rare in red-fronted lemur groups. Most relations between animals are very friendly. Here a pair of females rest together in a tree with their young.

◈ TOPIC LINKS

2.1 Creatures of the Night
p. 61 Together for life

2.3 Females in Charge
p. 78 Female dominance
p. 81 Lemur infanticide

2.4 The Last Refuge of the Lemurs
p. 85 Group-living lemurs

3.3 The Mating Game
p. 138 Sexual swellings
p. 140 Special friendships

4.2 Life in a Dispersed Society
p. 194 Reasons to be faithful

FEMALE DOMINANCE

Short breeding seasons are common among the lemurs of Madagascar, for example the breeding season of the sifaka, is a mere 42 hours long. Because food availability in Madagascar is seasonal, and baby rearing has to be squeezed into a limited period when conditions are good, such strict timing is vital. The short breeding season ensures that offspring are born when food is abundant and mothers can eat enough to produce plenty of milk. Any female who mates outside the breeding season is unlikely to raise her offspring successfully.

The difficulty that female lemurs face in obtaining enough food for their young may explain another aspect of their society. In almost all species, females are dominant to males, most unusual for a primate. Among the monkeys and apes males tend to rule the roost.

First in the queue

When feeding, female lemurs have first choice and males have to wait their turn. Female ring-tailed lemurs frequently take the place of males at good feeding sites, and often slap males on the nose and take food out of their hands. This female tendency to exert dominance over males seems to be linked to their greater need for energy.

Producing and rearing offspring is an costly business for all animals, but especially for female mammals. They alone have to carry and nourish the growing fetus, and feed and care for the baby until it is weaned. This is unlike the situation among birds, for example, where both parents may cooperate to incubate the eggs and feed the hatchlings.

Female lemurs face additional burdens in their struggle to provide for their young. First, lemurs have a slow metabolism for animals of their size. During pregnancy, females must

⭐ The diademed sifaka has an high mortality rate. Over 67 percent of the young die before reaching adulthood.

1. Because of their clinging and leaping form of locomotion, Sifakas have very short arms. On the ground they are unable to walk on all fours. Instead, they skip along rapidly on their powerful hind legs.

2. A crowned lemur mother and infant. Feeding their young is an energetic and demanding exercise for lemur mothers and may explain why they are dominant over males.

3. Female ring-tails get access to the best feeding sites and can even snatch food out of a male's hands. If males show any reluctance to part with food, females do not hesitate to give them a punishing slap on the nose.

increase their metabolic rate to sustain the developing infant, and this means increasing the amount of energy-rich food that they eat. Secondly, lemur fetuses grow more quickly than other prosimians. Newborn lemurs are about the same size as newborn lorises, but they are produced in half the time. Thirdly, all the females in a social group give birth at the same time, which increases competition for food. Milk production is the most energy-intensive part of the reproductive cycle, and female primates have to increase their food intake by up to 50 percent during this period. As a result, female ring-tails become aggressive during the suckling period and can often be seen fighting, chasing, and biting each other in contests over food. These squabbles waste valuable energy, making it even harder to obtain enough. The result is that female lemurs often face acute food stress throughout the suckling period.

Body size

If females were forced to compete for food with males as well as other females, it is doubtful they would fulfill their energy requirements. However, because female ring-tails are dominant to males, they are able to eat enough to provide for their rapidly growing infants. Reproductively, males may actually benefit from this arrangement. If the offspring are their own, then they have as much stake in them as the females do.

In most primates, males are larger than females. However, male and female lemurs are about the same size. This size similarity makes it easier for the females to boss around the males. Females may even prefer to mate with smaller males. Since the smaller males are easier to dominate, perhaps this makes good reproductive sense.

As well as benefiting females, it may also be in males' interests to remain small since the breeding season takes its toll on them too. Smaller males require less energy to keep mating, and it may be stamina, not fighting ability, that leads to high mating success in ring-tailed lemurs. Competition between male ring-tails for mates is physically demanding. Though it involves long chases and spectacular leaps through the canopy, it does not involve much active fighting. This favors a small body size, since smaller males are faster and more agile. Being large is only an advantage in physical combat.

Male and female black lemurs differ hugely in color.

WHY LOOKS MATTER

The black lemurs of Madagascar are not what they seem. While males are black, females are reddish-brown, with bright, cream-colored tufts on their heads. This color difference between the sexes is known as sexual dichromatism. Many lemurs show sexual dichromatism to some extent, but the black lemurs win for the most extravagant difference. The reason for the dramatic contrast between the sexes seems to be linked to the need for males to acquire high-quality mates.

The condition of a female's fur depends on her level of parasite infestation. Females with a lot of parasites tend to be duller in color than those with a few parasites. This means that males can use a female's color as an indicator of her health. By pairing with the most brightly colored, and therefore healthy, female, a male is choosing the mate most likely to produce healthy offspring.

It is interesting that, among lemurs, it is the females who are brightly colored. In most other animals, it is the male who is showy and who advertizes his quality as a mate. Why this is reversed in lemurs is not clear. However, it may be related to the harsh seasonal conditions of Madagascar and the heavy toll that reproduction takes on females. A male may want to ensure that a female will be able to cope with the rigors of rearing offspring before choosing her as a mate.

LEMUR INFANTICIDE

In many day-active, group-living lemur species, there is an unfortunate tendency toward infanticide. The reason for this seems to be that it helps males raise more offspring that are their own.

Male lemurs sometimes kill unrelated infants so that their mothers become ready to breed again. Females with infants usually do not become pregnant again until their offspring are mature. In the larger lemur species, such as sifakas, this can take as long as 2 to 3 years. However, if an infant dies, its mother can become pregnant up to a year earlier. Consequently, infanticide is a good option for a male who is new to the group since it allows him to start fathering offspring more quickly. On the other hand, it makes reproductive sense for fathers to be protective and stay close to mothers and their infants when there are other males around. As a result, lemur groups are composed of a number of male–female pairs so that males can watch out for danger and act accordingly. For example, male ring-tailed lemurs and

ruffed lemurs, are very hostile to strange males who try to join their group. Among ring-tails, fighting and chasing of strangers by both males and females is extremely common.

This watchfulness is not necessary in nocturnal prosimians because females these species hide their offspring in nests. This makes it hard for males to tell which babies are their own and therefore prevents effective guarding. It also limits the risk of infanticide because males cannot target particular female mates. In any case, nocturnal prosimians become pregnant again quickly after giving birth, and this reduces the benefit of infanticide. It also does not make sense to kill baby females, which mature quickly and are ready to mate almost as soon as their mother. Under these circumstances, all infanticide would do is reduce the number of fertile females available. As a result, permanent male–female partnerships are found only in the larger lemur species that carry their infants around with them, and not in those that leave them in a nest or parked on a branch while they feed. The one exception to this rule is the ruffed

lemur. This species has male–female partnerships but still parks its offspring during feeding. However, males remain with the parked babies and guard them while the female goes off to feed. In fact, ruffed lemurs may not be an exceptional, since it is clear that the males associate with females primarily in order to guard their babies, rather than to be with the females themselves.

Although their main interest is in protecting infants, male lemurs do show friendly behavior toward females and spend a lot of time grooming them. Males stay close to their partners at all times, even though this may force them to compete for food. When groups split up during the course of a day's foraging, the small sub-groups that form consist of male–female pairs who go off and feed together, with the female taking the lead. These sacrifices by the male are worth it since the benefit obtained with a healthy adult offspring, far outweighs the cost of losing a few tamarin pods to an assertive female.

1. Ruffed lemurs live in trees and never go down to the ground. They are fruit-eaters and thought to be important seed dispersers.

2. White-fronted lemurs live in small groups which contain a small number of male–female pairs. Here a male, distinguished by his white crown of fur, grooms a female using his specially adapted "tooth comb."

THE LAST REFUGE OF THE LEMURS

The lemurs of Madagascar show us what prosimians can achieve when left to their own devices. Isolated from competition with other primates, lemurs evolved into a bewildering diversity of species able to exploit almost every primate niche that Madagascar had to offer. Before humans arrived and drove many species to extinction, lemurs ranged in size from the tiny mouse lemur, who at 2 ounces (60 grams) is the smallest of all primates, to the massive *Megaladapis*, which was larger than a gorilla. There were species that specialized on every type of food available, from fruit and nectar to leaves, gums and grass seeds. Even today, after the loss of so many species, lemurs show an impressive variety of lifestyles, from the monkey-like behavior of ring-tailed lemurs to the bird-like behavior of the aye-aye, one of the world's strangest animals and the most bizarre primate. Monkeys and apes may be smarter, but the prosimians should not be underestimated.

AN UNSOLVED MYSTERY

No one knows for sure how lemurs first got to Madagascar. What we do know is that they arrived after Madagascar split from the African mainland. Lemurs could not have been present before Madagascar broke away from Africa because this event took place during the dinosaur era, millions of years before prosimians evolved.

So how did they get there? One way animals travel between islands is rafting. This happens when small fragments of land, often nothing more than large lumps of vegetation, float into the ocean. The ancestral lemurs that colonized Madagascar were probably small, perhaps resembling the tiny mouse lemurs of today. It would be easy for such small animals to be swept away on a raft of vegetation and survive a journey of thousands of miles since the raft itself would provide a tiny habitat containing everything the animals needed.

However the lemurs arrived on Madagascar, they were lucky they did. Their new home sheltered them from competition with the monkeys and apes, who proved to be the downfall of prosimian species on the mainland. The African prosimians could not compete with the more advanced ape and monkey species who dominated their forests. These prosimians were eventually forced to occupy the very narrow range of niches that we see occupied by the bushbabies and lorises of today, all of whom are solitary, nocturnal, and feed mainly on insects.

An ecological experiment

Apes and monkeys did not get the same lucky break that transported the ancestral lemurs across the ocean, so the apes and monkeys never made it to Madagascar. In the absence of competition from other primates, the lemurs flourished and diversified into over 40

1. A Madagascan rain-forest. Habitats such as this are home to many of Madagascar's lemur species, many of which are rare and endangered.

2. Madagascar is separated from the African mainland by some 240 mi (400 km) of ocean at the nearest point. How prosimians reached the island is not known.

0   495 miles (800 km)

AFRICA

INDIAN OCEAN

Madagascar

species. Therefore island of Madagascar represents a unique ecological experiment and gives us valuable insight into how these flexible animals have adapted to many different ways of life. The lemurs did not take a completely novel path while they adapted to their island niches. Instead, they evolved parallel to the monkeys and apes of mainland Africa, responding to the challenges presented by tropical African forest habitats in very similar ways.

1. Bamboo or gentle lemurs have specially adapted teeth for stripping the bamboo shoots that form the bulk of their diet.

2. A sifaka making a spectacular leap between the trees. It is assisted by its large, grasping hands and feet, and a long tail for balancing.

Lemur diversity

The lemurs of Madagascar can be placed in four main families. The first family is made up of the dwarf lemurs and mouse lemurs, who occupy the solitary, nocturnal niche typical of prosimians outside Madagascar.

The second family includes the indris and sifakas, large, day-active lemurs that live in small family groups. These are the largest of the lemurs and feed predominantly on leaves. The indri is the largest prosimian of all, weighing about 22 lb (10 kg). Indris and sifakas move through the trees by leaping from one trunk to another with the body in an upright position. An indri can leap up to 10 yards in a single bound.

The sportive lemurs and true lemurs make up the third family. Sportive lemurs are nocturnal and not sociable. Although males and females share a tiny home range together, they spend most of their time alone. They meet only 1 to 3 times a night, when they feed, rest, and groom together. Ring-tailed lemurs, mongoose lemurs, and bamboo lemurs are all true lemurs. These squirrel- to cat-sized creatures are more sociable than sportive lemurs and live in groups of up to 30. The different true lemur species have different diets. Ring-tailed lemurs are fond of fruit and leaves, while mongoose lemurs spend up to 84 percent of their feeding time in the dry season sipping nectar. Bamboo lemurs are partial to young bamboo shoots and leaves, as their name suggests.

Finally, we have the aye-aye, the sole surviving member of its family. This species is the most extraordinary of the lemurs. It seems to have evolved to fill the ecological niche of a woodpecker, perhaps because these birds are not found on Madagascar.

This wide range of species and lifestyles demonstrates just how successfully lemurs have evolved to fill the primate niches available on Madagascar. However, this is not the whole story. Lemurs were once even more diverse than they are now. Prior to the arrival of humans on the island around 2,000 years ago, there were giant lemurs, like modern sloths and koalas. Sadly, these slow giants were not equipped to cope with the changes brought by humans; as a result, more than 14 species became extinct. Today their existence is known only through fossil remains.

GROUP-LIVING LEMURS

The diversification of Madagascan lemurs into so many niches is an impressive feat. From this perspective, the most interesting species, and the one we know the most about, is the lemurs that have adapted to the same niche as monkeys. Like monkeys, these lemurs live in social groups and are active by day. However, there are important differences between these group-living lemurs and their monkey cousins, and these differences reveal a lot about the course that evolution has taken on Madagascar.

The lemurs whose lifestyle most resembles that of monkeys are the ring-tailed lemurs and sifakas. However even in these species,

the switch from nocturnal to diurnal is not complete. Strictly speaking, ring-tails and sifakas are cathemeral, and they are still partly active at night. This pattern of activity has distinct advantages. Cathemeral lemurs can feed more efficiently than nocturnal species because food is easier to find by daylight, because they can see. However because they can feed at night too, they avoid the overnight fast that strictly diurnal species must endure. There are disadvantages to being active during the day too, such as the increased risk of being seen by predators. Consequently, most cathemeral species that are active during the day live in permanent social groups, since this makes it easier to spot approaching predators. Also, unlike nocturnal species, they carry

 The aye-aye, which feeds on larvae, locates its prey by tapping on logs with its elongated middle fingers and listening for the response.

The aye-aye is a very odd primate.

THE AYE-AYE

With its scruffy black coat, bat-like ears, and large, protruding front teeth, the aye-aye is not a particularly attractive sight. It is, however, the largest of all the solitary nocturnal prosimians, and it possesses a number of unique adaptations. First of all, it has only 18 teeth, and primates usually have been 32 and 36. Apart from its large front teeth, which grow throughout its life like the front teeth of a rat, the aye-aye has only four molars or chewing teeth, on each side of the upper jaw, and only three on each side of the lower jaw. This is odd enough, but the aye-aye has an even more bizarre feature. The middle finger on each hand is elongated and thin. It bears a close resemblance to an old wizened twig. Finally, the aye-aye has claws on every digit except for the big toes, which have nails.

The aye-aye uses these peculiar features to obtain its preferred food of fruit and insect larvae. The large incisors are used to rip open tough-skinned fruits. They can even gnaw holes in coconuts. Once a fruit has been opened this way, the aye-aye uses its thin middle finger to scrape out the sweet fruit pulp. This finger also comes in handy for catching insect larvae. With large ears and keen hearing, the aye-aye can hear the faint movements of larvae burrowing under the bark of dead branches. When it finds a larva, it rips off the bark with its teeth and uses its stick-like middle finger to hook out the grub. In this respect, the aye-aye has come to occupy the ecological niche taken on the African mainland by woodpeckers.

1. A sifaka family rests in one of Madagascar's unusual cactus-like trees. Sifakas are among the largest of Madagascar's lemurs and are active by day.

2. Ring-tailed lemurs are the most sociable of the lemurs, living in groups of up to 30 animals. They are active by day and, unlike most other species, spend a lot of time on the ground.

Overleaf: White-fronted brown lemurs, one of the many subspecies of brown lemur. Brown lemurs are cathemeral, which means that they are active during both day and night.

their young with them at all times. It would be much too risky to leave young offspring alone in broad daylight.

At first glance, lemur social groups seem very like those of monkeys, but closer inspection reveals a number of differences. For instance, lemur groups contain an equal number of males and females and, in most cases, females are dominant to males. This is the reverse in monkeys, where females outnumber males by two to one and are subordinate to males. Another difference is that male and female lemurs are about the same size. Male monkeys are often twice as big as females. Finally, lemur groups tend to be much smaller, averaging around 20 animals, where monkeys can be found in groups of up to 100. Why should these differences exist if the lemurs have evolved to fill the same niche as the monkeys fill in Africa? Surely the same rules should apply to both groups?

Extinction and opportunity

The answers to these questions lie partly in the fact that, until about 2,000 years ago, there were more lemur species on Madagascar and a greater number of large, diurnal birds of

prey. Competition with giant lemurs meant that there was less ecological space to squease into for the ancestors of ring-tails and sifakas. Also the risk of being caught by one of the large birds of prey that ruled the daytime skies forced the lemurs to stay in the dark, where it was safer.

With the arrival of humans on Madagascar, and the wave of extinctions that followed, ecological space became available in the day-light world. The smaller lemurs invaded this world and took over the feeding and behavior niches they occupy today. The extinction of the large birds of prey allowed them to venture out by day and exploit the food resources that were now free due to the demise of the giant lemurs. However, it was not all easy for the newly diurnal lemurs. There were still ground-living predators to avoid and the lemurs formed groups as a defense mechanism. The ancestors of ring-tails and sifakas were pair-living animals, and they took the easiest route to group formation. Male–female pairs simply joined forces, giving rise to small groups containing equal numbers of males and females.

Holdovers from the past

Since the switch to daytime activity and group life happened recently in evolutionary terms, there has not yet been enough time for lemurs to adapt completely to their new monkey-like niche, and their social behavior contains holdovers from the past. The tendency of males and females to pair up is like the behavior of the nocturnal fork-marked lemur. Also the tendency for females to dominate the males when feeding is common in nocturnal species.

It is possible that a few thousand years down the line, lemurs will show different behavior as they become better adapted to the diurnal niche. However, some elements may remain unchanged. The heavy costs of repro-duction that females must bear in the harsh environment of Madagascar may continue to favor female dominance and small male size, and may mean that lemur groups remain unique in the primate world. At the moment, we cannot tell what will happen. It is another one of Madagascar's ecological mysteries. In any case, the issue of the most concern now is not how lemur social systems might change in the future, but whether lemurs will manage to survive at all.

LIVING UNDER THREAT

The amount of virgin rainforest cover in Madagascar has declined enormously in the last 40 years. In 1950, 12.5 percent of the island was covered by forest. In 1990, this had declined to 2.8 percent. Of the forest that remains, 23 percent is located within nature reserves but, unfortunately, this does not guarantee that it remains protected. For example, the Andranomena Reserve in western Madagascar, has fallen in size by 44 percent since 1950. The rapidly expanding human population of Madagascar requires increasing amounts of land for agriculture feed their families. The major threat to the forests, however, is the use of wood for fuel. Chopping down trees for fuel accounts for almost 80 percent of the wood removed from tropical forests globally and is the principal cause of deforestation in Madagascar.

The central plateau of Madagascar has been almost totally deforested and no primates live there today. Yet only a thousand years ago, every lemur species could be found in the central plateau. Now only the east and west coast forests contain lemurs, but even these animals too are under threat. As their forest habitat becomes increasingly fragmented, it becomes harder for the animals to travel between isolated patches of forest to find food and mates. The situation is so bad that the preservation of Madagascar's remaining forests is the highest primate conservation priority in the world. Almost all Madagascar's primates are endangered, including the aye-aye, the indri, the ruffed lemur, and the hairy-eared dwarf lemur. A number of species and subspecies are on the brink of extinction, such as the broad-nosed gentle lemur and the diademed sifaka. If no action is taken, it is unlikely that there will be a lemur left in 100 years.

Hopes of survival

How vulnerable a lemur species is to extinction depends largely on its lifestyle. True lemurs eat a wide variety of foods, they can be active both by day and night, and can occupy many different habitats. This flexibility means they will probably continue to flourish provided that their forest habitats stay larger than a certain minimum size.

Sportive lemurs, despite being less flexible than true lemurs, also have a reasonable chance of survival because they feed on the most abundant type of food – leaves. It is the highly specialized species that are likely to vanish first. The bamboo lemur, for example, thrives

Mongoose lemurs vary their activity pattern depending on the weather. They are nocturnal when it is dry and active during the day when it is wet and cold.

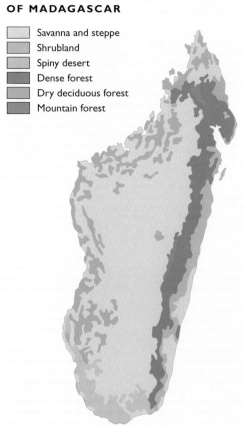

NATURAL VEGETATION OF MADAGASCAR

- Savanna and steppe
- Shrubland
- Spiny desert
- Dense forest
- Dry deciduous forest
- Mountain forest

1. As this map shows, the eastern forest of Madagascar is drier and spinier than the forest in the west, while the central plateau has been heavily deforested.

2. Like other sifakas, diademed sifakas are highly endangered by habitat destruction. They are also hunted for food. Their plight is made even more desperate by the fact that they are almost impossible to keep in captivity.

1

2

only in certain parts of Madagascar's moister forests. Loss of this restricted habitat would quickly drive the species to extinction.

The most endangered lemurs of all are those that live near the east coast of Madagascar, where the forests have become fragmented into a series of thin islands barely large enough to support viable populations. Sifakas and indris suffer most – because their forest habitat is shrinking, and they are also being hunted for food. It is almost impossible to keep these species in captivity successfully, so protection of their natural habitat is the only way to guarantee that they are not lost forever.

Unfortunately, there is no easy answer to Madagascar's conservation problems. The large human population needs space and resources, and this inevitably erodes natural habitats. The same conflict between people and wildlife occurs throughout the globe, but the problem is more acute here because Madagascar is an island, which means there is limited space for humans and animals to expand into. We can only hope that it is not too late and that a concerted conservation effort can save at least some of the lemurs for future generations. It would be sad indeed to lose the lemurs, since they are both a unique group of animals and a living link to our ancestral primate cousins.

1. The central plateau of Madagascar. This region has been most heavily affected by habitat degradation. As a result, lemurs are no longer found in this region of the island.

2. A pair of crowned lemurs in a habitat of eroded limestone. This species is found in the dry forests of the extreme north of Madagascar and, recently, in high-altitude, moist rainforest.

FAMILY PORTRAITS: PROSIMIANS

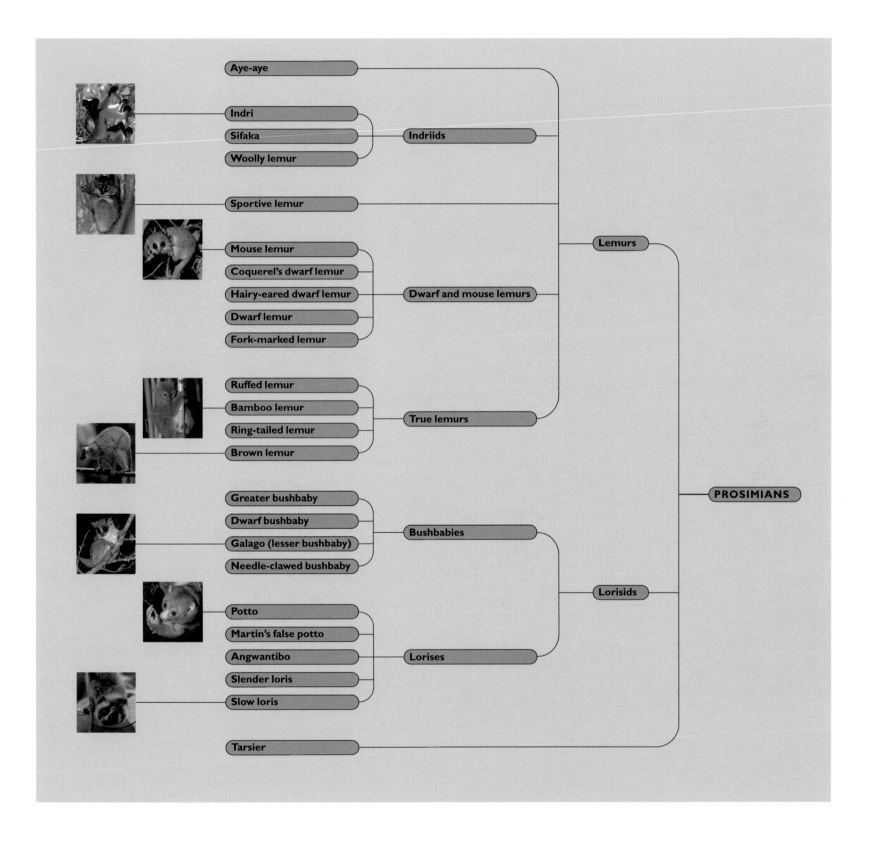

Aye-aye

Indri
Sifaka — Indriids
Woolly lemur

Sportive lemur

Mouse lemur
Coquerel's dwarf lemur
Hairy-eared dwarf lemur — Dwarf and mouse lemurs
Dwarf lemur
Fork-marked lemur

Ruffed lemur
Bamboo lemur
Ring-tailed lemur — True lemurs
Brown lemur

Lemurs

Greater bushbaby
Dwarf bushbaby
Galago (lesser bushbaby) — Bushbabies
Needle-clawed bushbaby

PROSIMIANS

Lorisids

Potto
Martin's false potto
Angwantibo — Lorises
Slender loris
Slow loris

Tarsier

INDRI

Indris are large, diurnal lemurs that are highly specialized for leaping and clinging to branches. They live in the hilly rainforests on the eastern coast of Madagascar. Indris feed on both fruit and leaves, but the proportion of each food type varies seasonally. They have very long feet and legs, but—unlike bushbabies and other species that move in this way—they do not have a long tail.

Indris live in small family groups consisting of a male, a female, and their offspring. They occupy large territories, which they defend vigorously against other groups. This is partly achieved by giving very loud, mournful calls early in the morning. This advertises their presence to other indri groups, and each group replies in turn to the calls. Female indris are dominant to males, especially in a feeding context. Females are able to forcibly displace males from choice feeding sites by kicking and biting them. Males have never been seen to retaliate when attacked by a female in this way.

The indri looks like a startled teddy bear. It lives in small family groups and defends its territory by using loud, mournful calls.

⊕ WHERE IN THE WORLD?

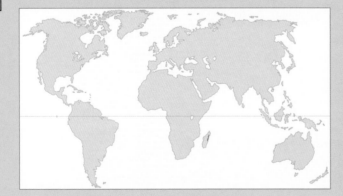

Indris are found only on the island of Madagascar. They are among the largest of all the lemurs.

FACT FILE

Distribution	Madagascar (rainforests of the east coast)
Species	Indri (*Indri indri*)
Body weight	Females: 15 lb (6.8 kg) Males: 13 lb (5.8 kg)
Activity pattern	Tree-living; day-active (diurnal)
Habitat type	Rainforest
Reproduction	First litter at age 4–7 years, then every 2–3 years; one offspring per litter
Average group size	2 (plus offspring)
Grouping type	Monogamous family groups
Maximum lifespan	Not known
Conservation status	Endangered by habitat destruction in its small and patchy range. Population numbers uncertain.

SPORTIVE LEMUR

The white-footed sportive lemur is a drab-colored animal. It is a leaf eater and often eats its own feces to extract all the nutrients from its food.

Known also as the "weasel lemur," the sportive lemur is a drab-colored animal found in many forest types throughout Madagascar. There are several species of sportive lemur, although experts cannot agree on how many there are. Up to seven different species have been estimated, on the basis of chromosome numbers, which vary between different populations of sportive lemurs.

Sportive lemurs are unusual because they do not have any permanent front teeth in the upper jaw. They also have a large caecum, or a blind sac found at the base of the large intestine, that houses bacteria that help digest the sportive lemur's leafy diet. In order to extract the maximum amount of nutrients from their food, sportive lemurs sometimes eat their own feces, like rabbits do), so that they can digest everything twice.

FACT FILE

Distribution	Madagascar
Species	Sportive lemur (*Lepilemur mustelinus*) Red-tailed sportive lemur (*Lepilemur ruficaudatus*) Grey-backed sportive lemur (*Lepilemur dorsalis*) White-footed sportive lemur (*Lepilemur leucopus*) Small-toothed weasel lemur (*Lepilemur microdon*) Milne-Edwards sportive lemur (*Lepilemur edwardsi*) Northern sportive lemur (*Lepilemur septentrionalis*)
Body weight	Females: 18–31 oz (550–935 g) Males: 18–30 oz (550–910 g)
Activity pattern	Tree-dwelling; nocturnal
Habitat type	All types of forest throughout Madagascar
Reproduction	First litter at around age 21 months; one offspring per litter
Average group size	1 (plus offspring)
Grouping type	Solitary. Male and female ranges overlap
Maximum lifespan	Not known
Conservation status	Threatened by habitat destruction

⊕ WHERE IN THE WORLD?

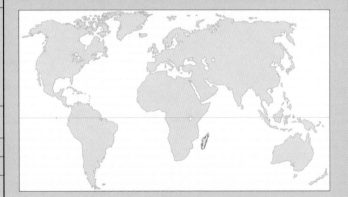

Found only on Madagascar, the sportive lemur has several species, which are distinguished by the number of chromosomes they possess.

✦ TOPIC LINKS

1.3 Primates Today
p. 37 Primate classification

2.4 Last Refuge of the Lemurs
p. 84 Lemur diversity
p. 90 Hopes of survival

MOUSE LEMUR

Mouse lemurs are among the smallest of all the primates. The smallest species, the western rufous mouse lemur, was discovered only in 1994 and weighs a mere 1 ounce (30 g). As their name suggests, mouse lemurs look very much like mice, with large, thin ears, a pointed snout and a long tail. However, their hands have very human-like proportions and give away their primate heritage.

Mouse lemurs are found only on the island of Madagascar. They feed mainly on insect matter, but may also eat fruit, flowers, buds, and leaves. They hibernate during the harsh dry season and store fat in their tails in order to see them through these periods. The tails undergo a fourfold change in volume, increasing their overall weight by 1.6–2.6 oz (50–80 g).

Mouse lemurs are strict seasonal breeders. Females are receptive to mating for only one day at the end of the dry season. They give birth at the start of the wet season when food is abundant. Like bushbabies, female mouse lemurs leave their offspring in nests while they forage.

Rather rodent-like in appearance, brown mouse lemurs (along with other mouse and dwarf lemurs) are unusual among the primates in that they hibernate for up to five months per year.

TOPIC LINKS

WHERE IN THE WORLD?

The mouse lemur is the smallest of the Madagascan lemurs, and is among the smallest of all the primates.

FACT FILE

Distribution	Madagascar
Species	Grey mouse lemur (*Microcebus murinus*) Brown mouse lemur (*Microcebus rufus*) Western rufous mouse lemur (*Microcebus myoxinus*)
Body weight	Females: 1–2 oz (30–65 g) Males: 1–2 oz (30–60 g)
Activity pattern	Nocturnal; tree-living, but may leap to the ground occasionally to feed on terrestrial insects
Habitat type	Most abundant in secondary forests. Also found in undergrowth and low levels of all forest types, including cultivated areas.
Reproduction	First litter at age 8–12 months, then every 12 months; litter size 2–3
Average group size	Single animals move around alone, sometimes with offspring
Grouping type	Solitary. Male and female home ranges overlap. Females may sleep together in shared 'dormitories'.
Maximum lifespan	15.5 years
Conservation status	Likely to be endangered (population numbers uncertain but known to be of concern)

BAMBOO LEMUR

The bamboo or gentle lemurs are specialist bamboo feeders. The three species—including this gentle lemur—all specialize on different parts of the bamboo plant.

As the name suggests, the bamboo lemurs are specialized for living in and feeding on bamboo. They are a distinctive genus of lemurs comprising three different species—one small species (the gentle lemur) and two larger species (the greater bamboo lemur and the golden bamboo lemur).

All three species feed almost exclusively on bamboo shoots and leaves, but each seems to specialize on a different part of the plant. The gentle lemur eats the new bamboo shoots, the greater bamboo lemur eats the pith from mature bamboo, and the golden bamboo lemur eats the growing shoots of a particular bamboo species that, interestingly, contains very high levels of cyanide. The three species all have a similar activity pattern: they are active during the day and move around their habitat by leaping and clinging to branches. They live in small family groups consisting of a male, a female, and their offspring (although family groups of the greater bamboo lemur often contain more than one breeding female).

FACT FILE

Distribution	Madagascar, in restricted area of southeastern rainforest
Species	Gentle lemur (*Hapalemur griseus*) Greater bamboo lemur (*Hapalemur simus*) Golden bamboo lemur (*Hapalemur aureus*)
Body weight	Females: 1.5–3 lb (670–1400 g) Males: 1.7–4.8 lb (750–2200 g)
Activity pattern	Tree-living; active at dawn and dusk (crepuscular)
Habitat type	Bamboo stands within forests
Reproduction	One offspring per litter
Average group size	3–6
Grouping type	Small family groups
Maximum lifespan	12.1 years (gentle lemur)
Conservation status	Extremely rare and on the brink of extinction; total population several hundred at most

⊕ WHERE IN THE WORLD?

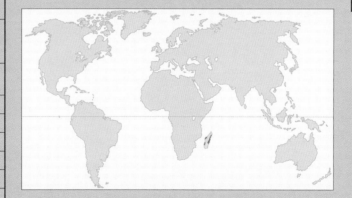

Bamboo lemurs have a restricted distribution in Madagascar. They are found only in bamboo stands within areas of forest.

✧ TOPIC LINKS

2.2 Scents and Sounds
p. 64 Scent glands

2.4 Last Refuge of the Lemurs
p. 84 Lemur diversity
p. 97 Hopes of survival

BROWN LEMUR

Brown lemurs are cat-sized primates found only on Madagascar. They are tree-living animals with a diet consisting of leaves, fruit, and flowers. Brown lemurs have a cathemera' pattern of activity—that is, they move around both by day and by night. They live in small groups of 7–12 individuals with approximately equal numbers of males and females. Unlike most other lemur species, brown lemurs do not show female dominance, nor do males appear to be dominant over females.

Although brown lemurs are classified as a single species, there are many different sub-species, and their distribution forms a ring around the island. Some subspecies have different numbers of chromosomes, but they are all, nevertheless, capable of interbreeding. In many of the subspecies, males and females are completely different colors, with females tending to be more brightly colored.

Brown lemurs are divided into a number of subspecies. Many of these show sexual dichromatism, which means that males and females show striking differences in color.

TOPIC LINKS

Scents and Sounds **2.2**
p. 68 Warning others

The Last Refuge of the Lemurs **2.4**
p. 83 An unsolved mystery

WHERE IN THE WORLD?

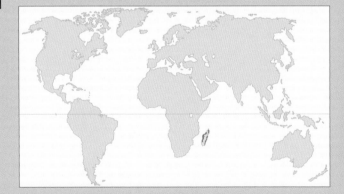

There are a number of subspecies of brown lemur in Madagascar. Their distribution forms a ring around the island.

FACT FILE

Distribution	Madagascar
Species	Brown lemur (*Eulemur fulvus*)
Body weight	Females: 1 lb (2.25 kg) Males: .99 lb (2.18 kg)
Activity pattern	Tree-living; cathemeral (day- and night-active)
Habitat type	Rainforest
Reproduction	First litter at age 20–24 months, then every 12 months; one offspring per litter
Average group size	9
Grouping type	Mixed multi-male, multi-female groups with balanced sex ratio
Maximum lifespan	30.8 years
Conservation status	Likely to be endangered (population numbers uncertain but known to be of concern)

GALAGO (LESSER BUSHBABY)

A senegal bushbaby. The lesser bushbabies are small, fast-moving primates that can leap large distances through the canopy. They have long, powerful legs and very long ankle bones.

The galagos, or lesser bushbabies, are a very diverse group of prosimian primates. There is still much debate about the exact number of species that should be included in the genus *Galago*. Galagos are confined to mainland Africa. They are fast-moving clingers and leapers with long leg and ankle bones that allow them to jump large distances through the forest canopy. They feed on insects, fruit and gum.

Litter size can vary quite substantially within a single galago species. For example, the South African lesser bushbaby (*Galago moholi*) is capable of producing up to two litters of twins in a single year, although in other years it may produce only a single offspring. These differences between years occur because of variation in the quality of the environment. The harsh, unpredictable nature of their savanna habitat means that *Galago moholi* does best by operating a 'boom or bust' reproductive cycle, producing lots of offspring whenever conditions are good but one or none when conditions are bad.

FACT FILE

Distribution	Sub-Saharan Africa
Species	Senegal bushbaby (*Galago senegalensis*) Somali bushbaby (*Galago gallarum*) South African lesser bushbaby (*Galago moholi*)
Body weight	Females: 5.8–6.7 oz (175–200 g) Males: 6.2–7.5 oz (185–225 g)
Activity pattern	Tree-living; nocturnal
Habitat type	Forests, savannas, open woodlands, and isolated thickets
Reproduction	First litter at age 9–12 months, then generally every 8 months; litter size 1–2 depending on species
Average group size	1 (plus offspring)
Grouping type	Single animals move around alone, sometimes with offspring
Maximum lifespan	16 years
Conservation status	Not currently endangered but threatened by habitat destruction

⊕ WHERE IN THE WORLD?

The bushbabies belonging to the genus *Galago*, or lesser bushbabies, are found throughout sub-Saharan Africa.

◈ TOPIC LINKS

2.1 Creatures of the Night
p. 55 Living in the dark
p. 58 Bushbaby society
p. 58 Male competition

2.2 Scents and Sounds
p. 70 When I'm calling you

2.3 Females in Charge
p. 74 Baby parking

POTTO

The potto is a species of loris. It is the largest of the African lorises, and also has the widest distribution, which stretches from Liberia in the west of Africa to Kenya in the east. Pottos are found in the canopy of primary and secondary forest and, due to their relatively large size, they favour quite sturdy branches. The potto has very unusual hands. Unlike other primates, the potto's thumb is rotated around so that it lies at 180 degrees to the rest of the fingers. The index finger is also reduced to a small bony lump, or tubercle. This gives the potto's hand a very wide span and provides it with a powerful grasping mechanism.

Prior to mating, pottos engage in some very energetic courtship. In addition to grooming, male–female pairs 'grapple' with each other. This playful wrestling allows secretions from the scent glands around the anus to be exchanged. Courtship is almost always followed by mating, which often takes place while both pottos hang below a branch suspended by their feet.

Pottos are slow-moving prosimians. During mating, however, they can get quite energetic and often couple while hanging upside down from trees.

🌐 WHERE IN THE WORLD?

The potto is the largest of the two African loris species, and has the widest distribution from West to East Africa.

FACT FILE

Distribution	West and Central Africa, Guinea to west Kenya
Species	Potto (*Perodictus potto*)
Body weight	Females: 27.8 oz (835 g) Males: 27.8 oz (830 g)
Activity pattern	Tree-living; nocturnal
Habitat type	Primary and secondary tropical rainforest
Reproduction	First litter at age 18 months, then every 12 months; one offspring per litter
Average group size	1 (plus offspring)
Grouping type	Solitary. Male and female ranges overlap
Maximum lifespan	10 years
Conservation status	Likely to be threatened by habitat destruction

SLOW LORIS

A common slow loris. The slow lorises are nocturnal prosimians. They are very slow in all respects, including their metabolism, which is 40 percent lower than expected for their body size.

Lorises are slow-moving primates that rely on concealment to avoid attack from predators. They have the widest geographic distribution of any prosimian family, with three genera in Africa and two in Asia. Lorises forage alone and rely mainly on scent for communication. Male home ranges are larger than those of females, and tend to overlap. When they are foraging, loris mothers leave their babies 'parked' on a branch and return to them later. Lorises do not build nests but sleep curled up on branches during the day. They give birth to a single offspring at a time.

Slow lorises are the larger and stockier of the two Asian loris genera. They are strictly nocturnal and feed mainly on fruits and gum. Slow lorises have very slow metabolic rates for their body weight—40 percent below that expected for an animal of their size.

FACT FILE

Distribution	Southeast Asia
Species	Common slow loris (*Nycticebus coucang*) Pygmy slow loris (*Nycticebus pygmaeus*)
Body weight	Females: 21–36.7 oz (630–1100 g) Males: 22.7–43.3 oz (680–1300 g)
Activity pattern	Tree-living; nocturnal
Habitat type	Continuous canopy and understory of primary and secondary rainforest and deciduous forest. Preference for dense vegetation.
Reproduction	One litter every 12 months; one offspring per litter
Average group size	Single animals move around alone, sometimes with offspring
Grouping type	Solitary. Male and female ranges overlap
Maximum lifespan	14.5 years
Conservation status	Not currently endangered but threatened by habitat destruction; adversely affected by even moderate levels of selective logging

⊕ WHERE IN THE WORLD?

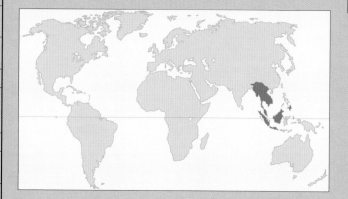

The slow loris is one of two Asian loris genera. Lorises have the widest distribution of any prosimian species.

◈ TOPIC LINKS

1.3 Primates Today
p. 37 Prosimians

2.1 Creatures of the Night
p. 54 Getting around
p. 58 Lazy loners

2.2 Scents and Sounds
p. 64 Urine marking

2.3 Females in Charge
p. 74 Baby parking

3

THE MONKEYS

MONKEY LIFESTYLES

The emergence of primates into daylight opened up a vast range of ecological opportunities. Freed from the constraints of the prosimians' nocturnal world, the monkeys were able to expand into new niches, not only in the tropical forests but also beyond, to the savannas, deserts, and mountain plateaus. The switch to daylight living led to a greater range of diets and lifestyles, from gum eaters to fruit-eaters to specialist grass-eaters. There are more ways to make a living in the daytime than at night, when poor visibility and reliance on smell limit the choice of food to be found. The change in lifestyle was accompanied by a change in the senses. Unlike prosimians, monkeys started to rely on their sense of sight. Their vision became sharper, their color perception richer. These improved visual skills help monkeys to select the ripest fruits or the tenderest young leaves, and allow them to keep a constant look out for danger.

Chapter opening: Hanuman langurs are widespread in India, where they are considered sacred.

NEW WORLD MONKEYS

The monkeys' adaptable nature means that they are widespread in both the Old World of Africa and Asia and the New World of South America. There are distinctive differences between the Old World and New World monkeys, but both show an amazing diversity of lifestyles.

The New World monkeys of South and Central America are known as the playtrrhines (▷p. 39). "Playtrrhine" means broadnosed, and the nostrils of these monkeys are wide and point to the side, unlike the narrow, downward-pointing nostrils of the catarrhines, Old World monkeys and apes that inhabit Africa and Asia. New World monkeys also differ from their Old World relatives by having a "prehensile" tail, one that can grip and acts as a fifth hand. All New World monkeys are forest animals. They do not occupy the diverse range of habitats of the Old World species. However, within their forest homes they show a wide variety of lifestyles.

In terms of lifestyle and behavior, the New World monkeys can be split into two main groups. The first is made up of the marmosets and tamarins, tiny, almost bird-like animals that flit rapidly through the branches, calling to each other with high-pitched chirps and trills. The second group consists of larger monkeys that are more diverse in their diet, appearance, and behavior. Some of these are predominantly fruit eaters, while others feed mainly on leaves or seeds.

Marmosets and tamarins

These squirrel-sized monkeys have fine, silky hair and an array of moustaches, manes, hair crests, and tufts. They are unique among the

1. Spider monkeys make good use of their "prehensile" tails, which they use like a fifth hand, to reach otherwise inaccessible places.

Colobus monkeys have no thumbs. Their name comes from the Greek word *kolobos*, meaning "cut short."

1. (opposite) Marmosets are small South American monkeys. This tassel-eared marmoset uses its claws to help it scamper up and down tree trunks.

Night monkeys are the only truly nocturnal monkey species.

monkeys because they have claws instead of nails on every digit except on the big toe. The claws help them maintain their grip as they dart up and down large tree trunks.

The marmosets are specialized gum-eaters. Their bottom teeth are adapted for gouging holes in bark to encourage gum to flow. After spending a few minutes feeding on the gum in each hole, they will often scent mark or urinate into it to establish ownership and deter other marmosets from feeding there. The pygmy marmoset is the most dedicated gum eater, spending over two-thirds of its feeding time on this one food type. The other marmosets feed mainly on fruit, and turn to gum only when fruit is in short supply. They also eat nectar, flowers, and small animals, such as snails, lizards, and frogs. Tamarins eat fruit too, and have a similar diet to marmosets, but they are not specialized for gum eating in the same way.

Marmosets and tamarins live in many different types of forest. They are found in tall, virgin rainforests, in dry forests, where the trees lose their leaves for half the year, and in patches of forest in the savanna regions of Amazonia. The highest numbers are found in virgin forests, where they do best. They also like areas with bushy vegetation and vine tangles as these provide the safest sleeping sites. These tiny primates often fall victim to large, monkey-eating birds of prey.

Competition between the marmoset species is intense and there is never more than one species in a particular habitat because of their specialization on gum. In contrast, different tamarin species often share the same habitat and, in some cases, join forces to defend it. The emperor tamarin, named because of its long, oriental-looking moustache and the saddleback tamarin, which gets its name from the area of paler hair on its back, are two such species. Mixed groups of these monkeys share a common territory,

 NIGHT LIFE

The night monkey of South America is the only truly nocturnal monkey. It feeds on fruit, insects, and leaves, and lives in family groups consisting of a male–female pair and their offspring. Like other nocturnal animals, night monkeys have very large eyes to see in the dark. However, unlike the nocturnal prosimians, they also have color vision, and their eyes lack the special reflective layer that makes prosimian eyes so sensitive. This strange mixture of features suggests that night monkeys evolved from day monkeys that returned to a moonlight existence. This was probably to avoid the dangers posed by birds of prey, such as hawks and eagles, daytime hunters who would find the small night monkeys an easy catch. Although they can see much better at night than other monkeys, night monkeys are not completely adapted to life in the dark. They tend to be most active when the moon is full and they can use its bright light to help them navigate around the home range. Males also take advantage of moonlit nights to claim their territories. On clear, well-lit nights, adult males patrol the boundaries of their range, giving a series of low, hooting calls to announce that the area is occupied.

1. Spider monkeys prefer to eat fruit. They have large home ranges and live in a fluid society similar to that of chimpanzees.

2. The slow and ponderous howler monkeys are specialized for eating leaves. They spend most of the day sitting and digesting their food.

move around together, and keep in touch by exchanging contact calls. Sharing a territory reduces the likelihood of predator attack and makes territorial defense more effective. It also makes foraging easier. Both species feed on trees and vines whose fruits ripen gradually over a number of weeks. The most efficient way to feed on these is to visit the plants once every few days and eat all the ripe fruit available. Waiting a few days before the next visit allows a new batch of fruit to ripen. By feeding together, the two species know exactly when to visit each plant and avoid wasted journeys to sites that have been stripped of fruit by rival tamarins.

Fruit eaters, large and small

South and Central America are home to a variety of fruit-eating monkeys. First of all, there are the capuchins, robust, stocky monkeys that move rapidly along the tops of branches. These are among the brainiest of the monkeys, with much larger brains than would be expected for animals of their size. They are mainly fruit eaters, but, because fruit is low in protein, they also eat insects, snails, and other small animals. They are inquisitive and destructive foragers, especially when searching for insects, and often waste resources as they move in search of their next meal. Some capuchin species are fond of palm nuts, which they smash open by banging them hard against branches and tree trunks to get at the edible kernels inside. Capuchins are the least specialized of the New World monkeys and have the widest distribution, living in most forested habitats from Honduras in Central America to the far southeast of Brazil.

Squirrel monkeys have a diet similar to capuchins but are smaller and more slender. Consequently, they are not as strong and are unable to pull open palm fronds or tear dead

bark from trees to find insects. Instead, they snatch caterpillars and grubs from the surface of leaves and branches. They eat more insects than capuchins, and have sharp, narrow teeth to crunch them up easily. Squirrel monkeys live in large groups of up to 40 animals. This is partly for defense against predators, and partly to withstand competition from other monkeys. A squirrel monkey group is too big for even larger monkeys to chase away.

The other small fruit eaters of the New World are the titi monkeys and night monkeys. In contrast to squirrel monkeys, these species live in small family groups and get their protein from leaves rather than insects. Night monkeys avoid competition with larger monkeys by living a strictly nocturnal lifestyle.

Larger than all these species are the spider monkeys. They are also fruit specialists and, like the titis, rely on leaves for protein. They are the largest of the New World monkeys and appear to fill the ecological niche occupied by chimpanzees in the forests of Africa. Like chimpanzees, spider monkeys have long arms and flexible shoulder joints that allow them to swing through the trees. However, unlike chimpanzees, they also have prehensile, grasping, tails for gripping branches. The tail is so strong that it can support an animal's entire weight, and spider monkeys are often seen dangling by their tails while using their hands to pluck fruit from branches below them. Woolly monkeys are closely related to spider monkeys and also rely on fruit as their staple diet. However, the woolly spider monkey, a relative of both woolly monkeys and spider monkeys, differs from its relatives because it depends more on leaves.

Leaf eaters and seed eaters

Howler monkeys are the New World's leaf specialists. They have powerful jaws and large molar teeth to finely grind leaves. They also

have enormous stomachs and an enlarged lower intestine in which vegetation is partially fermented, enabling them to extract the meager nutrients available in leaves. The need to spend a lot of time digesting means that howlers are less active than their fruit-eating counterparts. They may move less than 400 yards in an entire day, and spend up to three-quarters of their time just resting, so they are not the most riveting animals to watch. Although they are mainly leaf eaters, howler monkeys eat fruit that is less ripe than the fruit eaten by other monkeys. Howlers also eat fibrous fruits, such as figs and pods, which take a long time to digest. Like all New World monkeys, howlers have a prehensile tail, but they swing through branches. Instead, they move slowly along the tops.

The seed-eating monkeys, the sakis and uakaris, are the most unusual-looking monkeys. Sakis have furry, mask-like faces, while uakaris have bald, bright red heads. Uakaris live in the seasonally flooded forests of the Amazon and Orinoco river basins. Little is known about their behavior, but they seem to eat fruit and leaves as well as seeds. More is known about the sakis. An average of 60 percent of their diet consists of the seeds of unripe fruits. The amount of seed-eating varies seasonally, however. During the dry season, sakis spend up to 80 percent of their feeding time eating seeds, but this falls to as little as 10 percent in the wet season, when they switch to fruit. Some sakis can also crack open hard nuts. These species have strong jaw muscles, sturdy canine teeth, and a built-in nutcracker, a gap between the canines and the back teeth. To crack open a nut, they wedge it into the gap and bite.

3

4

5

3. Bald uakaris live in flooded forests of the Amazon and Orinoco river basins. They are fond of seeds, but also eat fruit and leaves. 4.

Saki monkeys are specialized seed eaters. They can spend as much as 80 percent of their feeding time eating seeds.

5. There are two sub-species of bald uakari, one with a bright red coat, seen here, while the other has a white coat.

 Black-and-white colobus monkeys sometimes eat soil. This provides them with minerals that would otherwise be lacking from their diet.

OLD WORLD MONKEYS

The monkeys of Africa and Asia, the Old World monkeys, have a similar range of diets and live in similar social groups to those of New World species, but they occupy a much wider range of habitats. This is largely because some of these species have made the transition from life in the trees to life on the ground.

Colobines

As with New World monkeys, a distinction can be made between the Old World species who are predominantly fruit eaters and those who prefer leaves. The African and Asian leaf eaters are known collectively as colobines. Like howler monkeys, they have special enlarged stomachs for fermenting vegetation, but the colobines' stomachs are more complex and efficient than those of howlers.

Colobines also have molars with sharp crests that slice leaves into very fine pieces, making it easier for the stomach bacteria to do their job. Most species prefer young leaves to tough, older leaves, and almost all include some other food besides leaves in their diet, be it flowers, fruits, or seeds.

There are 28 colobine species in Asia, and only nine in Africa. The Asian species are often called leaf monkeys or langurs, and they can be distinguished by differences in their coat color. They are found in a wide band that runs through India, China, Vietnam, Malaysia, and the islands of Borneo and Java. Most live in tropical forests, but some, such as the Hanuman langur of India, occupy more open habitats, including town centers.

The most unusual and the most endangered Asian colobines are the proboscis monkey of Borneo and the snub-nosed monkeys of China. The odd-looking

GUT REACTIONS

Although not as impressive as cows, which have five stomachs to digest grass, the leaf-eating colobine monkeys of Africa and Asia are also well designed for their job of breaking down leafy material. Colobines have a complex two-part stomach and a long gut that gives them a characteristic pot-bellied appearance. The top part of the stomach is separate from the lower, acid-filled section, and must be kept free of digestive acids because it provides a home for millions of bacteria that live there and ferment plant matter. These bacteria release vital, energy-rich nutrients from the leaves which would otherwise pass undigested through the body. The bacteria also break down toxic chemicals found in certain seeds. Since colobines have to spend long periods sitting around and digesting, they tend to be less social than monkeys who rely on fruit as their staple food. Colobines do not engage in as much grooming as these other species, and dominance relationships are more low-key. This is partly because there is little to fight over; leaves are so widespread that everyone gets his share, but it is also because the monkeys cannot spare the energy needed for fighting since it takes a lot of energy to digest the food sitting in their stomachs.

1. (opposite) Black-and-white colobus monkeys are able to survive on a small number of tree species and can live in small areas of forest. In order to supplement their diet, they often descend to the ground to eat soil and clay.

1. A group of Zanzibar red colobus gnaw on some charcoal. This helps them neutralize the toxins contained in their leafy diet.

2. The golden snub-nosed monkeys of China are beautiful animals. They live in mountainous conifer forests and can form herds containing up to 600 animals.

3. Red colobus are large, leaf-eating monkeys found across Africa from west to east. Both males and females transfer between groups, and the social system is fluid.

proboscis monkey gets its name from the male's enormous, tongue-shaped, fleshy nose. The females have much smaller, turned-up noses. Males are twice the size of females, with enormous pot-bellies housing their fermenting stomachs and long intestines. They live along river courses in mangrove forests and are often seen swimming, an unusual behavior for monkeys. The snub-nosed monkeys are closely related to proboscis monkeys and live in the mountain-ous conifer forests of China. The golden snub-nosed monkey lives in groups of 20 to 30 animals, but at certain times of the year these groups congregate to form large herds of up to 600 individuals.

African colobines live only in forest, and most are found in West and central Africa. They can be told apart by differences in coat color or by the length of their hair. The black-and-white colobus of East Africa can survive on the leaves of two or three tree species, so it never needs to forage far and occupies small areas. As a result, it is less vulnerable to habitat destruction than most primates and is often found hanging on in small fragments of forest. However, the western black-and-white colobus is more partial to seeds than leaves. This prefer-ence is a general feature of the West African colobines and seems to be related to the abun-dance of edible seeds in West Africa's forests. Another species with a penchant for seeds is the black or "satanic" colobus, whose diet consists almost exclusively of this type of food.

Other African species are more particular about their food than the black-and-white colobus. The red colobus, for example, has a definite preference for young leaves. Since these are a relatively scarce commodity, red colobus monkeys have to travel more than black-and-white, so they occupy a much larger area. Red colobus on the island of Zanzibar, just off the coast of Tanzania, have a much stranger dietary preference. These animals are often seen gnawing sooty lumps of charcoal. It appears that charcoal helps to neutralize the toxins found in the leaves that make up the monkeys' diet.

Guenons, vervets, and patas monkeys

The colobines of Africa share their habitat with the smaller, fruit-eating monkeys of the guenon family. There are many species in this widespread family, and each has its own distinctive coat and face marks (▷p. 114). Although their main source of food is fruit, guenons also eat insects or leaves to obtain protein. Small guenons, such as the redtail monkeys of East Africa, get most of their protein from insects. Larger species, such as the blue monkeys or diana monkeys, rely more on leaves because they are too big to get enough protein from insects alone. Different guenon species tend to catch different types of insect, and they vary in the techniques they use. This specialization seems to allow more than one species to coexist in a habitat without having to endure too much competition for food.

Not all guenons live in forests. Both the vervet monkey and the patas monkey are inhabitants of the savanna grasslands. Vervets are restricted to the small areas of forest that line the banks of rivers, a habitat known as gallery forest, and are equally happy foraging on the ground as they are in the trees. Though their varied diet includes the sap of acacia trees, they prefer fruit. The patas monkey, on the other hand, is a true savanna dweller. It lives in small groups in open habitats, and has evolved long legs that allow it to run quickly and evade the predators of the African plains.

4. A Sykes' monkey displays its impressive canines. Guenon groups usually contain a single male who has exclusive mating rights.

The Hanuman langurs of India are considered sacred by Hindus. They are named in honor of the monkey-god, Hanuman, and are fed offerings at temples on Hanuman's day.

 TEMPLE MONKEYS

Life can be tough for a monkey. Finding food and avoiding danger are full-time jobs, especially when habitat conditions are poor and little food is available. Some species are luckier than others, however, and perhaps the luckiest of all are the temple monkeys of India, especially the Hanuman langur. This species is considered sacred by Hindus, and gets its name from the monkey god, Hanuman. According to Hindu mythology, Hanuman accompanied the god Vishnu to Sri Lanka in search of Vishnu's wife, who had been kidnapped. While in Sri Lanka, Hanuman stole the mango plant and brought it back to India, where mangoes did not grow. He was punished for the theft and condemned to be burned. While trying to put out the fire, Hanuman's face and paws were scorched. Today, the striking black faces and paws of Hanuman langurs are a testimony to the monkey god's punishment. Thanks to their sacred status, they are not persecuted by humans, even though they often raid crops. On Hanuman's day, the monkeys are fed offerings at Hindu temples. And if a Hanuman langur suffers an untimely and accidental death, such as being electrocuted on power cables or run over by a car, it is given a full Hindu funeral by faithful worshippers.

GUENONS: NATURALLY DIFFERENT

The guenons are one of the most remarkable groups of modern primates. These small- to medium-sized monkeys have a fossil record that extends back a mere 2 million years, about as long as our own genus, *Homo,* has been in existence. Yet, unlike humans, who have only a single living species, the guenons are one of the most species-rich primate groups. Some 24 species are currently recognized, most of which belong to a single lineage, the genus *Cercopithecus.* This diverse group ranges from the tiny .68 pound (1.5-kilogram) talapoin monkey to the 22 pound (10-kilogram) patas, the largest member known.

2

1

1. Patas monkeys are savanna-living animals belonging to the guenon group. They have long legs and can run fast to avoid predators. 2.

Most guenons, like the De Brazza's monkey have distinctive facial markings that help distinguish species.

Frozen into diversity

Why are the guenons so species-rich? The answer seems to lie in the fact that the African forests were repeatedly broken up into small, isolated patches during the last 2 million years, while Europe and Asia froze under the ice ages. As the ice fronts edged down from the Arctic, the climates of Africa experienced cooler, drier periods that caused the luxuriant forests of central and West Africa to die. The forests survived only as small, isolated patches on each occasion. Within each patch, small populations of ancestral guenons survived. With little or no exchange of genes between patches, the isolated populations gradually diverged. By the time an ice age ended and the forests reunited, the guenon populations were sufficiently different not to mate with each other. With just a little more reproductive isolation, incipient species became full species. As each ice age came and went, this process was repeated across Africa, resulting in today's extraordinary diversity of species. However, only the vervet and patas monkey have successfully made a life in the open savanna.

Colorful cousins

The differences between guenon species are most strikingly reflected in the coloration of the fur, especially on the face. Some, such as the moustached monkey (*Cercopithecus cephus*) and the blue monkey (*C. mitis*) are relatively dull colored, but others, such as the diana monkey (*C. diana*) and De Brazza's monkey (*C. neglectus*), are quite spectacular. The patas is also known as the hussar monkey because its red, black, and white coat and neat white moustache reminded the European explorers who first saw it of a nineteenth-century cavalry officer, a perception enhanced by its bounding run across the savanna grasslands when disturbed. A newcomer to the family is the sun-tailed guenon (*C. solatus*), discovered deep in the West African forests as recently as 1986. How it remained undiscovered for so long in relatively well-known habitats is itself a mystery.

Adaptation and spread

While all the other species in the family are quite localized, with small geographical distributions, the patas and the vervet occur throughout much of sub-Saharan Africa. Both are unusual by guenon standards because they are adapted to life on the ground and prefer woodland and grassland habitats to forests, and all other guenon species are tree-living. This adaptation to more open habitats probably originated in an attempt by their respective ancestral populations to cope with the rapidly disappearing forests during an ice age. It also meant that their distribution was less restricted and that animals could migrate more easily between groups. This prevented the genetic isolation of populations that happened to their forest-living relatives.

Forming new species

The vervets (recently allocated their own genus, *Chlorocebus*) provide an example of how populations can diverge toward forming new species as they separate geographically. They probably originated in the vicinity of Lake Victoria in Uganda, and from there gradually spread both westward and southward through the savanna grasslands. Today, although adjacent vervet populations are clearly similar to each other, those at the opposite ends of these two arms of expansion are distinct. Different subspecies have formed and could, in time, evolve further into different species.

4. Blue monkeys have a wide distribution for a guenon species. They are widespread throughout equatorial Africa, and reach as far as the coastal forests of South Africa, where they are known as samango monkeys.

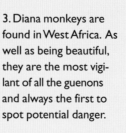

3. Diana monkeys are found in West Africa. As well as being beautiful, they are the most vigilant of all the guenons and always the first to spot potential danger.

Baboons

The other well-known monkey of Africa's grasslands is the baboon. This is an exceptionally successful and adaptable species group, found the length and breadth of Africa from the humid grasslands of West Africa to the mountain peaks of South Africa. Part of the baboons' success is their diverse and eclectic diet. They eat almost everything. They prefer fruit, but almost anything else will do. With hands like our own, baboons are good at digging for underground food that other savanna dwellers cannot reach, like roots, corms, and bulbs. They also eat meat. One population in East Africa became famous for the way its males hunted and killed small antelopes.

Baboons are highly specialized for a life on the ground. Tree-living monkeys have longer legs than arms which help them balance. When moving slowly along branches, they keep their long hind legs forward to carry most of their body weight. This allows them to raise their arms and feed on an all fours without falling over. Living on the ground demands more efficient walking, and this is achieved by having arms and legs that are about the same length. Consequently, baboons have much longer arms than forest monkeys, making their shoulders higher than their hips. They also walk with their fingers flat and the palms of their hands held vertical, which raises their shoulders further. As well as being better for walking on flat, and , this posture allows baboons to scan their surroundings for danger without craning their neck. Patas monkeys do not have this high-shoulder posture, and are forced to stand up on their hind legs to check for danger. Efficient walking comes at a price, however. Baboon feet are much flatter than those of the tree-living monkeys, and are less adept at gripping. In fact, the gelada baboon of Ethiopia finds it difficult to climb a tree, since it is specialized to life on the ground.

One baboon subspecies, the hamadryas, is adapted to life in the semi-deserts of northern Ethiopia and Arabia, and feeds mainly on grass seeds, roots, and bulbs. Hamadryas baboons are smaller than other baboons and have gray coats and pink faces. The gelada is another baboon species, but is one that is distantly related to the other types of baboon found in Africa. It is the only surviving member of a whole family of baboon species, the Theropithecines, that were successful during a period from 5 to 2 million years ago. One extinct species, *Theropithecus oswaldi* (▷p. 34), weighed over 200 lbs (100 kg), as large as a female mountain gorilla. A specialized grass-eater, the gelada lives only in the mountainous highlands of Ethiopia. Both hamadryas and gelada baboons have large and complex soci-

1. Savanna or common baboons are well known for their wide-ranging diets. They eat all plant and animal matter.

2. Chacma baboons, like this are eating a waterlily are found in the far south of Africa, and often rely on more unusual foods than their East African counterparts.

3

eties containing many levels. This social complexity seems to be an adaptation to their unusual lifestyles.

Baboon relatives

The forest-living mandrill and drill of West Africa look much like baboons, but these species may be more closely related to the mangabeys. Mangabeys are the largest of the tree-living monkeys, and are famous for the loud "whoop-gobble" calls of the males. These monkeys have large incisor teeth and can break into the toughest fruits. Although mangabeys have been studied in detail, little is known about the mandrill and drill. The mandrill is best known for the male's magnificent blue and red face and his bright blue bottom. Like baboons, mandrills live on the ground and are fond of fruit. Their huge groups contain up to 400 animals. The sight of them trooping across the forest floor must be impressive indeed. Unfortunately, very few people have ever managed to follow them.

4

3. Like all monkeys, baboons are highly social and live in groups of up to 150 animals. As a result, feeding competition within baboon groups can be intense.

4. Gelada baboons are found only in the highlands of Ethiopia and feed almost exclusively on grass. Male gelada, as shown here, possess impressive capes of fur.

Baboon males keep their large canine teeth razor sharp by grinding them against a specially adapted tooth in the lower jaw.

Macaques

Although the baboons are impressive in the range of habitats they occupy, the prize for world domination must go to the macaques. This is an enormously successful group of monkeys found in almost every habitat that you can think of, from the Atlas Mountains of Morocco to the temperate forests of Japan. There are 19 species of macaque, many of whom occupy some of the most extreme habitats of any primate. For example, the Barbary macaque is the only non-human primate found in Europe, with a small population found on the island of Gibraltar, while the Japanese macaque ranges further north and east than any primate species, other than human. The populations in the far north of Japan experience very harsh, snowy conditions in winter. They have enormously thick, furry coats to help keep out chills, and have also adopted a rather unusual behavior to beat the winter blues: they sit up to their necks in naturally occurring hot springs as a way of escaping the biting cold. By contrast, the long-tail macaque – also known as the crab-eating macaque – is the species that extends furthest to the southeast in Asia.

Macaques spend time on the ground as well as in the trees and, like baboons, have an omnivorous diet. Within Asia they also have a similar range of habitats and lifestyles to those enjoyed by guenons and baboons in Africa. Some species, such as the lion-tailed macaque of southern India, are very guenon-like in looks and behavior. Others, such as the rhesus, bonnet and Japanese macaques, are rather more baboon-like in terms of their adaptability and behavior.

Although macaques as a whole are a highly adaptable group of monkeys, species such as the longtail macaque, the rhesus macaque, the toque macaque, and the bonnet macaque are impressively successful. Unlike most monkeys, who fare rather badly in habitats modified by humans, these species thrive in such areas and achieve populations that humans find difficult to control, becoming known as 'weed species'.

Japanese macaques also thrive near human habitations. In some areas they are fed as a tourist attraction, adding a bit of primato-logical color to the annual cherry blossom season. As a result of this extra feeding, birth rates shoot up and groups increase rapidly in size. Troops of 1000 animals are not uncommon. These super-large groups are organized around a series of matriline families headed by a single female. The most dominant matriline also tends to be the largest, and females belonging to this family usually get first choice of the tasty tidbits provided by humans. When these groups get too large, however, social order inevitably breaks down and feeding time becomes a chaotic free-for-all.

1. Here, Japanese macaques play in the snow. These monkeys have extremely thick, furry coats that help keep out the cold.

2. A Japanese macaque sits out a snow storm. No other species of monkey is able to live this far north and endure such extremes of temperature.

3.2 GROUP LIVING

The defining characteristic of the monkeys is their intense social life. All monkeys live in groups, or "troops," of some kind, and within those groups individuals form strong bonds with each other. Many monkeys spend their days surrounded by close relatives, enmeshed in a complex network of relationships, some friendly, some more competitive in nature.

When they are not looking for food, monkeys socialize by grooming each other's fur, picking out dirt, dead skin, and parasites. Grooming is a valuable service for one animal to provide to another, and it also appears to be a pleasant and relaxing experience. However, these undoubted benefits are not the only reason that monkeys feel a compulsive need to groom each other. Living in a group can be tough, and many monkeys have to use their grooming services as currency to buy favors or access to things that help make life a little bit easier.

COMPETITION AND COOPERATION

The main reason that monkeys live in groups is to avoid being eaten by predators. This danger is greatest for animals that are active by day because they are easily seen by predators that hunt by sight. Nocturnal primates, on the other hand, are protected by the cover of darkness, so they forage alone and keep quiet to avoid giving themselves away. Social groups provide safety in two ways. First, if a predator attacks the group, the chance of any given animal becoming its target is smaller than if that animal were alone. A lone animal targeted by the predator would be much more likely to end up as dinner. Second, the more animals there are in one place, the more likely it is that one of them will spot a predator before it has a chance to attack. Since most predators rely on an element of surprise, they often give up the chase if they realize that their prey have detected them.

1. Living in groups helps protect monkeys from attacks by predators. The more eyes and ears on the look-out, the less likely the group is to fall victim to a surprise attack.

2. Here is an olive baboon group socializing. Grooming acts as the "glue" that ensures groups remain cohesive and protect individuals from danger.

★ In some areas of Japan, people put out food for macaques. As a result, the birth rate rapidly increases and super-large groups form, containing up to 1,000 monkeys.

1. Spider monkeys do not live in stable social groups. Instead, parties of animals come together and disband, depending on the size of the food resources available.

Getting enough to eat

Although group life provides safety in numbers, there is a price to be paid, coming in the form of competition for food. Since monkeys move around their home range together, they have to feed on the same resources, and often there is not enough to go around. Competition for food helps to explain why different monkey species behave so differently from each other and form varied kinds of social relationship. It also helps explain why separate groups of the same species sometimes have different social systems.

The social bonds between monkeys are not the ties of true friendship. Instead, they are a self-interested way for animals to keep one step ahead of the competition within the group. The value of bonding with other animals is stronger for females than males. Access to good-quality food is more important for females because it determines their ability to nourish offspring during pregnancy or when an infant is suckling. The nature of relationships between females varies much more widely than it does among males since different ecological conditions, and therefore different levels of competition, require different social solutions.

Female bonding

Many Old World monkeys live in what are known as female-bonded groups. Females born into such groups spend their entire lives within the group and form grooming relationships with their relatives. In some species, such as the vervet and redtail monkeys, the females are territorial and join forces to drive away rival groups. Other species, such as the diana monkeys, use the sole male who lives in their group as a "hired gun" to defend the territory on their behalf. Many species, including most baboons and some macaques, are not territorial, but might still be hostile to females of other groups.

Female-bonded groups tend to be found among those species that rely on patchy sources of food, such as fruit, rather than on widely distributed foods, such as grass. When food is patchy, the most powerful or aggressive individuals can monopolize it and prevent weaker monkeys from getting their share. The result is a social hierarchy. The largest or most aggressive animals, those who can push to the front of the line, sit at the top of the hierarchy and are dominant. Animals who give in to others are subordinate, or low ranking, and are positioned at the bottom of the hierarchy.

Rank inheritance

Females who are closely ranked in the hierarchy also tend to be closely related to each other. This is because of the way that young females achieve their dominant rank in the adult hierarchy. As they approach sexual maturity, young females begin to challenge adult females and behave aggressively toward them. They tend to direct these attacks at females who are lower ranking than their own adult female relatives. Their adult kin support them in their attempts at social climbing, ensuring that ranked lower females submit to these young upstarts. Young females do not behave aggressively to females who are higher ranking than their relatives since, even with their relatives' support, they cannot force the dominant female to submit. These young females are eventually able to dominate lower-ranking females without any aid from their relatives, at which point they become fully integrated members of the adult female hierarchy. And, since they are able to dominate those females who rank below their relatives but remain subordinate to those who dominate their relatives, they occupy a position in the hierarchy adjacent to their female kin. By continuing to bond with their relatives as adults, the females in this hierarchical society can form coalitions to fight for their share of food, and therefore stand a better chance of getting enough to eat.

Differences in dominance

The strength of a female hierarchy within a particular group depends on how much there is to fight over. Sometimes there is little to

2

dispute, either because food is widely distributed and not easily monopolized, or because there is enough for everyone. In these cases, there is a weak hierarchy, and social life is relatively peaceful. However, when there is plenty to fight over, hierarchies are pronounced, and fights are much more common because it is in the dominant animals' interests to ensure that everyone knows their place.

This difference between peaceful and aggressive groups is found throughout the primate world. Squirrel monkey females, for example, behave differently depending on where in South or Central America they live. In Costa Rica, where they feed on large fruit trees, there is little aggression or dominance. Dominant monkeys cannot monopolize whole trees, so females do not need to gang up with relatives to fight for their share. As a result, the groups are only loosely female bonded and the hierarchy is weak. By contrast, in Peru, where the food patches are smaller and more easily monopolized, dominance is more important and the monkeys

3

2. Unlike the other guenons, vervet monkeys live along riverbanks within the savanna. They are strongly female bonded and defend their territories against females from other groups.

3. In female-bonded monkey groups, females spend a lot of time grooming each other. Most grooming occurs between closely related individuals who are of similar rank.

are strongly female bonded. Differences in the level of female bonding are also seen between species. Bonnet and stump-tailed macaques tend to live in fairly calm, peaceful groups with little bonding between kin, for instance, while rhesus macaques live in very aggressive groups with extremely strict hierarchies, and have strong relationships with their kin.

Looser bonds

In general, groups with looser female bonding are more common among leaf-eating monkeys, such as howlers and colobus, since their food is freely available and therefore not worth fighting over. In such situations, the females do not form close grooming bonds since there is no need for kin to stick together. In fact, females sometimes transfer between groups. As a result, the females in any particular group are less closely related to each other than those in a female-bonded group, and social rank is not closely linked to kinship. Red colobus monkeys are an example of non-female-bonded monkeys. These large, leaf-eating monkeys are found across Africa from west to east. They live in large groups, and both males and females transfer between groups, resulting in a fluid social system.

Dominance in males

Male monkeys also form dominant relationships with each other and can be ranked in a hierarchy, but these tend to reflect competition for mates rather than for food. A male who is dominant to all the others in his troop will generally get the most matings, although the final say rests with the females.

In some species, such as olive baboons, males also form coalitions to help gain access to mates (▷p. 208). When a male is in a fight with another over a female, he might solicit the help of a third male, using a distinctive

2

3

1. Bonnet macaques are characterized by their peaceful, non aggressive groups. In contrast to those in many female bonded groups, the dominant females spend a lot of time grooming subordinate females.

2. Japanese macaque females square up to each other in a fight over leadership. The size of a female Japanese macaque's family determines her ranking within a group.

3. A male olive baboon shows his teeth to intimidate rivals. Most rivalry between males occurs over mating.

1. A chacma baboon submits to a more dominant animal. In most monkey groups, dominance relation-ships are highly ritualized and actual aggression is quite rare.

"head-flagging" signal. The other male will then come to his aid, help defeat the rival, and secure a mating with the female for his coalition partner. Some males are more useful as coalition partners than others. Those whose strength and rank mean that any male who pairs up with them has a good chance of winning a contest have been called "veto players," since they have the ultimate power to determine whether or not a coalition will work. Since their involvement in a coalition is necessary if it is to be successful, such males often get to mate with the female themselves as they will withdraw their support from a coalition partner if he does not let them occasionally reap the benefits of their involvement in the fight. Weaker males have no choice but to let these vital coalition partners mate with

females that they originally had their eye on because the long-term costs of losing the support of their partner far outweighs the short-term cost of letting another male "get the girl" on a few occasions.

Among savanna baboons, this political manuvering is found only in East African baboon males. Those found in South Africa do not manipulate each other this way, and mating with females is strictly determined by a male's size and dominant rank, rather than by who his friends are. The reason for this difference is still a matter of debate. It is possible that South African chacma baboon males are unable to form coalitions because they remain prisoners of their evolutionary past. They have not learned how to form coalitions even though they would benefit by doing so.

2. (opposite) A male olive baboon shows his enormously long, sharp canines. Competition between males for mates has led to the evolution of these fear-some weapons. Most baboon males bear scars from bites inflicted by other adult males.

FRIENDS AND ENEMIES

Despite the fact that feeding together might mean competing for the same food, different monkey species sometimes forage in mixed groups. In some cases, these associations are simply accidents—different species just happen to end up in the same tree. They might forage together for a while, but eventually they separate and go their own ways. In other cases, however, mixed groups are deliberate. These groups consist of particular pairs of species that spend up to 90 per cent of their time together and occupy a common home range. For example, pairs of tamarin species often behave in this way in Peru and Brazil, as do colobus and diana monkeys in Africa. The main reason for this seems to be that the larger groups afford better protection from predators.

1. Olive colobus are small and secretive monkeys. They form mixed-species groups with diana monkeys, and males defend their troop against other olive colobus males.

2. Red colobus groups often join together with diana monkey groups in order to gain extra protection against attack by predators.

Tamarins together

The tamarin species that group together feed on much the same types of food, such as fruits, particularly figs, nectar, and gum. This sometimes results in the larger species chasing off the smaller monkeys when access to food is disrupted. The association seems to be driven by the smaller tamarins, who are more vulnerable to attack by harpy eagles. By staying in a large group, where there are more eyes and ears to detect danger, they are less likely to be snatched by an eagle. As well as giving protection, sticking together has foraging benefits—by moving around as a single unit, the tamarins avoid wasted journeys to trees that have already been stripped of fruit.

Tagging along

In the Taï Forest of Ivory Coast in West Africa, red colobus monkeys form mixed groups with the larger and more aggressive diana monkeys—and with good reason. In many places, red colobus are the favorite prey of chimpanzees, and the vigilant diana monkeys are far better at spotting them than are colobus. Not surprisingly, then, it is mainly the colobus who maintain the association—when the dianas move, they follow.

The mixed groups are so important to red colobus that they have a strong influence on how females migrate between groups. Unlike most forest-living monkeys, red colobus females leave home to join new troops when

they reach sexual maturity, but males stay in the groups into which they are born. Migrating females are attracted to troops that defend the best territories, and, as far as females are concerned, the best territories are those that have a resident diana monkey group as well as plenty of food. Ecological competition between the two species is reduced by the fact that colobus are leaf-eaters, while dianas are fruit-eaters.

Keeping a low profile
The very small and secretive olive colobus monkeys of the Taï Forest also depend on diana monkeys for defense. Unlike red colobus, though, olive colobus live in groups of only 10 or so, and they are extremely quiet and shy. Why they live in such small groups is unclear, but it may help them to stay hidden from predators.

As with the red colobus, the need to stay near diana monkeys has a profound influence

on their social system. The main resource that a male red colobus defends against rivals is not food or mates but a group of diana monkeys. A male with a group of diana monkeys is much more attractive to females because his mating partners stand to lose fewer babies to predators.

Scavenging squirrel
Another reason why one species might stick close to another is to pilfer scraps of its food. This is the case with the squirrel monkeys and capuchins of Peru. The powerful jaws of the capuchins make them the only monkeys capable of breaking open the hard outer cases of palm nuts. Squirrel monkeys some-times forage with this species in order to catch bits of palm nut dropped by the feeding capuchins. Even so, the capuchins sometimes irritably chase the squirrel monkeys out of the tree when their attentions become too much to bear.

3. A young olive colobus female grooms a diana monkey. Olive colobus monkeys form mixed-species groups with diana monkeys to increase their protection from predator attack.

TOPIC LINKS

1.1 What is a Primate?
p. 22 Diet and distribution

3.1 Monkey Lifestyles
p. 108 Fruit-eaters, large and small
p. 112 Colobines

3.2 Group Living
p. 132 Contact calls

3.5 Family Portraits: Monkeys
p. 161 Tamarin

4.2 Life in a Dispersed Society
p. 189 Killer apes

1. Here Hanuman langurs are grooming. This activity can occupy a large part of a monkey's time. Some species spend over two hours a day grooming.

SOCIAL GLUE

When a monkey has been denied access to food or has faced aggression from a more dominant animal, a friendly encounter with a grooming partner can be most welcome. First and foremost, grooming helps relieve the stress of competition that builds within groups. This is important because high levels of stress reduce a female's fertility. The stress hormones produced in frightening or unpleasant situations can block the actions of reproductive hormones such as estrogen and progesterone. Without these hormones, females cannot release eggs from their ovaries or sustain pregnancy. Grooming counteracts

this effect by stimulating the release of opium-like substances that suppress the production of stress hormones and neutralize their effects.

Social stress is not just a problem for the low-ranking animals who are the most frequent victims of aggression. Dominance itself promotes stress. It has been observed that dominant female baboons in Gombe National Park in northern Tanzania, the home of Jane Goodall's famous chimpanzee clan, are much more likely to miscarry than low-ranking females, and this reduces the number of healthy offspring they can produce, despite the advantages that high rank brings in terms of access to food. Being dominant is not

necessarily easy for females, since they must strive to maintain their position, and being an aggressor appears to be almost as stressful as being a victim. Consequently, grooming helps females of all ranks. It relieves the "executive stress" of high rankers and soothes the low ranking recipients of aggression.

Grooming tactics

Low ranking females can make life easier for themselves by grooming more dominant animals. By doing so, they make the dominant female less aggressive, reducing the chance that she will attack the groomer in the near future. Grooming may also make a dominant female more willing to tolerate her subordinate near a source of food, enabling the subordinate to feed more easily. The ability to exchange grooming for favors from dominant animals means that high rankers tend to get a lot of grooming. This itself can create competition, as groomers vie for the attention of more dominant females. As a result, the most dominant females tend to be groomed only by other high rankers, and these prevent lower ranking females from gaining access.

Although all females would like to spend their time socializing with high rankers, in reality most end up grooming individuals who are ranked next to them in the social hierarchy. This does not mean that they do not try, however. Females can be adept at seizing opportunities to interact with animals who can provide them with the largest bene-

fit, or who have something that the other females would like to have. When subordinate female longtail macaques were taught how to obtain popcorn from a feeder unit while their higher ranking group mates were kept in ignorance, it was found that the knowledgeable females received significantly more grooming than they had prior to their training. Females were able to recognize that these subordinate females had special skills, and they used grooming as a way of making sure that they could remain close to the skilled individuals when they opened the feeder. A number of monkey species also increase the rate of grooming of new mothers in an effort to get access to the baby.

The high value placed on grooming means that choosing grooming partners judiciously is the most effective route to obtaining desirable

goals. There are some species, however, in which dominant females receive far less grooming than low ranking animals. Capuchin and bonnet macaques both show this pattern of grooming downward in the dominance hierarchy. Why they do it is not clear, but it may be that, in these species, grooming is used primarily as an appeasement gesture to reassure individuals that an animal has no aggressive intentions. Since low ranking animals are the ones in need of this kind of reassurance, dominant females spend more time grooming subordinates.

Grooming relationships are extremely valuable in helping females cope with the stresses and strains of group life, and females make great efforts to maintain these relationships in the face of other demands on their time. For example, when food is scarce and

Monkeys become blissfully relaxed during grooming sessions.

 GROOMING AND ENDORPHINS

When monkeys groom each other, chemicals known as endorphins are released in their brains. Endorphins are similar in their chemical structure to substances such as opium and seem to have much the same effect as these drugs. Monkeys literally get high on grooming. In humans, endorphins are produced in certain stressful situations to kill pain. The pulling and tugging of a monkey's fur during a vigorous grooming session seems to produce a level of mild pain sufficient to trigger endorphin release. Animals become visibly more relaxed during grooming and sometimes space out completely, and appear to be oblivious to their surroundings. Grooming is an activity performed between animals that are generally friendly with each other. A monkey needs to be able to trust its grooming partner if it is to relax so completely in the other's company. All monkeys are compulsive groomers, one could go so far as to say they are addicted, and for this reason, grooming can be used as a valuable currency to enable animals to get what they want. Most of the tactical social ploys used by monkeys in their daily lives involve grooming, and some species spend up to 20 percent of each day engaged in this highly pleasurable activity.

In monkey society, grooming is used as a "currency" to buy favors or access to food.

female baboons are forced to spend longer foraging, they will sacrifice their resting time in order to keep up their grooming commitments. Only when they are down to the absolute minimum of resting time will they cut down on grooming with their partners. Another reflection of the value of grooming relationships, and possibly the need to keep the peace, is the occurrence of "reconciliation." When two animals have a fight, they often engage in friendly behavior soon afterward, as though they are "making up" again. The usual explanation is that grooming relationships are valuable, and females have to make sure that they do not lose a valued partner over a silly fight. However, a more recent suggestion is that reconciliation simply allows animals to signal that the fight is over and they no longer risk attack from the other. Some species use common behaviors, such as grooming, to indicate that they are willing to

be friendly again, but in others there are specific behaviors that signal an end to hostilities. In stump-tailed macaques, for example, one individual will clasp another's bottom in a particular way to let them know that they are ready to make up.

Group size

Competition for food not only effects the social relationships in a group, but it also has a strong influence on the group's size. As a group expands over time, the area the animals must cover to find enough food grows larger, and squabbles over food become more common. Eventually, competition for food becomes unbearable and the monkeys split into two smaller groups. However, these new groups must still be large enough to give the animals protection against predators, so it can take a long time —sometimes years, for a

A squirrel monkey female calling to her "friends."

▶ CONTACT CALLS

Female squirrel monkeys in the forests of South America know how important it is to keep in touch and are one of the most vocal of the monkey species. When they are on the move, their rate of calling depends on the distance between females. The greater the distance and the harder it is for them to keep in visual contact, the higher the rate of calling. The calls females produce on these occasions are high-pitched "peeps," or squeaks. Females start making peeps whenever they lose visual contact with the rest of the group. When other group members hear these calls, they reply in the same manner, guiding the lost individual back to the group. Females also make calls known as "twitters." These signal when the troop should start moving and tell others to follow in the same direction. The final type of call that female squirrel monkeys use is the "chuck." This is not associated with movement, but is a way of maintaining social relationships. Females exchange chucks with their friends, and they chuck more frequently when they lose visual contact. Chucks may be a kind of distress call. Losing visual contact with friends makes the monkeys feel insecure, therefore they increase the rate of calling until they find their friends again and their distress levels drop.

1. Rhesus macaques grooming. When monkeys run out of time to groom all the other monkeys in their group, it can result in the group splitting up into smaller units.

group to finally split.

Grooming plays a role in this splitting process because it is the grooming bonds between animals that hold the group together. Grooming is often referred to as "social glue" for this reason. When groups are small and finding food is easy, animals can groom everyone they want. As a group grows larger, it becomes harder to keep these relationships going. This is partly because animals have to spend more time finding food, and partly because there is an increasing number of animals to groom. As a result, large groups tend to fragment into cliques of animals who all groom each other but spend little time with other group members. As time goes on, the cliques spend less time with each other and travel separately, although they continue to sleep together. Eventually, the combination of feeding competition and grooming-cliques becomes too much, and the group splits along the fault lines between the cliques.

Brain size

A further limit on how large a group of monkeys can become is the size of their brains. Over the course of primate evolution there has been a general increase in brain size, particularly in a structure called the neocortex, the "thinking" part of the brain. The neocortex forms part of the cerebral cortex and makes up the "gray matter" of the brain. It consists of a thin layer of cells that overlies the two cerebral hemispheres. Monkeys that live in larger groups tend to have a bigger neocortex and, therefore, bigger brains. It seems that a large neocortex allows animals to keep track of their many relationships with other members of the group. Living in a group requires a lot of social knowledge. Individuals need to know who is doing what to whom, and how their own actions fit in with this. Knowing exactly who to groom and when can make life much easier for animals and help them to avoid the worst effects of competition. Obviously, in a larger group, an individual needs to keep track of a greater number of relationships. Natural selection therefore favored brainier individuals with the ability to hold all this information in their heads and act on it appropriately. Over the course of evolutionary time, those primates with a tendency to live in larger groups gradually evolved larger brains.

THE MATING GAME

The most important outcome of a monkey's life is producing as many healthy offspring as possible. Males can achieve reproductive success by mating with many females, but competition between males for mates can be intense. Males need all their social skills to get ahead in the mating game. Females, on the other hand, are more concerned with parenting.

Compared to their prosimian cousins, baby monkeys develop slowly. As a result, they are dependent on their mothers for food and protection for a longer period of time. While an infant bushbaby can become a mother herself by the age of nine months, a baby baboon or spider monkey may still be suckling and just beginning to eat solid foods. Raising offspring to adulthood is a lengthy and costly process for female monkeys. Each offspring represents a significant investment of time and energy, and other animals may be called upon to help.

MALES AND MATING

Competition for mates can be intense in monkey society. Because females live in tightly knit groups, males often strive to monopolize a whole group for themselves. The same is not true of the prosimians, however (▷p. 75). Their short breeding seasons, in which all the females become fertile simultaneously, make it impossible for males to monopolize mating opportunities. The breeding cycle of monkeys is much more flexible, with different females becoming fertile at various times. This means a male only has to keep his eye on the females in his troop who are ready to breed. Even among those species that do have breeding seasons, such as vervet monkeys and macaques, the breeding season lasts months, rather than a few days or even hours, as in prosimians.

Seasonal breeders

If the number of females in a group is small, a male has no problem keeping his eye on them. However, as groups get larger, it becomes harder to do this. In species that are seasonal breeders, this can lead to influxes of males from outside the group. This behavior is characteristic of a guenon species, the blue monkeys. Since there is only one male associated with each group of female blue monkeys, there are always a number of lone males in the population. Most of the time, these males appear happy to live alone, since they do not have to compete for food. They avoid predators by moving as silently as possible and remaining concealed in the treetops. However, during the breeding season, the lone males become temporary members of blue monkey groups in order to seek mating opportunities.

 SPOT THE DIFFERENCE

In many monkey species, males and females are different. Males are often much larger than females, sometimes even twice the size. Most males also have enlarged canine teeth, which they keep sharp by grinding them against the other teeth. The sexes may also differ in fur color or length. Male gelada baboons have magnificent capes of long hair around their shoulders, while male black howler monkeys have a glossy black coat, in contrast to the olive-buff coat of the female. Some monkeys have more unusual adornments. The male proboscis monkey has an enormous, pendulous nose shaped like a tongue, while the male mandrill has a bright blue and red muzzle, a neat yellow beard, and a bright blue naked rump. Male vervet monkeys have a red penis and light blue testicles, which they flash at other males in the aptly named "red-white-and-blue display."

The difference between males and females is called sexual dimorphism, and is related to the competition between males for mates. This has led to the evolution of a large body size, teeth to improve their fighting ability, and capes or manes that help males look bigger and intimidate their rivals. Females also play a role in the evolution of sexual dimorphism by. For example, they prefer mates who are more brightly colored, as in mandrills, or those who have the biggest noses, as in proboscis monkeys.

A male vervet monkey reveals his brightly colored genitalia.

There is little the group male can do about this, but in some cases it does not matter because the females may be unwilling to mate with the outsiders. In other cases, females will mate with both the outsiders and the group male. To the group male, the main benefit of staying with his mating partners throughout the season is that it allows him to give his offspring greater protection than the outside males can. This might increase the number of his offspring that survive to adulthood and go on to have offspring of their own.

Rival males

In monkeys that are not seasonal breeders, such as baboons, mangabeys, and some capuchin species, this kind of male influx does not occur. If groups are small, a single male can defend all the females against the attentions of other males because, most of the time, the chances are that there will be only one fertile female to guard. Big groups create more of a problem, however. There may often be several females fertile at the same time, which makes it harder for the male to keep tabs on them. Other males then join the group, since they stand a good chance of mating. They tend to remain with the group permanently because different females come in and out of their fertile periods unpredictably. Males could miss many chances to mate if they employed a blue monkey-style strategy, which involves staying solitary for most of the time. The upshot of all this is that, when there are more than 10 or so females in groups of non-seasonal breeders, there will always be more than one male present, although females still always outnumber the

1. Hanuman langurs huddle together at a sleeping cliff. They commonly live in small groups containing a few females and a single adult male.

males by approximately two to one.

In ground-living monkeys, such as baboons, Japanese macaques, and some Hanuman langurs, males have another good reason to live in groups. It is too dangerous to live alone. In areas where predators are common, the number of males in monkey groups tends to be higher. It seems that males are sometimes prepared to put safety first, above mating.

Female loyalty

In small multi-male monkey groups, males fight for the right to mate with the entire group of females. In larger groups, they fight over particular females as they become fertile. In the former case, males often have battles over the ownership of the troop, and sustain horrific wounds. Bites, lacerations, broken bones, and cracked teeth are the inevitable result of these ownership contests.

In gelada baboons, which individual gains dominance can depend more on who the females decide to back than on the males' fighting ability. Geladas live in the highlands of Ethiopia and feed mainly on grass. Although they often form herds of up to 400, they are made up of a number of one-male units, each consisting of a male, plus around five or six adult females and their offspring. As a unit grows in size, the male may find himself with a loyalty problem. He does not have enough time to groom all the females, and the unit's dominant females tend to monopolize his attention. As a result, the low-ranking females in the unit are neglected and show increasing interest in outside males.

In some cases, a male known as a follower will form a grooming relationship with one or two of these neglected females and join the unit permanently. These follower males tend to be youngsters who lack the power to fight

with the dominant male and take over the unit. The follower and his females live peacefully within the unit and may eventually break off to form a new unit of their own. However, sometimes, the dominant male faces a challenge from a powerful older male. This is the time when female loyalty becomes critical since the new male can take over only if the females are willing to accept him. This is true even if the new male defeats the old one in a fight. If the established male has a strong grooming relationship with all his females, then their loyalty to him is more or less assured and the challenger will fail. However, if the established male has not been grooming all his females, they might defect to the new male, and the old male will be deposed. If this happens, he might be forced to leave the unit entirely – although in some cases an overthrown male sometimes remains as a follower, maintaining a relationship with a few females.

SEXUAL SWELLINGS

In order to signal that they are ready to mate, the females of a number of monkey species develop swellings on their rear ends. In some, this can be slight. In most species, however, the females develop a conspicuous, brightly colored swelling of the area around the sexual organs. The size of the swelling is controlled by the female sex hormones. It increases in size as the female approaches the time in her cycle when she is due to ovulate, reaching its peak at the point when the egg is released and she is at her most fertile. The reason for sexual swellings is still not fully understood. They probably relate to a female's desire for a good-quality mate and a safe upbringing for her offspring.

Fighting for favors

Among the reasons to explain sexual swellings is that females signal their fertility to incite male competition and ensure that they get a good-quality father for their offspring. If males are forced to fight over fertile females, only the best, most powerful males will triumph and be allowed to mate. This way females can take advantage of the male tendency to compete without too much effort on their part. This strategy seems to work well. In multi-male groups, subordinate males tend to mate with females in the early stages of swelling because dominant males show little interest at that point. However, as the peak of fertility approaches and females are most likely to get pregnant, dominant males assert themselves and tend to monopolize the females.

Who's the father?

A related reason why females might want to advertise their fertility is that it helps reduce the risk of infanticide. If all the males know that a female is fertile, and they all make sure to mate with her at some point while she is swollen, it becomes hard for a male to know exactly who has fathered a particular infant. This means that a male cannot risk killing an infant in order to speed up the rate at which a female becomes ready to mate again because he cannot be sure that he will not be killing his own offspring.

Fertility differences

It has also been suggested that female swellings are signals of quality, which males can use to find the best mate available. The size and color of a female's swelling might indicate how fertile she is and how likely she is to become pregnant. Young female

1

baboons, for example, tend to be much less fertile than older females. They go through a period of so-called "adolescent sterility" before they actually begin ovulating, and usually show swellings that are much smaller and darker in color than those of mature females. Adult males tend to ignore these females, who are mated only by smaller, juvenile males.

Other signs

Not all females indicate their fertility by swellings on their bottoms. For example, gelada baboon females, spend most of their time sitting down eating grass, therefore a sexual signal on their rear end would not be useful. Instead, female gelada have a number of small, fluid-filled vesicles or blisters, on their chests. These swell up and become brightly colored when the female is fertile, and signal her state in the same way as the perineal swellings of other species.

2

1. Male baboons engage in "consortships" with fertile females. During consortships, they have exclusive mating access to the female. In order to keep the female close by, males spend time grooming their consort partners.

2. The vesicles, or blisters, on the chests of female gelada baboons swell every month to signal their fertility to males. They also have vesicles on their bottoms, but since they spend most of their time sitting down, the chest blisters are the most visible, and therefore the most important, signal to males.

Male olive baboons use similar tactics to the gelada "followers" to ingratiate themselves with the members of a new troop. When male olive baboons reach sexual maturity, they leave their home troop and migrate to a new one, a practice that is thought to help prevent inbreeding. Young males arriving at a new troop are at a disadvantage. They do not know anyone, and the other animals are wary of them. Males therefore use their social skills to integrate themselves. A new male will remain on the periphery of the troop and make friendly overtures to one of the females. This gradually blossoms into a full-blown grooming relationship. This special friendship eventually allows the male to become an accepted member of the troop since it gives him the opportunity to interact with the female's friends. He may also gain mating opportunities since females sometimes prefer to mate with new males. The more socially skilled a male is, the smoother the process of integration. If males are too aggressive, females will avoid them both as friends and mating partners. Aggression may be a useful tactic when males compete with each other, but not when females are unwilling to accept them. For a male, success in the mating game therefore relies on a mixture of strength and subtle social skills.

1. All baboon infants are attracted to adult males, following them around and feeding on the scraps they leave behind.

2. Gelada males have to make sure they stay on the right side of the females in their harem. Their "loyalty" is essential if they are to prevent another male from taking over.

MONKEY MOTHERS

Mating is only half the story. While it is the most important concern for males, for females bringing up the babies is the main concern. Monkey infants are well developed at birth. Their eyes are open and they can cling tightly to their mothers' fur. Nevertheless, they are completely dependent on their mothers for food, and are uncoordinated and weak for the first month or so of life. Even once they have started moving around and feeding themselves, they are far from independent. Young monkeys rely heavily on their mothers until they are 12 to 18 months old. Prosimians, on the other hand, have often become parents by this age. Monkey mothers therefore have a full-time job on their hands. Like all working mothers, they have a tough time juggling the demands of their daily tasks and their infants.

Costs of motherhood

Female monkeys do not store fat, therefore they must increase the amount they eat to fuel milk production when offspring are born. However, finding time to obtain sufficient food can be a problem. New infants are a source of great interest to monkeys, and new mothers are often besieged by other animals that want to hold and play with the baby. As well as the attention directed toward the infants, new mothers receive much more grooming than normal. In female chacma baboons, this increased grooming is used to buy access to the baby since new baboon mothers are normally reluctant to let others handle their offspring. Unfortunately, all the extra attention comes at a time a female's need for food is greatest. The constant interruptions mean that new mothers cannot feed properly and often lose weight. To conserve precious calories, they spend as much time as possible resting.

★ Male squirrel monkey males put on a lot of weight just prior to the breeding season. This "fatted" condition helps them get through the exhausting period of mating and competition.

3. Here is a douc langur with infant. Langur females are very relaxed about allowing other females to handle and watch their infants. This might save them some energy and help reduce the costs of milk production.

4. Olive baboon females inspect the troop's latest arrival. Newborn infants are a source of great interest to all the other monkeys in a troop.

Aunts and babysitters

Some monkeys are more relaxed about their infants than baboons and have no qualms about letting others handle them. The offspring of vervet monkeys, colobus monkeys, and many of the Asian langur monkeys spend most of their early life being looked after by females other than the mother, a practice known as aunting. In these species, young females may use aunting to gain experience, which may help them be good mothers themselves when the time comes. The mother seems to benefits from babysitting since she saves energy that would otherwise be spent on carrying the infant. This energy saving probably leads to females producing their next offspring sooner than in species that do not allow aunting.

However, the champion delegators of motherhood responsibilities the marmosets and tamarins of South and Central America. These species give birth to twins, and the combined weight of the litter can be as much as 25 percent of the mother's body weight. This is quite a load for a female to carry, especially when most of her energy has to go into milk production. As a result, the female places all the responsibility for carrying offspring on to other members of the group, principally the babies' father. He hands the babies over to the mother to be fed, but other than that, they spend most of their time with him, or with another group member. In general, the other helpers tend to be related to the babies, older offspring helping to raise their young brothers and sisters. However, in some cases, unrelated male

2. Baboon infants spend the first weeks of life hanging upside down, clamped to their mothers' chests. By the age of 4 to 5 months, they have graduated to riding jockey-style on her back, where the view is much better.

3. Dominant females often remove infants from their mothers by force. The mother can do nothing except wait for the dominant female to get bored and let the infant go, hopefully unharmed.

1. By the age of 2 to 3 months, baboon infants begin to spend time away from their mothers and explore the world around them.

⭐ Proboscis monkey babies are born with bright blue faces. The color gradually fades over the first few months of the infant's life.

marmosets have been seen carrying infants find helping care for the young. While devoting time and energy to baby care may be the price they pay for staying in the group, it might also increase their chances of mating with the female when she is next ready to breed. Perhaps these males help out with raising unrelated offspring because it increases their chance of being the father next time around.

Since bringing up infants requires such a large group effort, the dominant female marmoset suppresses reproduction among the other females in the group. This makes sure that there is only one set of twins, hers, that needs looking after. It also means that everyone is free to help. The dominant female achieves this by producing pheromones in her genital scent glands and placing this special scent on tree trunks, branches, and even on

other females (▷p. 68). The pheromones disrupt the production of reproductive hormones in subordinate females and make them infertile. Since they are them unable to reproduce, the next best thing for subordinate females to do is help raise the dominant female's offspring. Since all the females are related, subordinate females will be helping to raise their siblings, nieces, or nephews, so at least they have some family interest in ensuring the offspring are raised successfully.

Clearing the way

As with the prosimians, monkey mothers are often at risk from infanticide by males keen to begin their reproductive careers (▷p. 81). Such behavior has been observed in many species, including baboons, blue monkeys, De Brazza's monkeys, and howlers. However, the

▶ TEMPER TANTRUMS

The sight of a young monkey having a temper tantrum is common in monkey groups. In some cases, tantrums happen because females are attempting to wean their offspring off milk and encouraging them to feed for themselves. Sometimes, however, tantrums have more to do with when infants are allowed to suckle rather than the amount of milk that the mother will let them have. During the first few months of life, infant monkeys cling tightly to their mothers' chests and suckle almost continuously. Since they are small and do not move much, the mother can continue with her own feeding uninterrupted. As infants grow larger and more active, suckling becomes a hindrance. The mother has to reach around the infant to feed herself, and this impedes movement and slows her down. Eating plenty is important for females who are breastfeeding and they need to keep their energy up. If the infant starts to get in the way she will push it away and refuse to let it suckle. At first, infants cannot understand what is happening and they throw tantrums in protest. However, after a few days, the infant gradually learns that the mother is not really rejecting it, but merely training it to suckle only when the mother is resting or grooming when the infant will not be in the way.

1. Tamarin females give birth to twins. In order to reduce the burden on the female, the father of the infants carries them, handing them over to the female only when they need feeding.

most notorious infant-killers, are the Hanuman langurs of India. These live in both one-male groups and multi-male groups, depending on the part of India they inhabit. In areas where one-male groups predominate, take-over fights are common and there is a high turnover of males within a group. Males generally last only a year or so as the head of a unit. Since a male's tenure within a one-male unit is short, infanticide makes good sense in order to bring females back into a fertile reproductive state.

Females with young infants are infertile because the suckling of their offspring inhibits the production of the hormones that cause the release of eggs from the females' ovaries. Once infants are weaned from their mothers, the inhibition stops and females are able to become pregnant again. In the normal course of events, this can take as long as 18 months to two years. For a male, who has only a year or so as head of a unit, this is too long to wait. The only way he can ensure that he will get the opportunity to father his own offspring is to kill any unrelated infants who are around at the time of his takeover hasten the mothers' return to fertility. however, females, have other ideas, and they often gang up and try to protect vulnerable infants. They are often able to keep aggressive males at bay for a few weeks or so, but the males are exceedingly persistent. The stakes are too high for them, and they refuse to give in and allow another male's offspring to survive. Even with all the female protectors, most infants eventually succumb, leaving their mothers with no choice but to mate with the dominant male in their group. This in turn helps recoup some of their reproductive losses.

2. Infanticide is very common among Hanuman langurs. It usually takes place when a new male deposes a resident male and takes over a group of females.

A silver-leaf monkey baby is paler than its mother.

 COLORFUL BABIES

Newborn monkeys often have bald faces and fur of a completely different color from that of adults. These "natal coats" differ widely between species and take about nine months to a year to acquire the normal adult color. While baboons are born with jet-black coats and bright pink faces and ears, dusky leaf monkeys bear infants whose delicate apricot color contrasts markedly with their mothers' brown coats. Banded leaf monkey babies are white with a dark stripe all the way down the back, and show up conspicuously against the orange of the adult coat. Stump-tailed macaques are also white at birth and gradually turn dark brown.

It is not certain why such dramatic differences in coloring occur. Perhaps the natal colors of the young act as a signal to trigger protective feelings in the adults so that they handle the infants gently during this vulnerable period of life. This theory would explain why the most striking differences in coat color are found among Asian leaf monkeys, where newborns are handled by every female in the group from the first day of life.

Overleaf: Female Hanuman langurs groom each other, while their offspring stick close by. Female langurs often gang up against infanticidal males in an effort to protect their infants. In most cases, however, the males succeed, despite the females' best efforts.

3.4 A UNIQUE INTELLIGENCE

The quick movements, bright-eyed expressions, and inquisitive nature of monkeys suggest they are highly intelligent creatures. While it is true that they have larger brains than most other mammals, the intelligence that monkeys possess is not an all-purpose kind of cleverness. The primate brain increased in size as a way of coping with the unique challenges posed by group living. Because of this adaptation, monkeys have methods of solving the types of problems that regularly crop up in the social world, such as making friends and avoiding enemies.

Social life requires brainpower because it is dynamic and fast changing. Individuals have to make quick decisions about how to act based on other group members' decisions, which may change without warning. Fast thinking is needed to keep up with the constant changes that occur in the life of a troop, but, more importantly, to stay one step ahead.

KNOWING WHO'S WHO

Getting by in a monkey group is a matter of who you know, not just what you know. A monkey group changes constantly as individuals come and go and move up or down the social hierarchy. Keeping up with who is around and knowing their rank is extremely important. Decisions about who to groom or fight may change daily because of unforeseen changes in the social setup. Most of a monkey's everyday life is, therefore, spent plotting and planning what to do, when to do it, and with whom. Staying on top of all this requires a well-developed brain and the ability to recognize not just who everyone is but also how they relate to everyone else.

Recognizing rank

The ability to recognize dominant relationships between other individuals without reference to oneself is the major difference between monkeys and other mammals, including prosimians. While many mammals can recognize who is a higher or lower rank than they are, only monkeys and apes can take this one step further and figure out the hierarchy between others and the implications of such relationships.

Scientists know that baboons can recognize rank relationships between others thanks to experiments in which baboon calls were recorded and played back to other members of the group. Adult females spent longer looking toward a loudspeaker when they heard something implausible, such as a high ranking female making a submissive grunt to a low ranker, than when they heard something plausible, such as a low ranker grunting to a high ranker. Looking at the loudspeaker for longer suggests that these baboons were puzzled by what they heard, and therefore that they recognized the individuals involved and understood the relationship between them.

Male bonnet macaques use their knowledge of rank relationships to form coalitions. During a fight, a male often needs the help of another male in order to defeat his opponent. Fighting males preferentially solicit help from the males who are higher ranking than themselves and their opponents because high-ranking allies increase their chance of winning. This shows that macaques not only know their own rank relative to other group members, they also know how other males rank in relation to each other.

Female bonnet macaques are just as canny. When two females are grooming, a dominant female may break up the pair in order to be groomed by one of them herself. Usually, the most subordinate female is the one to leave, but sometimes she stays put and her partner

1. A Japanese macaque male walks toward a human observer with the aim of checking her pockets for peanuts. All eyes are upon him as he approaches with the arrogant, bouncy walk of a high-ranking male. The animals in his path look wary and prepare to move out of the way.

1. Long-tail macaques are able to recognize the mother–offspring bond that exists between animals, even once offspring are adult themselves and no longer spend all their time in contact with their mothers.

leaves upon seeing the dominant female approach. This happens if the low-ranking female is more socially attractive, that is, if she spends a lot of time grooming and interacting in a friendly way with many other females. Each female must therefore be able to recognize not only rank relations between individuals, but also relative levels of social attractiveness. They can judge which grooming partner an approaching female is likely to prefer on the basis of these two different types of relationship.

Recognizing relationships

Monkeys not only recognize relationships based on rank or social attractiveness, they also recognize the mother–offspring relationships in their group. In an experiment on captive longtail macaques, females were shown photographs of mother–infant pairs in their group, mixed in with photographs of other familiar but unrelated pairs. The monkeys were able to distinguish which photographs showed mother–infant pairs, even when these included mothers with their adult offspring. Therefore, like human beings, longtail macaques seem to understand the relationship between mothers and their offspring as one that persists into adulthood, although the concept may not be identical to ours. In fact, it cannot be exactly the same because our concept of the mother–offspring bond relies on verbal language, which monkeys do not have. Nevertheless, the macaques' non-verbal representation of the mother–offspring bond does seem to correspond closely to our own.

 DOING THEIR MATH HOMEWORK

Monkeys are good not only at assessing social situations but also at counting. In an experiment, rhesus macaques were shown an eggplant being placed on the stage of a toy theater. A curtain was then drawn across, and either the eggplant was left as it was or another eggplant was secretly placed alongside it. When the curtain was drawn back, the monkeys spent longer looking at the stage if a second eggplant had been added. This suggested that the monkeys had some understanding of numbers. They were surprised to see two eggplants when there only should have been one. To test whether the monkeys could really tell the difference between one and two or just the differences in number, the experiment was performed again. This time, after the first showing, the single eggplant was either retained or replaced by one of roughly double the size. When these were both revealed, the monkeys looked at the different-sized eggplants for roughly the same amount of time. The monkeys who saw the double-sized eggplant did not seem to realize that anything had happened, since the number of objects remained the same. In other words, monkeys appear to be sensitive to the number of objects present, although other experiments suggest that the limit to this number is three.

Vervet monkeys also seem able to recognize mother–offspring relationships. When a recording of a screaming youngster was played to its mother and some other females, the mother looked intently toward the noise. However, the other females looked not toward the noise, but at the mother. This suggests that they recognized both the identity of the infant and its relationship with the female they were sitting next to.

Respecting bonds

Hamadryas baboons have been found to recognize a certain subtle kind of relationship that occurs between males and females. These baboons live in one-male groups, and the females often spend long periods grooming the group male. Other males recognize and "respect" these relationships. If a male sees another male and female grooming and socializing in a friendly way, he will not attempt to interact with the female, even if he subsequently gets the chance. However, if he sees the male and female together but not behaving in a friendly way, he will attempt to interact with and groom the female himself when given the chance.

Savanna baboons show no such restraint. Instead, they do their best to disrupt the bond between a consorting couple in the hope of gaining access to the female themselves. Indeed, males will often join forces to achieve this. Only relatively brainy species, such as baboons and macaques, engage in this kind of complex out manuevering of their competitors. Most males species rely mainly on brute force.

2. Female hamadryas focus all their social attention on the harem male. Other males who see this behavior "respect" the relationship and do not attempt to interact with the female themselves.

During a fight, vervet monkeys often redirect aggression onto un-involved third parties.

 TRIPARTITE RELATIONSHIPS

Recognizing the different kinds of relationships that exist in a social group is the mental ability that distinguishes monkeys from other mammals. This ability evolved not only to help monkeys form harmonious friendships with the other members of their close-knit groups, but also evolved to help them defeat their enemies. Many species use their knowledge of relationships to get at enemies that they cannot attack directly. Instead of fighting with their adversary, they redirect their aggression onto an innocent third party. For instance, rhesus macaques, baboons, and vervet monkeys frequently attack animals who are close relatives or friends of their enemies. In vervet monkeys, these family feuds go one stage further. A female vervet will often threaten another female simply because the relatives of each have been involved in a recent fight. Only monkeys more than three years old have been seen to do this, suggesting that young monkeys are not yet attuned to how revenge can be achieved indirectly, by exploiting the associations within this group, as well as directly.

CROP RAIDERS AND HARVEST HELPERS

The qualities of inquisitiveness and intelligence that have helped the monkeys achieve such a high level of ecological success can, on some occasions, lead to problems. In many areas of Africa, Asia, and South America, monkeys are significant pests. They wreck the carefully planted crops of subsistence farmers, raid the garbage cans on nature reserves, and have even been known to get into people's houses and help themselves to the contents of their cupboards. However, certain species have found ways to cooperate with humans so that both benefit.

1. Many macaque species thrive in urban environments. They often reach their highest densities in such habitats and can become pests.

2. Barbary macaque infants attempting to break through a fence. Often the rewards of finding human food are so great that monkeys will spend lots of time and effort trying to get access, despite attempts to keep them away.

Fast food

In many places, elaborate means of trying to exclude primates from human areas have been adopted. In the Kruger National Park in South Africa, for example, the tourist camps are surrounded by tall, electric fences. Unfortunately, the rich pickings inside the camps are so tempting that the baboons are actually willing to be shocked in order to get their hands on people's lunch boxes. From their perspective, this makes perfect sense. One slice of bread from a tourist's bag or a couple of yams from a farmer's garden can supply all their daily energy requirements. They would need to spend hours foraging on natural foods to acquire the amount of energy contained in a single banana.

Of course, tourists could help alleviate the problem of animals as pests through their own behavior. They could be more careful in the way they store food, making sure that doors and windows are firmly locked. Most importantly, they could resist the temptation to feed wild monkeys. Feeding gives the animals a taste for human food and encourages them to steal it whenever they get the chance. It is unfair to blame monkeys when they raid tourist tents or vacation lodges, when it is humans who put the idea into their heads in the first place.

Crop-raiding

Attacking crops is a different matter. Subsistence farmers do everything they can to discourage monkeys from coming onto their land and destroying crops. However, monkeys are clever and can quickly work out how to overcome the fences and other deterrents designed to keep them away. In light of this, there is often no alternative but to shoot the animals as pests. Part of the farmers' annoyance at the loss of valuable

crops springs from the fact that monkeys are wasteful feeders. Even in the wild, they might take only one or two bites out of a particular fruit before discarding it and moving onto the next one. Contrary to popular opinion, though, the monkeys are not being destructive merely for the sake of it, they are just bringing their natural habits into an unnatural setting.

Helping humans

However, some humans manage to have a more mutually beneficial relationship with monkeys. In some areas of Malaysia, for example, people have trained macaques to harvest coconuts from tall palms. The trainer sends the monkey up to the crown of the tree and it then throws down all the fruit it finds at the top. Since monkeys are much more agile than humans, harvesting fruit and nuts in this way is more efficient than if humans did the job all by themselves.

Capuchin monkeys, an intelligent South American species, have also been able to make themselves useful to humans. These small, agile monkeys are sometimes trained to help people who are paralyzed and confined to wheelchairs. They are able to pick up and carry objects, and can even "answer" the telephone, by bringing the handset to their owners.

3. A macaque harvests coconuts for its human owner. Although the monkey is well trained and does its owner's bidding, it has to be chained to prevent it from running off with the spoils.

4. Baboons are particularly adept at raiding crops and tourist sites, and their large size means that humans are often afraid to chase them off.

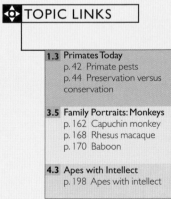

TOPIC LINKS

1.3 Primates Today
p. 42 Primate pests
p. 44 Preservation versus conservation

3.5 Family Portraits: Monkeys
p. 162 Capuchin monkey
p. 168 Rhesus macaque
p. 170 Baboon

4.3 Apes with Intellect
p. 198 Apes with intellect

LIMITS TO INTELLIGENCE

Although monkeys are good at recognizing relationships and responding to the behavior of others, they lag far behind humans in their mental abilities. Unlike humans, who realize it is possible to effect the thoughts and the actions of others, monkeys do not seem to realize that other individuals even have thoughts. Monkeys lack a "theory of mind," meaning they do not understand that others might have knowledge about the world that differs from their own. Put simply, this means that they are unable to understand another individual perspective when confronted with a situation in which the information available is not the same. For example, a vervet mother who is in a safe position does not warn her offspring of danger when she can see it and her offspring cannot. She seems unable to imagine a position other than the one she experiences.

Monkey see, monkey do?

In a similar way, monkeys do not understand that seeing is knowing. In an experiment in which a captive monkey watched food being

 Monkeys are able to count up only to three. They do not recognize any difference between bigger numbers of objects.

Olive baboon males in Kenya sometimes hunt gazelle kids. The meat is highly prized and everyone wants a share. Baboons do not share meat, so other animals have to resort to cunning tactics to get some.

1. (opposite) Baboon infants attract a lot of attention when they are first born. New mothers receive much more grooming than usual as other animals attempt to get close to the baby.

▷ TRUE DECEPTION?

Many observations of monkey behavior have been presented as evidence that monkeys use their enlarged brains and well-developed social skills to deceive their group mates to their own advantage. Consider this anecdote: a female baboon with a taste for meat sees that one of the adult males in her troop has caught a small gazelle calf. Since the male is one who is unlikely to give any of his carcass to another member of the troop, the female sidles up to him and begins grooming. Gradually, the male relaxes until he finally lolls back under the female's caresses. Instantly, the female snatches the carcass from the snoozing male and runs off with her prize.

But what is really happening here? Admittedly, it is tempting to conclude that the female baboon was grooming the male only to lull him into a false sense of security and get her hands on the meat. In reality, however, her true goal may have been to get as close as she could to the carcass, and grooming may have been the only way to get the male to tolerate her. When he fell asleep, he fortuitously presented the female with the chance to grab some meat. This might seem a "killjoy" explanation, but when dealing with issues such as deception, which involve intentions and other mental phenomena that are by their nature unobservable – we must be careful not to bring our intuitions about our own ways of thinking to bear. In most cases of so-called monkey deception, an explanation like the one above that avoids attributing any actual deception to monkeys provides an equally plausible account of their behavior. Most scientists now agree it is unlikely that monkeys actually intend to deceive their group mates.

1. Capuchin monkeys can be trained to use "tools" in captivity. They are adept at doing so, but it seems that they do not have a real understanding of how or why a tool works.

2. Baboons are very fond of birds' eggs, and ostrich eggs are, literally, the biggest treat of all. Despite their intelligence, chacma baboons do not understand how to crack an egg. They do so only by accident.

hidden in one of several boxes in full view of the human trainer, the monkey showed no understanding that the trainer knew where the food was hidden. Given a choice, the monkey was as likely to pick an ignorant trainer as a knowledgeable one to open one of the boxes and find the food.

Monkeys also lack the ability to recognize themselves in mirrors in the way that humans and chimpanzees can (▷p. 200), which suggests they lack a critical mental faculty that we take for granted, self-awareness. Instead, they always behave as though they are looking at another monkey. However, perhaps this is not solely due to their lower intelligence. To look another monkey in the eye is a threatening gesture, and this is exactly what monkeys see when they look in mirrors. Perhaps they fail to learn more about mirrors

and reflections because they are reluctant to continue exposing themselves to the threat of the "other" animal.

Although the ability to manipulate the thoughts of others is second nature to humans, and most of us could not imagine what life would be like without this ability, monkeys seem able to get by very well without appreciating that other animals also have thoughts. Instead, they pay a lot of attention to the social clues that other monkeys show in their behavior. These clues enable monkeys to predict what other animals are likely to do in a particular situation, without really understanding the thought processes that the animals are going through. In other words, monkeys are not good psychologists, but they are good students of animal behavior.

FOOD FOR THOUGHT

Although monkey intelligence is geared to coping with the social world, some species put their brainpower to other uses too. One such species is the capuchin monkey, the smartest of the New World monkeys. Capuchins are noted for the innovative techniques they use to find food. In the wild, they crack nuts by bashing them against tree trunks, and are destructive foragers, pulling apart birds' nests and ripping up dead bark to find insects. In captivity, they will readily use a wide variety of tools to get at food hidden in ingenious ways by their keepers.

Silly mistakes

Despite their ingenuity, capuchins are not as clever as they might first appear. One captive group was shown how to use sticks to push food out of a tube. The monkeys proved to be good at this task, but when presented with other tools to solve the same problem, their response revealed how little they really understood about what they were doing. Given a piece of string, the monkeys tried to use it like a stick to push the food out. They did not seem to realize that if a tool was going to be effective at poking, then it should be rigid. Next, they were given two short sticks. To reach the food, these had to be inserted one after the other into the same end of the tube. Again, the monkeys could not understand how to use the tools, and inserted one stick into each end of the tube. Eventually they hit upon the solution by accident, but they were unable to repeat their performance without irrelevant and counterproductive steps that slowed down their success.

South African chacma baboons show similarly "stupid" behavior when trying to open ostrich eggs. Baboons are fond of these nutritious treats and will raid ostrich nests when-ever they come across them. They appear to know that they need to drop an egg to break it, but not that the egg needs to hit something hard. Chacma baboons will sit for up to half an hour in an ostrich nest, repeatedly picking up and dropping an egg to no avail. Occasionally, the egg will hit another and crack open, it is then greedily devoured. However, the baboons do not learn how to repeat the trick, and return to another prolonged bout of picking up and dropping until the next egg breaks fortuitously.

Smart moves

Other monkey species have occasionally shown flashes of brilliance, however. Japanese macaques were shown how to retrieve pieces of apple from a hollow pipe by throwing stones through it to knock the apple out. The macaques picked up this technique easily and went on to invent their own technique of poking sticks into the tube. One female excelled by hitting on an even more ingenious method of retrieving the apple. She would find her infant, carry it to the tube and unceremoniously shove it into the pipe. When the baby grabbed the apple, the mother would yank it out and take the piece of apple away from the baby. Several other females picked up the shove-a-baby-through-the-pipe trick, but they tended to use any infant who happened to be handy. It was only the first, inventive female who singled out her own baby for the task.

Potato washing

Japanese macaques are well known for their innovative ways with food. A famous example is potato washing. In the 1950s, Japanese researchers fed sweet potatoes to a group of wild macaques to lure them onto a beach, where they were easier to observe. A young,

3. A white-faced capuchin monkey. Capuchins are the smartest of the South American monkeys. They have found ways to open hard-shelled nuts that defeat other species.

18-month-old female called Imo took her potato to the sea and washed off the sand before eating it. This behavior gradually caught on with other members of the troop, and soon most of them were washing their potatoes. At first, it was thought the other monkeys were copying Imo and that potato washing was a kind of cultural behavior, in much the same way that cooking with olive oil has become popular among humans. However, it soon became clear that the other animals were not really copying Imo, they were just following her to the water. Once there, they discovered the benefits of potato washing for themselves by accident. The fact that the potatoes were less gritty and therefore tasted better was enough to reinforce the behavior and encourage the monkeys to continue it.

Potato washing only really caught on among the juveniles. Five years after Imo started, 80 percent of troop members between two and seven years old were washing their potatoes, but only two of the 11 adult females were doing so. This changed over time, however. When the potato washers grew up, they passed the technique on to their own offspring, and the habit became increasingly common from then on.

There is no doubt that Imo was a very smart young macaque. When she was four, she invented another way of making life easier for herself. As well as giving the monkeys potatoes, the Japanese researchers had started giving them wheat grains. These took a long time to pick out of the sand, so the monkeys had to spend an even longer time on the beach. Imo was having none of this, however, and one day took a handful of sand and wheat and threw it in a small brook that ran by the beach. The heavy sand sank but the wheat floated, making it possible for Imo to pick the clean wheat grains from the water quickly and easily.

This technique, known as "placer mining," never caught on as much as potato washing. After five years, only 12 other monkeys were doing it. "Placer mining" may be harder to learn since it requires a more complex understanding of the relationship between objects. Washing a potato is simply a matter of holding a potato and dipping it in water – even the most naïve monkey could learn how to do this. "Placer-mining," on the other hand, requires that an animal "throws away" its food before being able to retrieve it. This makes the technique difficult to learn because animals are, understandably, reluctant to let food out of their clutches once they have got hold of it. Perhaps only the very brightest animals could understand that the reward for throwing their food away was greater than for resolutely hanging on to it.

1. Imo, a young Japanese macaque, invented potato washing. This technique was soon being used by others.

2. Researchers believe that other monkeys learned potato washing by trial and error rather than from copying Imo.

FAMILY PORTRAITS: MONKEYS

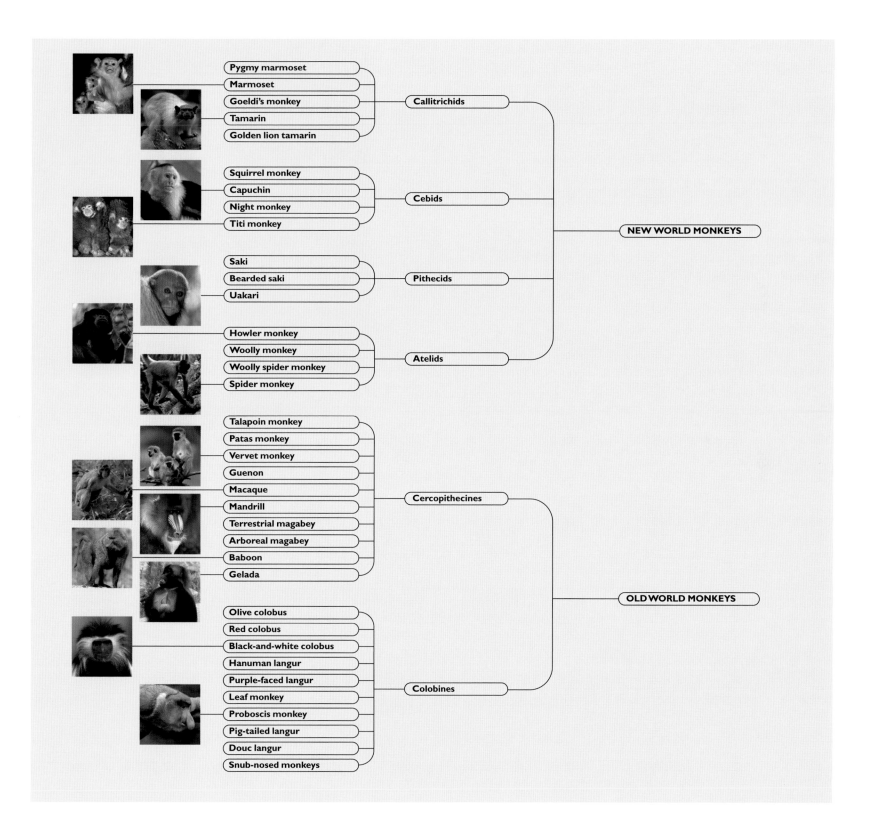

Pygmy marmoset
Marmoset
Goeldi's monkey
Tamarin
Golden lion tamarin
— Callitrichids

Squirrel monkey
Capuchin
Night monkey
Titi monkey
— Cebids

Saki
Bearded saki
Uakari
— Pithecids

Howler monkey
Woolly monkey
Woolly spider monkey
Spider monkey
— Atelids

NEW WORLD MONKEYS

Talapoin monkey
Patas monkey
Vervet monkey
Guenon
Macaque
Mandrill
Terrestrial magabey
Arboreal magabey
Baboon
Gelada
— Cercopithecines

Olive colobus
Red colobus
Black-and-white colobus
Hanuman langur
Purple-faced langur
Leaf monkey
Proboscis monkey
Pig-tailed langur
Douc langur
Snub-nosed monkeys
— Colobines

OLD WORLD MONKEYS

MARMOSET

Marmosets are the smallest of the South American monkeys, with the pygmy marmoset being the smallest monkey of all, weighing a mere 3.3 oz (100 g). They are generally brightly colored and can appear very birdlike in their movements and vocalizations. Marmosets are specialized for feeding on the gum produced by trees. They have very large, chisel-shaped incisors—like those of rodents—which they use to gouge holes in bark and allow gum, sap, and resin to flow out. They also have claws instead of nails (except on their big toes), which helps them to cling to tree trunks more effectively.

Unlike most other monkey species, marmoset males and females do not differ either in size or coloration. They live in small family groups and give birth to twin offspring. The male carries the babies for most of the time, handing them over to the mother only when they need to be fed.

Silvery marmoset and twins. Females marmosets give birth to twins, but males do most of the carrying so that the females can save their energy for milk production.

TOPIC LINKS

WHERE IN THE WORLD?

Marmosets are small South American monkeys. They are common throughout much of Brazil and Amazonia.

FACT FILE

Distribution	South America (throughout Brazil and Amazonia)
Species	Silvery marmoset (*Callithrix argentata*) Tassel-eared marmoset (*Callithrix humeralifer*) Common marmoset (*Callithrix jacchus*) Buffy tufted-ear marmoset (*Callithrix aurita*) Buffy-headed marmoset (*Callithrix flaviceps*) White-faced marmoset (*Callithrix geoffroyi*) Black tufted-ear marmoset (*Callithrix pencillata*) Pygmy marmoset (*Cebuella pygmaea*) Goeldiís monkey (*Callimico goeldii*)
Body weight	Females: 3.3–10 oz (100–300 g) Males: 3.3–10 oz (100–300 g)
Activity pattern	Tree-living; day-active (diurnal)
Habitat type	First litter at 12–24 months, then every 6 months; two offspring per litter (except for Goeldiís monkey—single offspring)
Reproduction	First litter at around age 21 months; one offspring per litter
Average group size	2–13
Grouping type	Family groups of male and female plus offspring; may also include a number of adult "helpers"
Maximum lifespan	12–13 years
Conservation status	Several species endangered by widespread habitat destruction

TAMARIN

All tamarins have a striking appearance, with bright fur, crests, and manes. This ochraceous bare-faced tamarin is found in Amazonia, Brazil.

Tamarins are among the smallest of the New World (South American) monkeys. They are brightly colored, with a variety of crests, manes and moustaches; there is little difference between the sexes in either size or coloration. Tamarins feed on insects, fruit, and gum and are able to exploit marginal or disturbed habitats. Tamarin females give birth to twin offspring, and males play a significant role in caring for the young—primarily by carrying them around. Without this help, it is unlikely that females could cope with the extra energy demands of lactation.

Tamarins show flexible patterns of social organization. They are most often found in polyandrous groups, where a number of adult males live and mate with a single reproductive female. However, they are also found in groups consisting of several reproductively active adults of both sexes. In most cases, non-reproductive animals help the parents to carry and rear their offspring. Among monkeys this form of cooperative breeding is found only in the marmosets and tamarins.

FACT FILE

Distribution	South America (throughout Amazonia into the Guianas, Colombia and Central America)
Species	Black-and-red tamarin (*Saguinus nigricollis*) Saddle-back tamarin (*Saguinus fuscicollis*) Tripartite tamarin (*Saguinus tripartitus*) Moustached tamarin (*Saguinus mystax*) White-lipped tamarin (*Saguinus labiatus*) Emperor tamarin (*Saguinus imperator*) Golden handed tamarin (*Saguinus midas*) Inustus tamarin (*Saguinus inustus*) Barefaced tamarin (*Saguinus bicolor*) Cotton-top tamarin (*Saguinus oedipus*) Geoffroy's tamarin (*Saguinus geoffroyi*) White-footed tamarin (*Saguinus leucopus*)
Body weight	Females: 11.5–19.5 oz (345–585 g) Males: 12–19.1 oz (360–575 g)
Activity pattern	Tree-living; day-active (diurnal)
Habitat type	Primary and secondary rainforest; some species prefer edge habitats between forest types
Reproduction	First litter at age 15–23 months, then every 11–12 months; two offspring per litter
Average group size	4–6
Grouping type	Polygynous (several males, one female) and polygynandrous (several males and females)
Maximum lifespan	13 years
Conservation status	Several species endangered by widespread habitat destruction and live capture for export

⊕ WHERE IN THE WORLD?

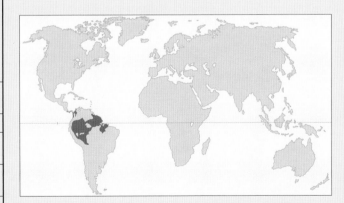

Tamarins are small, brightly colored South American monkeys. They occur throughout Amazonia and up into Central America.

◈ TOPIC LINKS

3.1 Monkey Lifestyles
p. 105 New World monkeys

3.2 Group Living
p. 128 Friends and enemies

3.3 The Mating Game
p. 143 Aunts and babysitters

CAPUCHIN MONKEY

Capuchins are the "organ-grinder monkey." They are stocky and robust in build and have quite short, prehensile tails. Although capuchins feed mainly on fruit, the protein in their diet comes from insects, and they have been observed to come down to the ground to eat snails. Capuchin monkeys live in female-bonded groups: the females remain in the groups they are born into, while males transfer between groups when they reach sexual maturity. In brown capuchin monkeys, females prefer to mate only with the dominant male in the group. When fertile, they follow the dominant male around for up to four days, mating with him repeatedly.

Capuchins have very large brains in relation to their body size and are highly inquisitive, active primates. Tufted capuchins are particularly skilled at obtaining foods that are unavailable to other species, and have been seen to crack open palm nuts by bashing them against tree trunks. In captivity, capuchin monkeys have been taught to use tools successfully.

Capuchin monkeys are lively and inquisitive animals. Their mental and physical abilities have made them useful to humans.

⊕ WHERE IN THE WORLD?

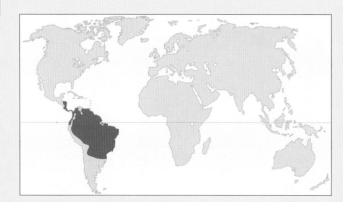

Capuchins are found throughout South and Central America. They live in the canopy of all types of tropical forest.

FACT FILE

Distribution	South and Central America
Species	Black-capped or tufted capuchin (*Cebus apella*) Brown or wedge-capped capuchin (*Cebus nigrivittatus*) White-fronted capuchin (*Cebus albifrons*) White-capped capuchin (*Cebus capucinus*)
Body weight	Females: 4–5.5 lb (1.9–2.5 kg) Males: 7–8 lb (3.2–3.7 kg)
Activity pattern	Tree-living; day-active (diurnal)
Habitat type	Canopy of all types of tropical forest
Reproduction	First litter at 4–6 years, then every 14–26 months; one offspring per litter
Average group size	10–35
Grouping type	Mixed multi-male, multi-female groups
Maximum lifespan	40 years
Conservation status	Likely to be threatened by widespread habitat destruction and hunting

TITI MONKEY

Titi monkeys are small and monogamous.. Pairs defend their territories by means of long dawn duets that can last as long as 15 minutes.

Titi monkeys are small, monogamous South American monkeys. They have long, fluffy tails—male and female dusky titi monkeys twine their tails together as a way of social bonding. Titi monkeys give birth to a single offspring; a week or so after the birth, the responsibility for carrying the baby falls solely on the male.

Different species of titi monkey prefer different habitat types. The yellow-handed titi monkey prefers high forest and lives in the canopy, while the dusky titi prefers the understorey and is often found in bamboo thickets. All titi monkeys are quite strongly territorial. Adult male and female pairs defend their territories by means of long dawn duets that can last up to 15 minutes. Neighboring titi groups then reply with duets of their own. Titi monkeys will aggressively defend their territories if they are intruded upon by other groups.

FACT FILE

, Distribution	South America (Amazonian areas of Brazil, Venezuela, Colombia, Peru, southeastern Brazil)
Species	Dusky titi (*Callicebus moloch*) Yellow-handed titi (*Callicebus torquatus*) Beige masked titi (*Callicebus personatus*)
Body weight	Females: 2–3 lb (955–1400 g) Males: 2–2.7 lb (1000–1300 g)
Activity pattern	Tree-living; day-active (diurnal)
Habitat type	Mature high forest, lowland forest, bamboo thickets
Reproduction	First litter at age 2.5–3 years, then about every 12 months; one offspring per litter
Average group size	3–4
Grouping type	Monogamous family groups
Maximum lifespan	Not known
Conservation status	Endangered by widespread habitat destruction

⊕ WHERE IN THE WORLD?

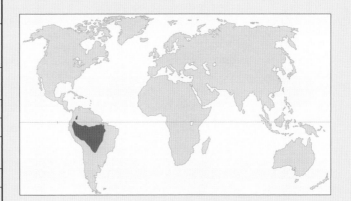

The titi monkeys of South America have several different species, which all prefer different types of habitat.

✥ TOPIC LINKS

3.1 **Monkey Lifestyles**
p. 108 Fruit-eaters large and small

UAKARI

Uakaris are South American monkeys. The black-headed uakari is found in dry forest around the black-water rivers of the Upper Amazon, and is very rare. The other species, the bald uakari, comprises two subspecies, both found in the flooded forests of the white-water rivers of the Upper Amazon. Bald uakaris have bright scarlet faces and completely bald heads, with the two subspecies differing in coat color: one has a bright red shaggy coat while the other has a white coat.

Uakaris specialize in eating fruits with hard outer shells that other monkeys are unable to bite through, and have special dental adaptations for this. Both black-headed uakaris and bald uakaris live in large groups of 20–30 animals containing a number of males and females. White bald uakaris sometimes split up into smaller foraging parties, which often spend many days apart before rejoining again.

The white or bald uakari has a shaggy white fur coat, which provides a striking contrast to its bright red head.

⬥ TOPIC LINKS

Monkey Lifestyles   **3.1**
p. 109 Leaf-eaters and
seed-eaters

🌐 WHERE IN THE WORLD?

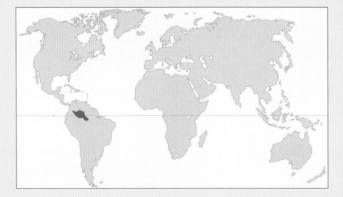

Uakaris are extremely unusual South American monkeys. They have a very restricted distribution in the Upper Amazon.

FACT FILE	
Distribution	South America (Amazonia)
Species	Black-headed uakari (*Cacajao melanocephalus*) Bald uakari (*Cacajao calvus*)
Body weight	Females: 6–6.2 lb (2.7–2.8 kg) Males: 7–7.7 lb (3.2–3.5 kg)
Activity pattern	Tree-living/semi-terrestrial; day-active (diurnal)
Habitat type	Black-headed uakari in black-water forest, bald uakari in white-water flooded forest (both can live only in undisturbed forest)
Reproduction	First litter at about age 4 years; one offspring per litter
Average group size	Black-headed uakari: 15–25 Bald uakari: 5–30
Grouping type	Mixed multi-male, multi-female groups
Maximum lifespan	Not known
Conservation status	Possibly endangered

HOWLER MONKEY

Like other howler monkeys, the black howlers produce some of the loudest calls in the animal kingdom. They have a specially adapted bone in their throats called the hyoid, which acts as a resonating chamber and increases the volume of their calls.

Howler monkeys are large, South American leaf-eating monkeys. The species differ in appearance mainly in their coat color. In each species, males and females are different in size, the males larger, and some are sexually dichromatic—that is, males and females are different colors. Female howler monkeys give birth to a single offspring, and infants are frequently cared for by females other than their mother. Male howler monkeys have been seen to commit infanticide when immigrating to a new troop.

Howler monkeys derive their name from the loud territorial roaring they use to defend their home range areas. The call is exceptionally loud and carries for many miles. The hyoid bone in the throat of howler monkey males has evolved into a large hollow chamber that helps sound to resonate, and therefore increase the volume of the call. Howler monkeys sometimes engage in prolonged vocal battles in which both males and females participate. If necessary, aggressive calling is backed up by physical attacks.

FACT FILE

Distribution	South America (southern Mexico to northern Argentina)
Species	Red howler (*Alouatta seniculus*) Black-and-red howler (*Alouatta belzebul*) Brown howler (*Alouatta fusca*) Mantled howler (*Alouatta palliata*) Mexican black howler (*Alouatta pigra*) Black howler (*Alouatta caraya*)
Body weight	Females: 9.5–14 lb (4.3–6.4 kg) Males: 14–25 lb (6.4–11.4 kg)
Activity pattern	Tree-living; day-active (diurnal)
Habitat type	Primary rainforest, secondary forests, dry deciduous forests
Reproduction	First litter at age 3.5–4.5 years, then every 22 months; one offspring per litter
Average group size	6–15
Grouping type	Mixed multi-male, multi-female groups
Maximum lifespan	13 years
Conservation status	Endangered by habitat destruction and hunting; some species (e.g. brown howler monkey) close to extinction in some areas

⊕ WHERE IN THE WORLD?

Howlers are among the largest of the South American monkeys. Their distribution ranges from southern Mexico to northern Argentina.

◆ TOPIC LINKS

3.1 Monkey Lifestyles
p. 108 Leaf-eaters and seed-eaters

3.3 The Mating Game
p. 135 Spot the difference

SPIDER MONKEY

Spider monkeys are the largest of the South American monkeys. They are long-limbed, with a prehensile tail that is used as a "fifth limb" when feeding. Males and females are very similar in size and coloration, making it difficult to tell the sexes apart (the fact that female spider monkeys have very large, pendulous genitalia further adds to the confusion). Most species of spider monkey lack a thumb—swinging through the trees requires hands to act like hooks, and a thumb is unnecessary for this.

Spider monkeys are ripe fruit specialists, although they are known to eat large amounts of leaves during periods when fruit is less available. They live in fairly large groups of up to 12 or so individuals, in a "fission-fusion" form of social organization. The groups split up into smaller parties for foraging during the day, and only rarely are all the animals in a group found together.

Spider monkeys are large and agile, like this black spider monkey. They all have a very flexible social system, with small parties joining together and splitting up throughout the day.

⊕ WHERE IN THE WORLD?

Spider monkeys are ripe fruit specialists. They are found from the Yucatán Peninsula of Mexico to Argentina.

FACT FILE

Peninsula of Mexico	*Distribution*	South America (from Yucatán through Amazonia)
Species		Black-handed spider monkey (*Ateles geoffroyi*) Brown-headed spider monkey (*Ateles fusciceps*) Black spider monkey (*Ateles paniscus*) Long-haired spider monkey (*Ateles belzebuth*)
Body weight		Females: 16–20 lb (7.3–9.2 kg) Males: 18–20 lb (8.3–9.1 kg)
Activity pattern		Tree-living; day-active (diurnal)
Habitat type		High primary rainforest
Reproduction		First litter at age 4–5 years, then every 22–50 months; one offspring per litter
Average group size		15–18
Grouping type		Mixed multi-male, multi-female fission-fusion groups
Maximum lifespan		20 years
Conservation status		Some species and subspecies endangered through habitat destruction and on the verge of extinction in some locations (e.g. brown-headed spider monkey in Ecuador)

VERVET MONKEY

Vervets are highly successful African monkeys. They are seasonal breeders, becoming fertile just once a year, and give birth to a single young.

Vervet monkeys are guenons who have made it out of the forests and onto the savanna. However, they are not quite as well adapted to this environment as baboons or patas monkeys, and tend to be restricted to areas of riverine or swamp forest. Unlike most other guenons, vervet monkey groups usually contain more than one adult male. The males have ritualized dominance relationships, which help keep the peace and prevent competition over mates disrupting group life.

Vervet monkeys have longer pregnancies than other guenons (165 days compared to 140 days for blue monkeys) but the infants develop much faster after birth. It seems likely that the increased dangers from savanna-living predators may have led to this difference.

Vervets were originally placed in the genus *Cercopithecus* with the other guenons, but experts have recently decided that vervets are different enough to be placed in their own genus, *Chlorocebus*.

FACT FILE

Distribution	South America (throughout Amazonia into the Guianas, Colombia and Central America)
Species	Vervet, green or grivet monkey CLARIFY HERE (*Chlorocebus aethiops*)
Body weight	Females: 6.6 lb (3.0 kg) Males: 9.5 lb (4.3 kg)
Activity pattern	Semi-terrestrial; day-active (diurnal)
Habitat type	Savanna woodland, riverine forest, semi-arid savanna
Reproduction	First litter at 4–4.5 years, then every 16 months; one offspring per litter
Average group size	10–40
Grouping type	Multi-male groups; territorial
Maximum lifespan	31 years
Conservation status	Not currently threatened or endangered, except for regions of South Africa

⊕ WHERE IN THE WORLD?

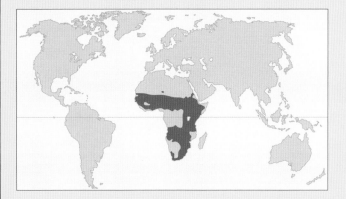

Vervet monkeys are found in areas of gallery forest along rivers. They are widespread throughout sub-Saharan Africa.

◈ TOPIC LINKS

1.1 What is a Primate?
p. 21 Size and diet

1.2 Primate Origins
p. 33 Ancient to Modern

1.3 Primates Today
p. 42 Primate pests

3.1 Monkey Ecology
p. 114 Guenons: Naturally different

3.2 Group Living
p. 123 Differences in dominance

3.3 The Mating Game
p. 135 Spot the difference

3.4 A Unique Intelligence
p. 150 Recognizing relationships
p. 151 Tripartite relationships

RHESUS MACAQUE

Macaques have the widest geographical distribution of any primate genus, and within the genus rhesus macaques take the prize for the widest species distribution. Rhesus macaques occur from Pakistan and Afghanistan in western Asia to China and Vietnam in eastern Asia. On the Indian subcontinent they range from the north to the far south. Rhesus macaques are able to coexist with humans and exploit human-modified environments with great efficiency. As a result, they reach their highest densities in places where they overlap with humans.

Rhesus macaques are seasonal breeders and, in good conditions, can produce one offspring per year. In colder environments, such as the temperate forests of China, rhesus macaques live in larger groups, have larger home ranges, and lower reproductive rates than populations living in more tropical habitats. In harsher habitats, most females do not breed every season and can only produce an offspring once every two years. Rhesus macaque females have strict dominant hierarchies and high-ranking females can be aggressive. Females are also aggressive toward other groups and join together to defend their resources against outsiders.

Rhesus macaques are known as a "weed" species because they do so well in human habitats. In India they often inhabit temples and are fed offerings by visitors.

🌐 WHERE IN THE WORLD

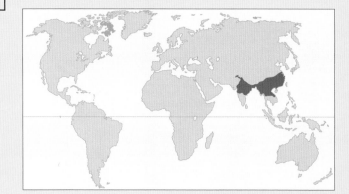

Rhesus macaques are found across Asia, from Pakistan in the west to China and Vietnam in the east.

FACT FILE

Distribution	Asia from Afghanistan to Vietnam, including Indian subcontinent
Species	Rhesus macaque (*Macaca mulatta*)
Body weight	Females: 12 lb (5.4 kg) Males: 17 lb (7.7 kg)
Activity pattern	Semi-terrestrial; day-active (diurnal)
Habitat type	Tropical and temperate forests
Reproduction	First litter at age 3.5–5.5 years, then every 12–24 months; one offspring per litter
Average group size	40
Grouping type	Mixed multi-male, multi-female groups
Maximum lifespan	21.6 years
Conservation status	Not endangered

MANDRILL

The male mandrill has very striking facial markings. When males are sexually active, these colors become even brighter than usual. The male also puts on weight and becomes "fatted."

Mandrills are ground-living forest monkeys that are similar in appearance to baboons, although they are not especially closely related. Mandrills live in dense primary forest, which makes it hard to observe them and little is known about their behavior. Male mandrills have impressive red, white, and blue facial markings. These colors are also present around the genital region, and the bright blue rump of mandrill males is distinctive.

Mandrills eat mainly fruit, seeds, nuts, and shoots. Males feed largely on the ground, mainly due to their large size, which makes moving through the trees difficult. The smaller females and juveniles are often seen feeding up in the middle layer of the forest canopy. Mandrills frequently move around in large groups of up to 700 individuals. These large groups are unlikely to be stable, however, and probably break up into smaller groups while foraging. When a lone male joins a group and becomes sexually active, it becomes "fatted," putting on weight, while the coloration on its face and rump becomes brighter.

FACT FILE

Distribution	West Africa
Species	Mandrill (*Mandrillus sphinx*)
Body weight	Females: 28 lb (12.9 kg) Males: 70 lb (31.6 kg)
Activity pattern	Ground-dwelling (females and juveniles also partly tree-living); day-active (diurnal)
Habitat type	Primary rainforest
Reproduction	One offspring per litter
Average group size	250–700, although these may be composed of sub-groups comprising 40 or so individuals
Grouping type	Mixed multi-male, multi-female groups
Maximum lifespan	29 years
Conservation status	Endangered by habitat destruction and hunting

WHERE IN THE WORLD?

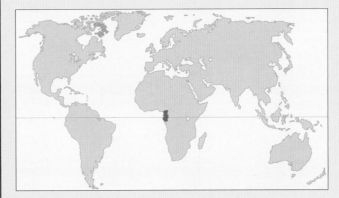

Mandrills are large, forest-living monkeys. They are found throughout sub-Saharan Africa in a wide variety of habitats.

TOPIC LINKS

1.1 What Is a Primate?
p. 14 What makes primates special?

1.2 Primate Origins
p. 34 The rise of the monkeys

3.1 Monkey Lifestyles
p. 117 Baboon relatives

3.3 The Mating Game
p. 135 Spot the difference

BABOON

Baboons are the largest and most successful of the African monkeys. They are found in habitats as diverse as the deserts of Namibia and the tropical forests of western Uganda. Baboons are sexually dimorphic. The females are only half the size of males, and males also have much larger canine teeth. Both these differences are related to high male–male competition for mates.

Baboons are sometimes placed into five separate species, but since all species can, and do, interbreed, it is becoming more common to consider them as a single species divided into a number of subspecies. The yellow, anubis, guinea and chacma varieties of baboon, known as the "savanna" baboons, all live in large, mixed-sex groups ranging in size from 40 to 80 individuals. However, guinea and chacma baboons are behaviorally different from the other savanna baboons, and recent genetic evidence indicates that they might have split off earlier from the Papio lineage and evolved independently of the other species. The hamadryas baboon is very different from the savanna baboons. It is found in desert habitats; |is smaller, with a gray coat and pink facial skin, rather than a brown coat color; and has a complicated, multi-level society based on single-male groups.

Male baboons are twice the size of females and have more pronounced muzzles.

WHERE IN THE WORLD?

Baboons are the most successful of the African monkeys. They are found throughout sub-Saharan Africa in a wide variety of habitats.

FACT FILE

Distribution	Sub-Saharan Africa from Ethiopia to South Africa
Species	Yellow baboon (*Papio cyncocephalus cynocephalus*) Anubis baboon (*Papio cyncocephalus anubis*) Guinea baboon (*Papio cyncocephalus papio*) Chacma baboon (*Papio cyncocephalus ursinus*) Hamadryas baboon (*Papio cyncocephalus hamadryas*)
Body weight	Females: 22–33 lb (10–15 kg) Males: 37–66 lb (17–30 kg)
Activity pattern	Ground-dwelling; day-active (diurnal)
Habitat type	Desert, savanna grassland, woodland, forest, and mountain habitats
Reproduction	First litter at age 4–6 years, then every 20–38 months; one offspring per litter
Average group size	22–80
Grouping type	Mixed multi-male, multi-female groups
Maximum lifespan	Not known
Conservation status	Not endangered

GELADA

The red patch of bare skin on the gelada baboon's chest is a distinctive feature of this species.

Gelada baboons are a distinctive genus found in the high-lands of Ethiopia. They are the only surviving species of a group that was highly successful between 5 million and 100,000 years ago. Gelada baboons are the most terres-trial of all the monkeys and have become so well adapted to life on the ground that they are unable to climb trees. Instead, they are specialized grass eaters, with a distinctive habit known as "shuffle feeding." They sit upright, plucking grass blades with their hands and shuffling forward on their bottoms as they deplete the small area in front of them.

Gelada live in single-male groups consisting of around 10 individuals. These groups frequently join together to form larger bands and herds of up to 600 individuals. Male gelada are much larger than females, and have strik-ing mantles of long hair around their head and shoulders. Female gelada have a number of small white blisters or vesicles on their chests that swell up during their fertile period.

FACT FILE

Distribution	Africa (Ethiopian highlands)
Species	Gelada baboon (*Theropithecus gelada*)
Body weight	Females: 26 lb (11.7 kg) Males: 42 lb (19 kg)
Activity pattern	Ground-dwelling; day-active (diurnal)
Habitat type	Mountain grassland
Reproduction	First litter at age 4–6 years, then every 24–38 months; one offspring per litter
Average group size	One-male groups: 10; bands: 30 –300; herds: up to 600 individuals
Grouping type	One male with several females
Maximum lifespan	Not known
Conservation status	Threatened by human activity

⊕ WHERE IN THE WORLD?

The gelada baboon is found only in the high-land plateaux of the Simen Mountains in Ethiopia.

◈ TOPIC LINKS

BLACK-AND-WHITE COLOBUS MONKEY

Black-and-white colobus are large, strikingly beautiful monkeys. The three species of black-and-white colobus can be distinguished easily by differences in their coat patterns. They are all leaf- and seed-eaters and live in a wide range of forest habitats across Africa, from primary rainforest to isolated patches of dry forest. Black-and-white colobus live in small single-male groups. The male produces a loud roaring call that is used to defend his territory and his females against other males.

All black-and-white colobus monkeys are arboreal, or tree-living, although they may occasionally come to the ground to feed on soil. This provides them with essential minerals otherwise lacking in their diet. Like other colobus monkeys, they have highly specialized stomachs to allow them to ferment and detoxify their food. Black-and-white colobus monkeys can survive in small areas, because their diet consists of leaves from just a few species of tree with abundant foliage, therefore whereever these trees occur they can thrive, while other species are unable to survive.

Like all colobine monkeys, black-and-white colobus monkeys have a complex stomach that is specially designed for fermenting and detoxifying plant matter.

WHERE IN THE WORLD?

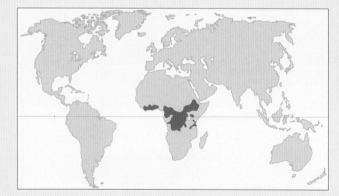

Black-and-white colobus are large, African leaf-eating monkeys. They are found across central Africa from west to east.

FACT FILE

Distribution	Africa
Species	Guereza or eastern black-and-white colobus (*Colobus guereza*) King colobus or western black-and-white colobus (*Colobus polykomos*) Angolan colobus (*Colobus angolensis*)
Body weight	Females: 16.5–20 lb (7.5–9.2 kg) Males: 21–30 lb (9.7–13.5 kg)
Activity pattern	Tree-living (may occasionally come to the ground to feed on soil); day-active (diurnal)
Habitat type	Wide range of forest types throughout sub-Saharan Africa
Reproduction	Litter every 12–18 months; one offspring per litter
Average group size	12–15
Grouping type	One male with several females
Maximum lifespan	Not known
Conservation status	Threatened by habitat destruction and hunting

PROBOSCIS MONKEY

Proboscis monkeys form part of a group known as the odd-nosed monkeys, and one glance at a male proboscis monkey is enough to tell you why. This large, red monkey from Borneo has an enormous, pendulous nose shaped like a tongue. Females have smaller, cuter, turned-up noses, and weigh half as much as males.

Proboscis monkeys are found in areas of forest along rivers or coastline. They sleep in trees along the riverside at night to gain extra protection from predators. They are good swimmers and can frequently be seen crossing rivers this way. Like other colobine monkeys, about half their diet consists of leaves, the rest made up of fruit and seeds. Proboscis monkeys have an interesting social organization. They live in moderate-sized groups containing either males and females, or solely males. However, about two-thirds of their time is spent as part of a "band," where a number of male–female groups and all-male groups associate together to form one larger group.

Proboscis monkeys are found in mangrove forests and are one of the few primates known to swim.

FACT FILE

Distribution	Borneo
Species	Proboscis monkey (*Nasalis larvatus*)
Body weight	Females: 22 lb (9.8 kg) Males: 45 (20.4 kg)
Activity pattern	Tree-living; day-active (diurnal)
Habitat type	Coastal and riverine forest
Reproduction	One offspring per litter
Average group size	Foraging party size varies from 2 to 63
Grouping type	One male with several females
Maximum lifespan	Not known
Conservation status	Endangered by habitat destruction

⊕ WHERE IN THE WORLD?

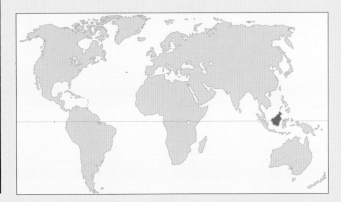

Proboscis monkeys are found in the mangrove forests of Borneo in Southeast Asia.

◆ TOPIC LINKS

3.1 Monkey Lifestyles
p. 110 Colobines

3.3 The Mating Game
p. 135 Spot the difference

THE APES

The dawn mists part reluctantly on the slopes of the Virunga volcanoes in Rwanda. As the sky lightens, a huge, silverback male gorilla stirs in his sleep. Around him, his little group of three females and a younger adult male doze fitfully, huddled in the warmth of their night nests. Tucked in beside the females are their young, one of whom peers warily around and then clambers off the nest to find his half sister. He peers intently at her, an outstretched hand inviting her to play.

Gradually, the sun rises, drawing the chill from the ground. The group stirs one by one, adults rolling over and stretching legs cramped by the nest's confinement. A few quiet grunts simper through the still air, and another replies. A female begins to feed on the wild celery that carpets the forest floor. A new day begins in the endless cycle of eating and dozing that sustains life in the cool mountain air.

Previous page: Like all apes, orangutans are among the most endangered primates because they breed slowly.

AN ANCIENT SUCCESS STORY

The apes achieved their evolutionary peak between 20 and 10 million years ago, when 30 species roamed the vast tropical forests of Africa and Asia. During that period, they represented one of the great success stories of primate evolution. They had evolved into a diverse group, occupying almost every ecological niche now filled by Old World apes and monkeys combined, and they varied in size from the 6 lb (3 kg)cat-sized *Dionysopithecus* to the enormous *Gigantopithecus* (▷p. 32), 613 lb (275 kg) in weight and the largest primate ever to walk the Earth. The apes held sway over their Old World forest empire, dominating the primate communities. During their heyday, 90 percent of the anthropoid species in Africa were apes.

Then, around 10 million years ago, a rapid drying and cooling of the world's climate began to kill off the rich forests that had clothed the tropical landscapes for so long. The forests shrank, eventually contracting to the areas they occupy today, and savanna grasslands spread to take their place. The apes of the Old World went into terminal decline, out-competed by a range of newly evolved monkey species that thrived in the new habitats.

Survivors

By 5 million years ago, only a handful of ape species were left. Many of these were hominids, members of a lineage that would eventually give rise to modern humans. Today, the once glorious ape family is represented by just five species of "great ape," including humans, and 8–9 species of gibbon, the "lesser apes." The great apes include the orangutan, found only in Sumatra and

Borneo; the gorilla of tropical Africa; two species of chimpanzee, both confined to central and West Africa; and ourselves. The gibbons live only in Southeast Asia, where they range from Bangladesh and the Indo-China peninsula to the islands of Indonesia and Borneo.

Apart from humans, the surviving ape species live in small pockets in the tropics and are confined to forests or forest edges. Although deforestation and hunting have taken their toll, the real trigger to the apes' decline was the dramatic reduction in forest area that occurred, especially in Africa, during the last 10 million years. The apes, as a

1. A chimpanzee cuddles its inquisitive infant. Chimpanzees are as much at home in the trees as they are on the ground.

family, have been slowly squeezed into ever-smaller remnants of forest.

Recent history

We have little idea how far the original range of the African apes extended, but we do know that, until as recently as 10,000 years ago, around the time humans invented agriculture, orangutans lived on the mainland of southern China. Even further back in time, the animals that were almost certainly their ancestors, the decidedly orang-like sivapithecine apes, were found all over southern Asia, from China in the east to Europe in the west. The gibbons, too, were once much more widespread. Gibbon-like apes were once found throughout southern Europe and eastward through Asia into China. Today, none of these species is found outside the confines of Southeast Asia's forests, and even there, populations continue to dwindle. The orangutan teeters uncomfortably toward extinction, its population reduced to a few thousand.

The gorillas and chimpanzees of Africa are more of a mystery. The fossil record from forested areas is poor over the last 5 to 6 million years, mainly because forests do not provide good conditions for fossilization. In fact, the gap between Africa's prehistoric apes and the modern species is so great that it almost seems as if the modern apes appeared from nowhere. This curious feature of ape evolution stands in marked contrast to the fossil record for human lineage. Because our

Patterson/Gimlin, © 1968 Dahinden

Bigfoot caught on film at Bluff Creek, California, in 1967.

An alleged yeti scalp discovered in a monastery in Nepal.

 ## DOES THE YETI EXIST?

Rumors of giant ape-like creatures that roam the wild places of our planet are far from uncommon. The most famous of these is the yeti, or abominable snowman, of the Himalayan mountains. The 1951 Everest expedition came back with photographs of footprints. A dried scalp with long reddish hair, purportedly from a yeti, was also found in a monastery.

Other similar tales of ape-like creatures come from the forests around Lake Malawi in central Africa, and from the tropical forests of Borneo, where the creature is known locally as the *orang pendek*, to distinguish it from the *orang utan*, and the *orang asli*. the name for the tribal forest people of the area. From the pine forests of the northwestern US comes Bigfoot, or Sasquatch, famous for being the only apeman to be caught on film. Sadly, the film is almost certainly a hoax.

Of these creatures, Bigfoot is perhaps the least plausible. Aside from modern humans, who have been present in the Americas for only about 20,000 years, no primates are known to have lived in North America for the last 30 million years. The yeti too seems to be a myth. Even the lush, warm forests of the tropics can support only small, dispersed populations of great apes. Simple calculations show that, in the cold and impoverished habitats of the Himalayas, life would be impossible for so large an ape. Perhaps the yeti is a whispered folk memory from the time when orangutans lived on the Chinese mainland, to the east of the Himalayan foothills, a mere 10,000 years ago.

In contrast, the stories from Malawi and Borneo could have some factual basis. An isolated population of chimpanzees left behind as prehistoric forests contracted might have been the origin of the Malawi hairy giants. And who knows what might have been lurking, orang-like, in the forests of Borneo until recently?

ancestors adapted early on to more open savanna habitats, where bones fossilize more easily, our own evolutionary tree is by far the most complete among contemporary primates. However this, too, vanishes into obscurity as we trace our ancestors back into the forests from which they emerged around 5 million years ago.

What the fossil record cannot tell us, the record hidden in our genes can (▷p. 40). Comparisons of the DNA of modern humans and our ape cousins reveals that chimpanzees and humans share a common ancestor who lived in African forests around 5 million years ago. The two species of chimpanzee, the bonobo, or pygmy chimpanzee, and the common chimpanzee, split from their shared ancestor much more recently than this, about a million years ago. Further back in time, the human–chimp lineage diverged from the line that led to the gorilla about 6 million years ago, a million years before the human and chimp lineages separated. Therefore the chimpanzees are very much our sister species, and the gorilla a more distant half sister.

1. A male orangutan rests at Gunung Leuser National Park, Indonesia. The orangutan is the most endangered of the great apes.

2. Modern genetics has revealed the shared evolutionary paths of humans and other ape species.

3. A baby gorilla rests casually on the back of a silverback male. Gorilla males often seem indifferent to the behavior of their offspring.

EVOLUTIONARY PATHS

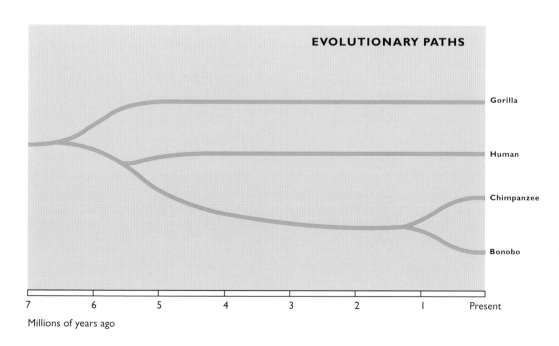

Gorilla

Human

Chimpanzee

Bonobo

| 7 | 6 | 5 | 4 | 3 | 2 | 1 | Present |

Millions of years ago

DISAPPEARING FORESTS

All over Africa, Asia, and South America, ancient forests are being cut down to satisfy the unending demand for timber and farmland. It has been estimated that during the 1980s alone the world lost 8 percent of its tropical forest cover, and almost half of each year's loss occurs in just two countries, Brazil and Indonesia. Many African countries, too, have lost as much as half of their original forest cover in this century. In Uganda and Nigeria the estimate is even higher. Some 90 percent of their tropical forests are thought to have disappeared. The impact of deforestation is enormous, especially on species such as great apes that are particularly dependent on forest habitats.

1. Shifting cultivation fills the gaps in the forest left by logging in land-hungry countries, but this practice prevents the forest regenerating.

2. The chainsaw wreaks havoc on tropical hardwood forests. In a few hours, a man can fell a tree that took several hundred years to grow.

Struggling to survive

It is not known how big the great ape population of Africa might have been in the past, but if the animals' geographical range coincided with the distribution of the original forests in West and central Africa, their story must be a grim one. This is especially likely to apply to the gorilla and the common chimpanzee, whose ranges lie in those areas, notably West Africa, that have been most severely hit by deforestation. The bonobo chimpanzee, which is found only in the Congo, has perhaps suffered less from its effects to date. However, the civil war that has raged in that country for the last decade is likely to have severely reduced many bonobo populations.

Ultimately, apes are likely to suffer more than monkeys from deforestation, for three reasons. One is their size because it is harder for an animal as large as the gorilla to hide when the forest has been cut down. Therefore, it is more likely to come into conflict with people. The second reason is also related to size. Being large has given the great apes a perhaps undeserved reputation for aggressiveness, and both gorillas and chimpanzees have been accused of stealing and eating human babies. People inevitably fear them and will kill them simply to be rid of what they think is a dangerous enemy. The ready market for ape meat is often another incentive to kill. Third, deforestation forces apes to range over a larger area in order to supply their daily food requirements. However, if the area is too large, it can lead them into crop raiding and increased contact with humans.

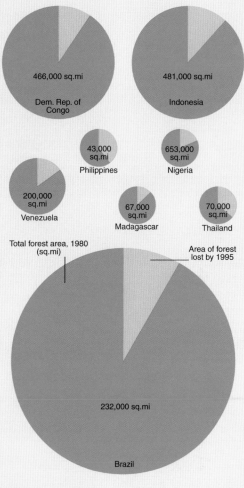

466,000 sq.mi

Dem. Rep. of Congo

481,000 sq.mi

Indonesia

43,000 sq.mi

Philippines

653,000 sq.mi

Nigeria

200,000 sq.mi

Venezuela

67,000 sq.mi

Madagascar

70,000 sq.mi

Thailand

Total forest area, 1980 (sq.mi)

Area of forest lost by 1995

232,000 sq.mi

Brazil

3

4

Timber logging

Most deforestation is due to logging for timber. Even where forests are not completely felled, considerable damage can be caused by the roads that are built into the forest to provide access to the timber. Long after the logging companies have moved on elsewhere, these roads continue to provide access to the forest for slash-and-burn farmers. As a result, yet more forest is cut down. Logging roads also provide access for hunters, who use the road networks to sell their bushmeat to a wider market. Increased supply leads to increased demand, a vicious circle that serves to make hunting even more worthwhile.

Debt crisis

Perhaps the most worrying finding about deforestation comes from a recent survey in sub-Saharan Africa. The acreage of forest lost per year has a monetary value that matches the countries' repayments on debts to foreign banks. It seems, therefore, that African countries are selling off their natural heritage to pay the interest on overseas loans. Apart from losing one of their main natural resources, they are also losing the primates that live in those forests.

3. Forest fires can denude thousands of square miles of tropical forest. Some fires are set deliberately to clear farmland. Others may be caused by lightning.

4. Countries worldwide are losing forest at different rates. These diagrams show the decrease in forest area over a 15-year period, from 1980–1995. (Source: FAO)

TOPIC LINKS

1.3 Primates Today
p. 43 Life on the knife edge
p. 46 The bushmeat trade

2.4 The Last Refuge of the Lemurs
p. 90 Living under threat

3.4 A Unique Intelligence
p. 152 Crop raiders and harvest helpers

4.1 Planet of the Apes
p. 177 Survivors

APE ANATOMY

The apes' flat chests, unlike the dog-like chests of monkeys, the structure of their teeth, their bigger brains, lack of a tail, and more human-like appearance all serve to distinguish them clearly from the monkeys (▷ p. 40). Apes and monkeys last shared a common ancestor 25 million years ago, and in some ways living apes more closely resemble that ancient ape-monkey ancestor than the Old World monkeys, who have changed considerably in the intervening years (▷p. 32).

Flat Chested

After their split with the monkeys, apes evolved a number of adaptations to their forest niche that turned out to be important later in the story of human evolution. Perhaps the most significant of these was the flat chest familiar in our own bodies. This seems to have been an adaptation to a way of life based on climbing trees, as opposed to running along branches in the way most Old World monkeys do. The great apes also have short legs and long arms compared to other primates. The long arms are used to haul the body up when climbing a tree, while the feet are used to grip the trunk, providing a platform to stand on so that the arms can reach further up. This "shimmying" style is effective in allowing such heavy-bodied animals to shift from walking on the ground to climbing in trees. It is easy to see that this style of movement predisposes apes to walking on two legs, and many apes often do walk short distances on two legs when on the ground. Therefore our ancestors were "pre-adapted" to develop the two-legged style of walking that eventually became a human hallmark.

Great apes have a peculiarity in the way they hold their hands when walking on all fours. Most monkeys walk with the hands flat so that the weight of the shoulders is borne on the outstretched fingers. By contrast, the great apes walk on their knuckles. Each species does it in a slightly different way. Chimpanzees walk on the backs of their knuckles. Gorillas walk on the backs of the last two joints of the fingers. Orangutans walk on their fists. All these forms of knuckle-walking look extremely awkward, and we have no idea why the differences occur.

Swinging through the trees

Perhaps because of increasing competition with Old World monkeys, the gibbons took the long-armed, flat-chested body plan one stage further, gaining the ability to hang by their arms from branches. This gave gibbons access to a niche that neither monkeys, who walk or sit on top of the branches, nor other apes, who are too heavy, could reach. Modern gibbons are about half the size of their ancestors from about 10 million years ago. Thanks to their low weight, they can hang from even the outermost branches of the highest trees, safe from tree-climbing predators, such as leopards, and with unrestricted access to the fruits that grow at the ends of fine branches.

Two further adaptations locked the gibbons securely into this niche. When apes first evolved flat chests, their shoulder blades moved from the sides of the chest to the back. This had the important effect of freeing the shoulder joint and allowing the arm to swing all the way around. In contrast, monkeys, like dogs, have restricted movement in their

1

2

1. A silverback lowland gorilla male uses its short legs as a platform from which to pull itself up a tree trunk.

2. A chimpanzee walks across the forest floor, tucking in its fingers to walk on the back of the knuckles.

3. (opposite) A young orangutan displays its acrobatic skills high in the forest canopy. Unlike the other great apes, orangutans seem to have four arms.

1. The gibbon's body is perfectly adapted to allow it to occupy a terminal branch niche in the forest canopy.

Suspended from the thin branch tips, it is safe from predators while feeding.

shoulders and cannot easily rotate their arms. The great apes' ability to rotate the arm allows them to reach up above their heads when hauling themselves up tree trunks, something monkeys cannot manage. In gibbons, evolution has freed the ball-and-socket joint of the shoulder and the joint at the wrist even further. Their wrists, in particular, are so free that a gibbon can rotate its arm through 360 degrees without having to let go of the branch. If humans were to try the same thing, we would find that we can turn about 270 degrees, two-thirds of a circle, but no more. It is almost as though the gibbon's arm has been disconnected from the rest of its body.

This extraordinary flexibility, combined with the flat chest, allows gibbons to move in a unique and spectacular way. As anyone who has seen them in a zoo or the wild will know, they swing underhand from branch to branch and can travel at enormous speeds through the treetops in this way. Also, the way they achieve this is as impressive as what you see. A gibbon uses its body as a pendulum to gain momentum when moving. As it swings below the branch, it pumps its legs up and down, much as children will work their legs when building up speed on a swing. The whole process is a remarkable example of how evolution can adapt a body plan that developed for one purpose, climbing tree trunks, to something entirely different, swinging.

Chimpanzees have the largest testicles for body size of any primate alive today. Those of the gorilla are the smallest.

LIFE AND DEATH

When the venerable chimpanzee Flo died at Gombe National Park, northern Tanzania, in 1972, she became the first non-human primate to have an obituary in a major newspaper, the UK's *Sunday Times*. Flo was born around 1929 and was approaching her mid 40s when she died. She was one of the first chimpanzees at Gombe to accept the presence of the young Jane Goodall more than 40 years ago when Goodall started her work there. Flo was by then already a mature mother, and her first infant, Faben, was a boisterous young male in his teens. When Flo died, she was a grandmother.

The great apes are among the longest living of the primates. In captivity, the average lifespan of chimpanzees and gorillas is only a few years short of our own. They can match a respectable 50 years to our 70-year average. Such longevity has its costs, however. As a general rule, everything is slowed down in long-lived species. Like humans, chimpanzees have extended childhoods, reaching puberty at around age 10. In humans, puberty is typically reached at around 16 to 18 years old in traditional hunter-gatherer populations, but much earlier in well-fed Westerners. Where most monkeys give birth every year or two, great apes give birth only once every 4 to 5 years, virtually the same interval as in traditional human populations. Typically, human and chimpanzee mothers have only 5 to 6 children in a lifetime.

Slow reproduction has its benefits too, of course. It gives youngsters more opportunities for learning, and has favored the evolution of greater intelligence and longer lifespans. However, it also bears with it the seeds of its own destruction. In the face of sudden catastrophic environmental change, the species does not reproduce fast enough to evolve new adaptations that suit the new conditions. The fate of all species caught in this invidious bind is to go extinct. It might have been this factor that finally killed the dinosaurs. The great apes are now bearing the brunt of the same evolutionary shortcoming. Only those species capable of adjusting fast enough at the technological level have any chance of escaping the inexorable decline into extinction. So far, humans have been the only ape species capable of surviving. But how long will we manage to stave off our own eventual fate?

2. A newborn lowland gorilla baby clings to its mother's back as she travels through the forest. Newborn baby primates have a strong grip, which can still be seen in newborn human babies.

2

Jane Goodall, doyenne of primate studies, has been following the fortunes of her beloved chimpanzees at Gombe, Tanzania, for over 40 years.

 GOMBE: A LIFETIME OF RESEARCH

In 1960, the young Jane Goodall began, somewhat uncertainly, to follow the wild chimpanzees of the Gombe, a national park on the wooded slopes above the eastern shore of Lake Tanganyika. It was hard and frustrating work, since the shy chimpanzees could travel fast and far in the hilly terrain when they wanted to be rid of this slender ape who had attached herself to them. It was to be the better part of five years before the chimpanzees were sufficiently habituated to allow her to follow and observe them continuously.

Nearly half a century later, we look back on a wealth of data painstakingly recorded by Jane Goodall, her Tanzanian field assistants, and a privileged group of postgraduate students from all over the world who earned their research degrees by studying different aspects of the chimpanzees' behavior and ecology. The chimpanzees themselves became the stars of many TV documentaries.

Gombe represents one of the longest continuous studies of a single large mammal population in which the lives of individual animals have been intimately documented, their births and deaths, friendships and fights, their rises and falls in the social hierarchy. It was at Gombe that termite fishing and toolmaking were first documented, and infanticide and murder were first seen by shocked observers.

LIFE IN A DISPERSED SOCIETY

While we associate monkey society with large groups and intense social relationships, the apes seem altogether much less social. Gibbons are monogamous, while the great apes are typically found alone or in small groups of no more than six or seven individuals. It seems a paradox that the most intelligent of the primates should have so impoverished a social life. Appearances, however, can deceive. In reality, ape society can be unexpectedly complex beneath the surface. This is especially true of the chimpanzees, who live in a dispersed society, technically known as a fission–fusion social system. Here, individuals form a community with special relationships with each other, yet they do not necessarily spend all their time together. Rather, they are able to maintain their relationships with other members of the community even though they might not see each other for weeks or even months at a time. This is very reminiscent of human behavior.

APE LIFESTYLES

Apes are typically fruit-eaters, although, like all primates, they do eat a variety of foods, including meat. To be sure, the siamang (the largest of the gibbon family) and the gorilla (the largest of the great apes) eat more leaves than do most other species; even so, their diet is as much orientated towards fruit as are the diets of their smaller cousins. This preference for fruit, particularly for ripe fruit, limits the apes' ecological flexibility. Unlike monkeys, apes cannot digest fruits that are not fully ripened because they lack the digestive enzyme needed to break down the bitter-tasting chemicals called tannins that trees use to protect fruits until the seeds inside are ready to germinate. For all apes, ourselves included, eating unripe fruit is unpleasant, induces stomachache if we eat too much, and causes sickness and diarrhea if we persist despite the warning signs.

Foraging for fruit

Dependence on fruit has shaped the foraging behavior of apes, and, as a consequence, their social lives. Because apes are generally large, they need a lot of food each day to survive; but fruits are a very patchy resource. In the tropics, trees often fruit out of synchrony, something we in temperate latitudes, with our strongly seasonal climates, do not expect. The result is that, although there is probably always a tree in fruit somewhere in the forest, it may be a considerable distance from the last one. To make ends meet, apes are forced to spread out and forage either alone or in small groups.

Chimpanzees are by far the most mobile of the apes, typically traveling 3 miles (5 km) or

1. Apes are fruit-eaters, but, unlike monkeys, cannot digest unripe fruit. Here a female orangutan reaches for a durian fruit—a treat, despite its offputting smell.

more in the daily round of foraging. Orangutans and gorillas are more sedentary and rarely travel more than .6 miles (1 km) a day. This partly reflects feeding preferences and how patchy their food supply is. Gorillas rely heavily on leafy herbaceous plants to give them enough energy for the day, and since these are common and widespread, gorillas can munch away sedately without having to travel too far. Orangutans are more solitary in their lifestyle. This is because the forests of Southeast Asia are dominated by trees called dipterocarps, the fruits of which are inedible because of their heavy chemical defences. Since about a third of the trees in their habitat belong to the dipterocarp family, orangutans are forced to disperse more than other apes.

Fair-weather friends

In the more mobile chimpanzees, sociability is strongly influenced by how much fruit a tree carries. During the dry season, when fruits are scarce, chimpanzees often forage alone or in small parties. During the fruiting season, when more large trees are in fruit, and especially when "bonanza" species such as figs are fruiting, large groups often form as animals converge on what are sometimes called supermarket resources. Chimpanzees may even invite their friends and relatives to join them when they discover a new bonanza tree in fruit. By drumming on tree buttresses and making loud pant-hoots that reverberate around the forest, a chimpanzee can cause heads to turn several miles away. Soon, lines of chimpanzees converge excitedly on the source of the sounds.

1. A chimpanzee forages for fruits in the forest canopy.

2. A mountain gorilla amid the rich herbaceous vegetation of the Virunga volcanoes in Rwanda.

3. A young chimpanzee pant-hoots in order to summon his friends.

THE DISPERSED SOCIETY

The need to spread out to find food has serious consequences for ape society. These primates do not live in the large, intensely social groups so characteristic of Old World monkeys (▷p.120).

The gibbons set the scene by being monogamous, a living arrangement that is rare among primates (▷p.194). Female gibbons eschew the close friendships seen among female monkeys. Instead, each forages alone in a separate territory, accompanied only by her male and her dependent offspring. Female territories never overlap, and neighbors may be hostile towards each other when they meet at territory boundaries.

Female orangutans and some chimpanzee females are also territorial, but their territories are less strict. The ranges of these females overlap to some extent, and females may ignore each other when they meet. In other cases, such as the bonobo, females may forage together and form groups containing as many as 10 females and their offspring. Males, in turn, are social only if female groups are large.

Gorillas appear more social than most apes, living in small, permanent groups. However, even their groups turn out to be marginally different from those of the monogamous gibbons. The typical gorilla group is just two or three breeding females and one or occasionally two adult males.

Chimpanzees are the only primates that hunt vertebrate prey on a regular basis. Red colobus monkeys are their favorite prey.

 KILLER APES

Chimpanzees are the only species of primate other than humans who hunt other mammals in an organized, deliberate fashion. Their favored prey seems to be red colobus monkeys, perhaps because these are moderately slow and easy to catch in trees, and not too aggressive when caught. In areas where colobus are not found, small forest antelopes, such as duiker or young bushbuck, are the preferred alternative.

Chimpanzee hunting is an all-male activity. Hunts often start with a single individual noticing a prey animal. If the target is a group of monkeys in a tree, the hunter will soon be joined by others, who spread out in the surrounding trees to block the monkeys' escape routes. Then, one or two chimpanzees will make a sudden dash to try to catch a victim. As the monkeys flee, they may run straight into the arms of one of the waiting chimpanzees.

A hunt attracts considerable interest from all the chimpanzees in the vicinity, who watch from the sidelines and make a cacophony of shrill hoots as the hunt progresses. The sharing of meat after the hunt is almost ritualistic. Everyone wants a share, and those who have parts of the carcass become targets for begging from those who do not. Hunting is very much a seasonal activity, tending to occur at times of the year when plant foods are in short supply, notably the dry season. This suggests that meat is a kind of emergency food. Therefore, even though meat is only a small part of the diet of those chimpanzee populations that are known to hunt, it may be essential for survival in poor-quality or seasonal habitats.

1

2

Male attachments

The social behavior of great ape males seems to be driven by how many mating opportunities they can obtain. Female great apes typically give birth every 4 to 5 years. After giving birth, a mother is unable to conceive again while the infant is dependent on her, since, like humans, suckling causes suppression of the hormones that control the menstrual cycle. Because intervals between successive births are long, opportunities for mating are rare—all the more reason for males to jealously guard their mating opportunities. In many cases, this means defending the territories of a number of females.

Male orangutans are the least social of the great ape males. Their females are too dispersed to make it worthwhile being permanently social, so each male tries to establish a large territory containing the territories of a number of females. An established male defends access to his females as best he can. Since a male who spent all his time with one female would be wasting mating opportunities that might exist elsewhere, orangutan males prefer a kind of roving strategy, whereby they hope to bump into sexually active females more often if they keep searching alone.

Chimpanzee males find themselves in a more complicated situation because the wide range of habitats they occupy means that female grouping patterns vary. In some areas, such as Gombe in Tanzania, females typically forage alone. In richer forest habitats, such as the Taï Forest in Ivory Coast, West Africa, females travel in groups, and in the dense forests of the Congo River basin, female bonobos travel in even larger groups. What the males do depends on how big the female groups are, because the chance of finding mateable females increases with group size. When female groups are large, male chimpanzees associate with them. When females forage alone, the males tend to rove around alone, like orangutan males.

1. Chimpanzees are highly social and, when members of a community meet up while foraging, a great deal of social grooming often follows.

2. Orangutan males develop massive fatty flanges on either side of the face when they mature. These form part of the power display in rivalries between males.

3. Once-captive chimpanzees released on to an island in West Africa clamber in the mangroves at the water's edge in anticipation of their daily food delivery.

4. Mountain gorillas forage at leisure among the herbs and groundsel plants of the Virunga volcanoes, Rwanda.

Chimpanzees are the only primate species, apart from humans, who are known to deliberately engage in genocide.

1. (opposite) A lowland gorilla group at Odzala National Park in the Republic of Congo. The group has left the safety of the forest to forage for favorite foods in the open.

The gorilla provides us with evidence at the other end of the spectrum. Female gorillas tend to associate in groups of two or three. Although male chimpanzees might not consider such small groups of females worth much attention, male gorillas have a different view and do form permanent social groups with the females. This is mainly because gorillas are less mobile than chimpanzees and travel a much shorter distance each day. Unlike male chimpanzees, male gorillas would be unable to rove around wide areas in search of mates.

Brotherhoods

This is not to suggest that chimpanzees are not social. Male chimpanzees band together, often in a "brotherhood" of closely related males, to defend large territories against other male brotherhoods. The large territory gives the members of a brotherhood access to the many females who range within it. Such valuable mating opportunities are defended against all rivals, even to the point of launching apparently deliberate extermination raids against the males of neighboring communities. At Gombe in the late 1970s (▷p. 185), scientists watched in astonishment as the males in one community attacked and wiped out the males in an adjacent community one by one. Similar cases of mass murder were later reported from other chimpanzee populations. Our days of belief in their innocence were brought to an abrupt end—the animals we had thought of as gentle denizens of the forest had turned into monsters.

▷ NEST-MAKERS

The great apes are unusual among the anthropoid primates in that they all make nests in which to spend the night. The orangutans and chimpanzees make their nests in trees, but the gorillas typically make theirs on the ground. Nestmaking is something of a ritual at the end of each day. The nests are made by bending tree branches or other foliage inwards to make a kind of leafy platform on which the animal lies. Each member of a group makes its own nest, except for infants who invariably share their mothers' nests.

Why the great apes make nests remains a puzzle. Although many of the smaller prosimians use nests, these tend to be much less formally constructed affairs tucked into the safety of treeholes. Prosimian nests also tend to be used repeatedly over many weeks and months, whereas ape nests are used only on the day they are made and then abandoned. Nests might offer two advantages—concealment from predators, and warmth during cool nights. Chimpanzees sometimes also make day nests when it rains. Orangutans will hold a large leafy branch over their heads as an umbrella during heavy rain storms, a behavior that might well have its origins in nestmaking.

A chimpanzee relaxes in a night nest perched precariously in the tree canopy. The nest is made by folding in branches to make a leafy platform.

REASONS TO BE FAITHFUL

Monogamy is extremely rare among mammals, with only about 5 percent of species adopting it on a regular basis. The reasons for this are speculative, but the female's self-sufficiency during gestation, and subsequent ability to feed her offspring unaided, make the male mammal all but redundant and therefore more likely to stray. The exceptions to this include tamarins, marmosets, and the dog family. These species have a cooperative approach to rearing their young, probably because it allows more offspring to survive.

1. Infanticide by males is a particular problem for primates because of their long inter-birth intervals. Monogamy, which is prevalent among gibbons, may be one solution to this problem.

2. A female chimpanzee with infant shows agression towards a male. In polygamous species, such as chimpanzees, males compete for the privilege of mating with the females. Only dominant males are reproductively successful.

Parental cooperation

Cooperative rearing by a male–female pair is an effective strategy for birds because most nestlings require a diet of animal matter, rich in protein and energy, for rapid growth. Since males and females are equally good at procuring this, it pays to cooperate in rearing the young. Doing so allows both sexes to rear more offspring than if one sex left all the rearing to its partner.

By contrast, the mammalian system of internal gestation followed by lactation makes the male mammal all but redundant after fertilization. Only the dog family, including wolves and jackals, are universally monogamous. Here, the male helps the female by bringing meat back to the den and regurgitating it half-digested as weaning food for the pups.

Monogamy in primates

Among primates, gibbons are one of the few species to lead a monogamous life. However, their reasons for doing so are puzzling. Unlike male marmosets, birds, and dogs, male gibbons do little to help with rearing the young. They neither carry nor feed them, nor, it seems, do they defend a feeding territory for the females. Although male gibbons are actively territorial, their main concern is to prevent rival males from coming onto their territory and mating with their female. Therefore, something very substantial must make monogamy worthwhile for the male gibbon, as he would father many more offspring if he opted for the roving strategy of other male primates, such as orangutans. The deterrent to leading a polygamous life seems to be the risk that his offspring will be killed by other males.

Killing for fertility

Infanticide is a particular problem among primates. Because of their large brains, they have a long gestation period, and a lengthy infancy, during which the infant is completely dependent on the mother for nutrition. As in

all mammal species, the mother is unable to conceive while she is suckling an infant. Her fertility returns only when the youngster is nearly weaned and the mother's hormones revert to normal. This means that males who take over a female from another male have to wait a long time before the female is ready to breed again.

Infanticide has the effect of bringing the female back into breeding condition right away. It is therefore a highly profitable strategy for males, since a long wait for a female to return to fertility can take up a significant proportion of a male's reproductive life, which is limited when polygamy is the order of the day. The problem is much less acute for females, as they have a much longer reproductive life. If a female spontaneously aborts

a fetus or loses an infant to infanticide, the evolutionary consequences are less serious for her than for a male. However traumatic the loss may be at the time, she is likely to be pregnant again soon.

Male protection

By staying close to the female from one conception to the next, the male gibbon ensures that each offspring he sires makes it through to the point at which it is no longer at risk of infanticide. This is also a convenient arrangement for the female, since it saves too many of her reproductive cycles being disrupted by harassment from other males. Females may also be able to exploit their males' intolerance of intruders to ensure that no one else eats the food on their territory.

3. In monogamous species, such as these white-handed gibbons, males and females live together in separate territories which they defend against intruders.

SEX AND THE SOCIAL WHIRL

The social life of gorillas and orangutans is sedate and low-key. Neither species is renowned for indulging in wild displays of emotion, although both can be spectacular when angry. Theirs tends to be a quiet, undemonstrative lifestyle. Chimpanzee social life could hardly be more different. Whether they range in small groups, like the woodland chimpanzees of Gombe, or in large groups, like the forest-living bonobos, chimpanzees live life on the edge, experiencing constant tension. Dominance relationships between males are hard fought and can become a constant distraction in an otherwise sedate community life.

In chimpanzee society, the males largely stay put throughout their lives. Females, by contrast, often move from one community to another, though to do so more than once in a lifetime is perhaps rare. It is not entirely clear why they should change community in this way, although one reason may be to avoid inbreeding with their close male relatives. However, the fact that they do move has interesting implications for the spread of genes within chimpanzee communities. At Gombe, female genes from one community have been detected as much as 370 miles (600 km) away in other communities. Each female might move only 6 to 9 miles (10–15 km) away from the territory into which she was born, but when her daughter, granddaughter and so on later do the same, the wave of genes traveling

outward in successive generations can reach great distances. At this rate of travel, a distance of 370 miles (600 km) represents about 50 or more generations of migrations. With a chimpanzee generation lasting 15–20 years, that takes us back some 750–1000 years into history.

Insights from genetics

The science of genetics has given us unexpected insights into the hidden life of the chimpanzee. When scientists analyzed the genes of chimpanzees living in the Taï Forest of the Ivory Coast, they discovered that the genes carried by individual males were more widely distributed than one would expect if males stay for life within the territories of

1. Freud intimidates a rival male by swinging on a sapling in his bid to become the dominant male of the Gombe community.

2. Pygmy chimpanzees (bonobos) are renowned for their use of sex as a means of social bonding. Here an adult female has sex with a two-year-old infant.

birth. Since the males clearly do stay in their home territories, the only conceivable explanation is that females sometimes slip into the community next door to mate. Thus, it was the females who were responsible for moving male genes around the forest.

Although male great apes are as assiduous as the males of any species in attempting to prevent their females from straying, the harsh fact of life is that females do not necessarily share the males' interests in these delicate matters. If there's a better male next door, well…

An obsession with sex

The bonobos have taken this loose living to an extreme, and have abandoned any pretence at the niceties of prim society. For bonobos, sex is flamboyant and universal. It is used as a casual greeting and as a means of cementing a friendship, just as we might engage in conversation. No one is excepted. Males mate with males, females mate with females, and both mate with juveniles and sometimes even with infants. And, as with us, sex may be used in extortion—a male may sit at the base of a fruit-laden tree and allow up only those females who mate with him first.

The apes share one other curious feature of sexual behavior with us: while all other primates mate in the usual dog-like position, apes occasionally mate face to face, as we do. Of all the apes, it is the bonobo chimpanzee, so like us in many other ways, that does this most often. Why the ape lineage should show this curious shift from the normal mammalian sex position to an unusual face-to-face mode, we are unable to explain. Perhaps it has something to do with the fact that our relationships are more intimate and intense, and the responses we see in a partner's face provide us with deeper and more meaningful clues about their attitude towards us and so enrich our experience.

2

APES WITH INTELLECT

Primate brains have evolved to be larger for their body weight than those of any other group of animals. The evolutionary pressure favoring this increase in brain size seems to have been the need to live in larger groups with more complex social organization. Not surprisingly given their especially large brains, we are particularly impressed by the great apes' intelligence. When we give them puzzles to solve, they do much better than other species. Also, we are impressed by their sensitive and reflective behavior, both as they interact with each other and as they watch us while we study them. Chimpanzees, at least, share about 98 percent of their DNA with us, so how much do they share of our mental world? This thorny question has both fascinated and frustrated scientists for more than a century. It is such a difficult question to answer precisely because it is difficult to study the mind behind the behavior, even in humans.

THE SOCIAL BRAIN

Mike, one of the males at Jane Goodall's study site at Gombe, managed to become the top-ranking male by an unusual and surprising tactic. Being small for a male, he would not have been able to fight his way to the top of a hierarchy based on physical power. However, one day Mike noticed that the empty kerosene cans in Jane Goodall's camp clattered when they fell. So he took to throwing cans around, a tactic that scared off his rivals, not least because being hit by a large metal can hurts. They soon learned to give him a wide birth and allowed him to dominate them.

Such opportunistic exploitation of situations to achieve one's ends is the hallmark of chimpanzee intelligence. To be able to exploit other individuals in the subtle way Mike did requires an understanding of how others will respond to his actions. This is a more complex issue than first impressions might suggest, for it gets at the heart of what we think of as consciousness.

Know thyself

One of the fundamental aspects of human consciousness is that we have a sense of self-awareness. We know who we are, and we can reflect on our own inner thoughts. This is a difficult phenomenon to study experimentally. We can examine how we think by introspection, reflecting on our own thoughts, but we cannot study other species in the same way. It is even difficult to study other human beings in this way. We can ask them whether they experience certain feelings, but when they answer, we have no guarantee that what they have described is the same as what we experience. Language is a poor medium for conveying inner thoughts and feelings.

One way to find out whether apes have self-awareness is to see whether they can

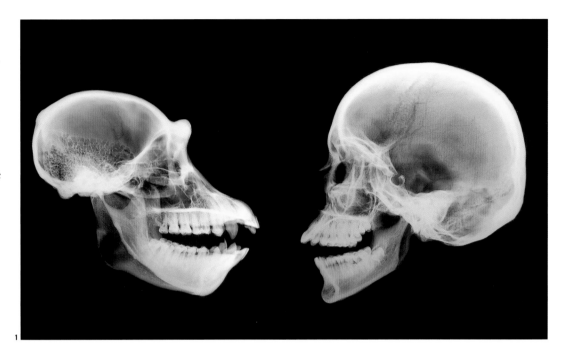

1. X-rays reveal just how much larger human brains (right) are than those of chimpanzees (left).

2. Chimpanzee Mike learned to intimidate rival males at Gombe by throwing empty kerosene cans around. It enabled him to become the dominant male, despite his small size.

★ Apes are the only animals to share with humans the ability to recognize themselves in mirrors.

1. Unlike other primates, chimpanzees can recognize themselves in a mirror, and can use mirrors to ensure that otherwise unviewable parts of their bodies are clean.

2. Pygmy chimpanzees or bonobos have a restricted distribution in the rainforests of the Congo. Some scientists believe that they are more similar to humans than common chimpanzees.

recognize themselves in a mirror. Most animals, such as dogs and cats, fail to realize that the animal facing them in a mirror is in fact their own reflection. They treat the image as though it were another cat or dog. They snarl and spit at it, and try to run behind the mirror to attack the offending animal that snarls back at them.

Scientists studying animal behavior soon came to see the ability to recognize a reflection in a mirror as the benchmark for the concept of self. An animal that recognized itself clearly had some sense of its own identity, a sense of the self as distinct from others. This led to a very simple test. You allow an animal to become familiar with mirrors by placing one in the cage. Later, you give the animal a general anesthetic and put a dot of paint on its forehead while it is unconscious. Then you wait to see whether, when it comes around from the anesthetic, it notices the mark on its forehead. If it does, and shows this by picking at the spot using the mirror to guide itself, then you infer that it has a sense of self.

All the great apes pass this test successfully, although so far no monkey of the dozen or so species tested has passed the test (▷p. 156). The conclusion is that apes have a sense of self, but monkeys do not. However, is the ability to recognize oneself in a mirror really indicative of self-consciousness? It is, of course, indicative of something that apes can do and monkeys cannot. However, what this is remains difficult to decipher.

Mind-readers

A more promising avenue to explore is to ask whether apes have a "theory of mind," otherwise also known as the ability to mindread. All this means is that an individual can imagine what is going on in another individual's mind. The ability to understand another's mind in this way is essential for a number of decidedly human phenomena, including the ability to lie effectively, to write novels, and even to be religious. To lie convincingly, I have to know what thoughts my words will produce in your mind. To be able to write a novel, I, and you, the reader, have to be able to imagine the thoughts and motives of a cast of characters. To believe in a god, I have to suppose that there is a divine being whose intentions may influence events, and whose mind I can influence by prayer.

To do all of these requires the ability to reflect on other individuals' thoughts as well as our own. Psychologists generally take the ability to understand that someone else can hold a false belief as the benchmark for a theory of mind. Children develop the ability to recognize that someone else can believe something different from themselves at about four years of age. Prior to this, they assume that what they believe to be true must be what everyone else believes. The crucial issue, then, is whether any primates share this ability with us.

It is difficult to test for a theory of mind in animals since they cannot speak to us. None the less, two studies have looked for this ability in chimpanzees, and some other tests have looked for related skills, such as the ability to understand the difference between knowledge and ignorance in another individual, and the ability to understand that someone else might be able to see something we cannot, or not see something we can.

From the results, chimpanzees seem to be able to distinguish between individuals who have knowledge about a situation, for example, where food is hidden, and those who do not. However, the evidence that chimpanzees, the only species tested up to now, understand false beliefs and therefore have a theory of mind, is more equivocal. So far, one test has been positive, and one negative. And even the positive result was somewhat marginal.

A life of low cunning

Chimpanzees are nothing if not devious. In one experiment, a low-ranking chimpanzee was shown some fruit hidden in a large outdoor compound. He was then taken back to join the others in their indoor accommodation. Later, all the animals were released back into the outdoor enclosure. Instead of rushing off to where it knew the fruit was hidden, the low-ranking chimpanzee loitered near the door while all the others set off to their favorite corners of the compound. Only once everyone was settled did he surreptitiously set off to retrieve the fruit. He knew that had he gone straight over to the fruit, his unusual behavior would have attracted everyone else's attention and one of the more powerful animals would soon have relieved him of the hidden fruit. Deception of this kind is well established in chimpanzees, although this is not the case in monkeys (▷p. 155).

3. At around four years of age children develop the ability to imagine that other individuals see the world differently from the way they do.

CONVERSATIONAL APES

Long before the fictional Dr. Doolittle entered our cultural consciousness, the idea of being able to talk to animals had long fascinated human beings. Language is so second nature to us that we found it hard to believe that other animals did not also have languages. All we had to do was to understand what their chatters, grunts and barks signified, and off we would go into the uncharted waters of another species' world. The apes, with their self-evident similarities to us, held out the greatest hope for realizing this project.

1. Several chimpanzees have been taught sign languages based on those used by people with speech or hearing difficulties. However, it remains uncertain whether they simply copy their trainers or actually construct sentences.

Teaching chimpanzees to talk
Some early attempts to teach chimpanzees to speak a human language, invariably English, were at least partially motivated by these considerations. The two most famous experiments were carried out in the 1950s and 1960s. Both raised an infant chimpanzee as part of a normal human family alongside the scientist's own child of the same age. Alas, both projects failed miserably. The best that either of the chimpanzees could manage was half a dozen whispered words that bore an imperfect resemblance to the English words they had been taught. Worse, the human child simply learned to copy the chimpanzee's bad table manners rather than the chimpanzee learning to copy the child's cultural behavior.

Sign language experiments
The reason why these projects failed soon became evident. The chimpanzee larynx is set too high in the throat to allow the animals to produce the full range of human vowels and consonants. Even if they understood language, they could never prove it by speaking to us. There followed a number of projects that tried to teach sign languages to chimpanzees on the grounds that apes naturally use gestures when communicating with each other. The most famous of these projects involved the chimpanzee Washoe, who was taught American Sign Language as an infant. She became quite proficient, with a vocabulary of about 100 signs, after many years of practice. However, even her abilities seemed modest compared to those of young children, who are capable of learning one new word for every 90 minutes of their waking day between the ages of three and six years. In any case, Washoe's performance remained shrouded in dispute. Some scientists claimed that all she did was to repeat the signs that her handlers used. Other scientists pointed out that Washoe's language production was limited to asking for things she wanted, which was mostly food and drink. Children, on the other hand, soon start using language to ask questions about the world, such as "What's that?" and "Why?"

Talking with symbols
The next phase of experiments involved use of symbolic languages. In one study symbols representing question words like what? and where?, descriptive words like red and round, concept words like bigger than and on top of, object words like apple and drink, and names like Sue and Austin were placed on a computer keyboard. The apes constructed simple sentences by pressing keys in order.

Success of a kind
These projects proved much more successful, with Kanzi, a young bonobo, learning a vocabulary of several hundred concepts and regularly engaging in "conversations" with his

2. Kanzi, the bonobo, communicates with his trainer using a "keyboard" containing more than 100 symbols.

3. Human children learn to speak effortlessly when very young. A natural skill at imitation is probably essential.

handlers. What is most remarkable about Kanzi is that he was never formally taught these signs. He learned them as spontaneously as an infant would, while watching his mother being trained to use the keyboard. His own proficiency on it is spectacular. He can carry out complex instructions given in English, and reply via a keyboard connected to a voice synthesizer. Even so, many doubt whether he has true language in the human sense. Once again, the main problem is that he can use only two- or three-word "sentences," most of which concern his immediate wants. His proficiency seems to be at about the same level as a two-year-old human child.

◆ TOPIC LINKS

2.2 Scents and Sounds
p. 70 Vocal signals

3.4 A Unique Intelligence
p. 148 A unique intelligence

4.3 Apes with Intellect
p. 208 Should apes have human rights?

4.4 An Ape on Two Legs
p. 214 The humour factor
p. 223 Cains's children

4.5 Family Portaits: Apes
p. 229 Chimpanzee
p. 230 Bonobo
p. 231 Human

USING TOOLS

Ever since their ingenious behavior was caught on film, the termite-fishing chimpanzees of Gombe in Tanzania have been famous. Fishing for termites is a delicate operation. The chimpanzee feeds a long grass stem into the entrance hole of a termite nest, jiggles it around for a few moments, and then slowly withdraws it inch by inch, taking care not to dislodge the precious cargo of soldier termites clinging tenaciously to it. Once out, the termites are swept rapidly into the mouth and a sweet, nutritious snack is enjoyed.

Chimpanzees are among the few animal species to partake in this delicacy, since termites barricade themselves deep within their concrete-like mud mounds to avoid such a fate. Most animals are not strong enough to break open their fortresses. Even humans, who savor termites as much as any other species, have to wait until the termites form their huge mating swarms outside the nest, but that happens on only a few days each year. Chimpanzees have solved the problem by fishing, an activity that requires great patience and skill.

Chimpanzee toolkits

All over central Africa, chimpanzees can be found using tools to obtain food. As well as their termite-fishing rods, they use a number of other simple tools. In Gombe they employ wads of chewed leaves like sponges to dip for water trapped in deep cavities in tree trunks. Leaves are also used for wiping blood or mucus off fur, much the same way we use tissues.

1. Chimpanzees are expert tool users. Here one uses a thin stem to withdraw termites from a termite nest, a feat that requires patience and delicate skill.

Chimpanzees eat more than 30 species of plants that are known to have medicinal properties. Many of them are also used as medicines by the local human population.

An altogether more adventurous game is dipping for ants. Chimpanzees dip the ends of thin sticks and chewed twigs into the marching columns of African safari ants. As soon as the soldier ants have gripped the intruding implement with their powerful jaws, the twig is withdrawn and pulled quickly through the hand to gather the ants. These are swiftly transferred to the mouth and rapidly chewed. Unlike the modestly armed termites, soldiers of the notorious safari ants can deliver a ferocious bite with their fearsome jaws, so fast action is essential if the chimpanzee is to avoid bites in painful places. A stick held too long in the ant column, or a foot placed too near it, will result in ants racing on to the chimpanzee. Ant-dipping is a skill that is learned fast or not at all.

Nutcrackers

In the Taï Forest of Ivory Coast, chimpanzees have developed a completely different local tradition, nutcracking. The oil palm tree is found all over tropical Africa and produces a rich nut that is highly valued by humans for its oily flesh. However, the meat of the nut is enclosed in an unusually hard outer case. Most animals cannot eat oil palm nuts simply because they are so well protected. Humans and chimpanzees are the exception, and both have solved the problem in the same way. They use hammers to crack the nuts.

When one of the Taï Forest chimpanzees decides to do some oil palm nutcracking, it looks for a suitable hammer. This is often a stone of a particular shape and weight that can be held firmly in the hand, but sometimes a piece of wood will do. Next, the chimpanzee gathers some nuts and heads for a spot where

Eating *Aspilia* in Mahale.

 HERBAL MEDICINE

Like all animals, chimpanzees in the wild acquire parasites, either from the food they eat or from vegetation as they brush past. Internal parasites are often the hardest to detect and deal with. Worms and other parasites in the gut can become so debilitating, even for humans, that they constitute a serious threat to life. At best, they use up food and tax the body's immune system.

Like humans all around the world, chimpanzees have learned that some plants possess natural medicinal properties. The chimpanzees of Gombe and Mahale in Tanzania swallow the bristly leaves of *Aspilia* and other plants. At Mahale, chimpanzees with heavy parasite loads chew *Vernonia* pith. Research has shown that chimpanzees who swallow these leaves or chew on the bitter pith will subsequently have fewer parasites. *Aspilia* and other species of leaves swallowed whole by apes across Africa appear to physically expel worms from the gut while *Vernonia* juice contains numerous compounds that are toxic to worms. In fact, about 25 plant species sometimes eaten by chimpanzees are also taken by humans to treat a variety of medical problems ranging from stomachache to worms and amoebic dysentery.

there is something to use as an anvil. This might be a rock embedded in the ground, the buttress root of a tree, or even a branch. Once settled, the chimpanzee balances a nut on the anvil and hits it with the hammer until it cracks. This can be tricky because each oil palm nut has to be carefully steadied between thumb and finger until just before the hammer comes down, otherwise it will roll off the anvil. Sometimes, the anvil may be unsteady and might have to be propped with another stone.

Good hammers are rare, and the chimpanzees of the Taï keep a close eye on where their hammers are. Anvil sites are of course fixed, since they tend to be trees or large rocks. The problem is that hammers can move, or, at least, other chimpanzees can move them from one site to another hundreds of yards away. It seems that when the chimpanzees happen to pass an anvil site, they take note of which hammers are present and remember this. That they are keeping track of the location of the hammers is also suggested by the fact that, when they visit a nut tree, they often collect the nearest suitable hammer on the way, even though this might require a slight detour.

In order to study this behavior in more detail, scientists painted numbers on all the hammer stones in one part of the Taï Forest, and then carefully plotted their locations day by day. At the same time, they recorded which hammers the chimpanzees collected when they went nut collecting. By measuring the distance between the nut tree and all the hammers available, the scientists were able to show that the chimpanzees carefully balanced the size of the hammer against the distance they had to carry it. Heavy hammers were carried shorter distances than lighter hammers.

It has been suggested that the chimpanzees learn how to use these hammers by carefully watching their mothers. It has even been suggested that mothers teach their offspring the correct technique, giving them easy bits of nut to finish cracking, or holding the youngsters' hands in the right way. However, it is by no means clear that the juvenile chimpanzees are doing anything more than working the technique out for themselves, having noticed that the adults are doing something interesting that occasionally produces titbits to eat. The fact that the chimpanzees seem to be slow at learning how to crack nuts lends some

1. In West Africa, some chimpanzee populations have learned to use stone hammers to crack the super-hard nuts of the oil palm.

2. Risking painful reprisals, a chimpanzee at Gombe uses a stem to collect safari ants to eat. One false move would result in ferocious attacks by the ants.

3. A chimpanzee in Liberia, West Africa, smashes a coconut on a stone anvil. Such behavior has never been seen among the chimpanzees of central or East Africa.

4. Sultan, the star of Wolfgang Köhler's studies of ape intelligence, lengthens a pole to reach some food.

support to this view. It can take as long as three years of patient trial and error to become proficient. Teaching ought to be faster.

Tricks with bananas

Inevitably, chimpanzee tool use and tool making have been subjects of considerable interest, not least because they raise questions about the abilities of our own tool-using ancestors. Tools provide us with a window into the chimpanzee's mind.

One of the earliest studies of tool use was carried out by the German psychologist Wolfgang Köhler. At the outbreak of the First World War in 1914, Köhler happened to be in the Canary Islands off the west coast of Africa. Because these islands belong to Spain, Köhler was interned as an enemy alien. His captivity was of a rather gentlemanly nature, as befitted the times, and Köhler was allowed to busy himself in innocent pursuits at the local zoo. Here he became intrigued by the intellectual skills of the chimpanzees.

Köhler set the chimpanzees a number of tasks, such as how to reach a banana outside the cage when given two sticks that were each not quite long enough. Sultan, a young male, solved the problem once he had been shown that the two sticks could be slotted together to form a single long one, a significant achievement that astounded the observers.

These experiments remained classics for many years, though looking back on them now, we are perhaps less persuaded than Köhler and his contemporaries were. Impressive as his apes' performances were, their problem-solving achievements were far from spontaneous. Nowadays, Köhler's observations would not be regarded as such conclusive evidence of truly insightful tool-using behavior.

None the less, apes can use tools in an apparently insightful way. Kanzi, the language-trained bonobo (▷ p. 202), can light a barbecue and cook his own sausages.

PRIMATE POLITICS

Apes sometimes play politics, manipulating each other to further their own selfish interests with as much apparent guile as humans. However, are we right to read human-like thoughts and intentions into such behavior? A revealing example comes from a chimpanzee colony at Arnhem Zoo in the Netherlands.

Yeroen had been the dominant male of the chimpanzee colony at the zoo. Being top male brought many privileges, but none was more precious to Yeroen than sexual access to the females. However, Yeroen was getting on in years, and his younger rival Luit was showing a distinct interest in replacing Yeroen as top

male. Eventually, Luit's persistence paid off and he was able to displace Yeroen.

However, Luit had reckoned without the cunning and experience of old age. After his demotion, Yeroen began making overtures to Nikkie, the youngest of the group's three adult males. Then, whenever Nikkie got into a fight with Luit, Yeroen came to Nikkie's aid. It was not long before the combined efforts of the two males overturned Luit's dominant position in the group. Yeroen seemed prepared to allow the powerful young Nikkie to dominate him and become top male. Although the price Yeroen paid was to be second male, as Nikkie's ally he still had access to some of the females, so he was better off than he had been with Luit at the top. Luit, meanwhile, slumped

into third position, where he was denied any opportunity to mate.

Nikkie, however, was not entirely happy about this arrangement. Every now and then, the sight of Yeroen mating with "his" females became too much for him and he attacked the old male. Being no match for the younger male, Yeroen would back off. However, when Nikkie later got into a scrape with Luit, Yeroen would sit on the sidelines and watch. His refusal to help made Nikkie vulnerable, for Nikkie was no match for Luit in a one-on-one contest. Yeroen's pointed reminder of who pulled the strings was usually all Nikkie needed to reinstate the old male's mating privileges, at least until the next time Nikkie was overwhelmed by jealousy.

Apes' greater intelligence and sensitivity makes them much less tolerant of being caged than many other primates. Like humans confined in cages, they become depressed and disorientated.

 SHOULD APES HAVE HUMAN RIGHTS?

Customs of ancient origin oblige all humans to follow a moral code that governs how they may treat other members of the tribe. This code, embodied in Judaeo-Christian cultures in the Ten Commandments, accords all the members of the tribe with certain fundamental rights and obligations. In many traditional societies, such rights were not always extended to members of other tribes, who were regarded as legitimate prey to be enslaved, killed, or robbed of their women or belongings. However, today, in our more civilized world, we endeavor to accord human rights to everyone. The right to life, to freedom from persecution, and so on, are enshrined in United Nations declarations. To be sure, human rights are as often breached as upheld, as we have seen in the episodes of genocide that so dishonored the history of the twentieth century.

Many have asked whether other species ought to be accorded the same rights. The great apes, being most similar to us, have been frequent contenders. The main argument against giving humans rights to apes is that such rights are contractual among humans, and presuppose sufficient intelligence to understand the nature of the contract. Yet we all agree that human babies and the mentally handicapped should not be denied human rights, despite the fact that they too cannot understand the obligations of a mutual contract. We offer them membership of the club by acting as their guardians. We could just as easily do the same for apes.

Understanding Yeroen

This typical instance of the complex interplay of chimpanzee social life is easy to interpret in anthropomorphic terms. Yet it remains far from clear just how much Yeroen's actions were underwritten by deliberate scheming. Examples of what seems like clever behavior impress us, and we fall prey to our natural tendency to interpret animal behavior in terms of intentions. There is a crucial issue here because the African great apes are very closely related to us, so if anyone shares our emotional world it must be them. But how can we be sure that they really do? We cannot read their inner minds and feelings.

There are two opposing schools of thought on this issue. The "behaviorists" insist that we should confine our discussions to what can be objectively observed, that is, behavior. Since we cannot observe inner feelings and experiences, it is meaningless even to ask whether other species have them. We know that we have them, and we can be sure that some animals, insects and bacteria, for example, do not, but where is the point of transition along this continuum?

Behaviorists argue that caution demands that we draw the line at humans and leave it at that. On this view, all behavior must be explained on the basis of learned patterns. The opposite point of view insists that, while it is difficult to know exactly where to draw the line, we can be reasonably sure that those species closest to us in evolutionary and neurological terms probably do share something of our inner world. Besides, assuming that these animals have an inner world provides a much simpler explanation of their behavior than a strictly behaviorist interpretation. However, while the non-behaviorist view may seem ultimately more fruitful, we are still left with the problem of finding out what is going on in minds other than our own.

1

2

1. Yeroen and the young male Nikkie form a coalition against the new dominant male, Luit, at Arnhem Zoo in the Netherlands. (Photograph courtesy of Frans de Waal, from *Chimpanzee Politics*.)

2. Yeroen in contemplative mood. When the wily old Yeroen demoted his rival, Luit, did he consciously intend to use Nikkie to do so? (Photograph courtesy of Frans de Waal, from *Chimpanzee Politics*.)

AN APE ON TWO LEGS

The sky above loomed dark and threatening as clouds of ash and sulphurous fumes spread from the distant volcano. The rumbles and explosions spawned by the volcano rolled across the plain to where two adults and a child stumbled wearily across the ash-covered landscape. It had been a bad night. The noise had disturbed their sleep, and daylight had brought no respite. They were anxious to get as far away as possible. A group of antelope, startled by a sudden explosion in the mountain's deep interior, crossed their tracks at full tilt. The date was 3.5 million years ago. The three figures were australopithecines, our ancient ancestors. A short while after they passed, a light rain fell and turned their footprints into concrete, to be buried under more layers of ash and dust. There they remained, hidden from view and the ravages of time, until 3.5 million years later when they were accidentally discovered by the fossil-hunter Mary Leakey.

THE ANCESTORS' STORY

We have been so successful as a species that we might be pardoned for thinking our presence on the stage of life was somehow ordained and inevitable. However, we have not always had it so easy. Our species has reached the dawn of the 21st century through a long and circuitous series of accidents, near misses, and downright luck. So tenuous was the thread that held us in place at times that it is almost a miracle we are here at all. Our story is that of the waif who became a millionaire more by luck than judgement.

The hard evidence

The ancestry of humans is unusually well documented. We have a large number of fossils that can be organized into a reasonably coherent sequence through time. Even though palaeoanthropologists continue to argue about the details, the broad pattern is clear. At some point around 5 million years ago, one group of perfectly ordinary apes began to make increasing use of the more open woodlands that bordered their forest home. It was a last-ditch attempt to cope with the deteriorating forest conditions brought about by change in the climate.

Species that venture into unfamiliar habitats invariably run great risks. They lack both the physiological tools as well as the ecological knowledge to cope effectively with new environments. They survive only if they adapt rapidly enough to the new conditions, and they only adapt quickly if many die, weeding out the less well adapted and leaving better-suited individuals to breed. In times of great mortality, a species' survival can hang in the balance. This is the story of that one successful attempt to break free from the inevitability of extinction that faced most of the other ape populations.

1. The 3.5-million-year-old tracks of a larger and a smaller australopithecine frozen forever in the volcanic ash at Laetoli, Tanzania. The tracks appear to be those of a child and two adults, one walking in the footprints of the other.

First steps

Our story begins with a group of great apes known as australopithecines, or "southern apes." These are the earliest known ancestors of humans to appear in the fossil record after the split between our own lineage, hominids, and that of chimpanzees, which occurred some 5 million years ago (▷p. 179). The australopithecines were only slightly different from the great apes of today. They had a similar brain size and probably similar dietary requirements. However, they did differ in one crucial respect. Australopithecines walked on two legs like we do, rather than on four like chimpanzees or gorillas. We know this from the remarkable 3.5-million-year-old footprints that Mary Leakey found in volcanic rock at Laetoli in northern Tanzania. It is clear from the shapes of the prints that their feet were more humanlike than apelike, and therefore already adapted for a striding gait.

Fossil bones of australopithecines reveal that they had already evolved some of the anatomical features that characterize modern humans. One of these is a bowl-shaped pelvis. Great apes, like all other primates, have a long, narrow pelvis. Their guts hang from the pelvis and spine, and are supported below by skin. However, when the body is tilted upright, a long pelvis is unable to support the guts, or unborn babies in the womb. The guts flop forward and down. To prevent that happening, and to provide a more solid platform on which to balance the trunk, the australopithecines evolved a bowl-shaped

pelvis within which baby and guts nestle.

The striding walk so characteristic of modern humans was not fully developed at this stage, but the australopithecines' form of upright walking was sufficiently similar to ours to require the same kind of long legs as we have. Other great apes have comparatively short, weak legs and long, powerful arms for climbing tree trunks. We humans have the opposite—weak arms and long, muscular legs designed for walking long distances.

The australopithecines' ultimate success as a species is attested to by the fact that they colonized virtually all of the savanna and woodland habitats of Africa south of the Sahara. Moreover, they subdivided into a number of different species over the 3 million years of their existence. We have no idea exactly where they originated, but the earliest fossils are all from the eastern corner of Africa—modern Tanzania, Kenya, and Ethiopia.

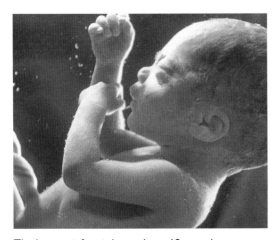

The human infant is born about 12 months prematurely because its head would not pass through the mother's birth canal if it were born at the same stage of development as the infants of other primates.

 ## THE COSTS OF BEING BIGHEADED

Evolution is a hodgepodge affair that rarely produces perfection. It builds on what is already there, modifying and adapting existing parts rather than creating novel components. The result is an often imperfect design, especially when evolution has been as fast and relentless as it has been in our case.

One example is the weakness of our backs. In the industrialized world, more working days are lost from back pain and back injury than from any other cause. This is because the lower backbone is not really strong enough to carry the full weight of our trunk and head, despite 4 million years of walking on two feet. Our backs are a compromise between stability and flexibility. To make them completely resistant to dislocation would require a heavier and less flexible spine. Running and throwing spears would then become more difficult.

Another example is the fact that human babies are born 12 months early. Given the size of our brain, humans ought to have a 21-month pregnancy, judging by comparison with other primates. Our 9-month pregnancy is a compromise between the earliest point at which the baby can survive outside the womb and the width of the birth canal through the pubic bone. Because the birth canal has narrowed due to changes in the skeleton that let us walk upright, a baby with a fully developed brain would have a head so large that it would be unable to pass through. Instead, we give birth early and the baby completes its brain growth outside the womb.

This explains why human babies are so helpless at birth compared to those of other monkeys and apes, and why premature babies are so much at risk. Even full-term babies are already on the margin of survival. It also explains why birth complications are more common in humans than other primates. The baby's head can only just fit through the birth canal as it is.

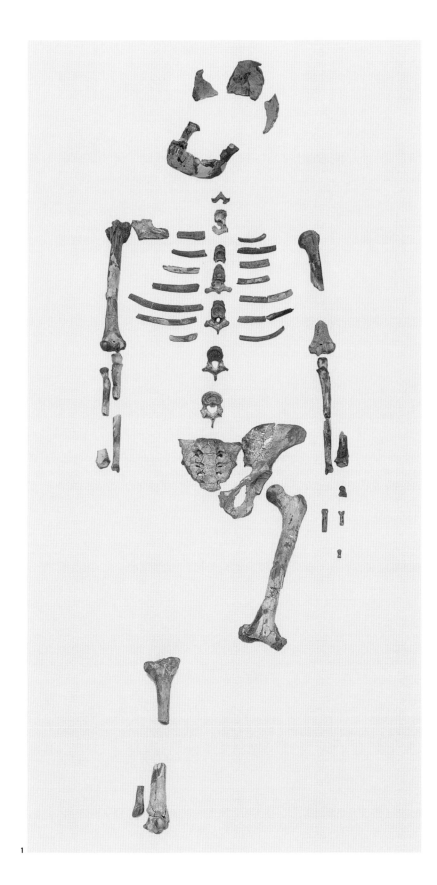

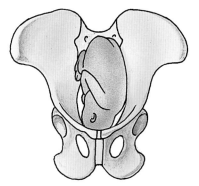

Chimpanzee

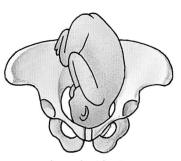

Australopithecine

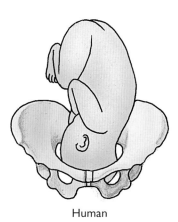

Human

2. The pelvis of a modern human is bowl-shaped to provide a stable platform for our two-legged striding walk, and is remakably narrow compared to the size of a human baby's head. Chimpanzees and australopithecines, or early humans, have more cylidrical pelvises, through which their smaller babies pass more easily.

1. The most complete skeleton of an australopithecine. Known as Lucy, she lived about 3 million years ago in the Afar Desert of northeast Ethiopia.

THE HUMOR FACTOR

Grooming forms a special part of social life for monkeys and apes. It is the glue that bonds their social groups together. However, grooming is a time-consuming activity, and only a few individuals can be groomed at once. Even among humans, physical expressions of intimacy, such as stroking and patting, cannot easily be directed at two individuals at the same time. For our ancestors, this created a serious problem. Their environment demanded ever larger social groups, but their system of bonding would not allow it. When numbers exceeded the ideal group size for grooming, the groups became unstable and broke up. To overcome this limitation, our ancestors needed another mechanism for social bonding— one that would bridge the gap between the time available for social interaction and the amount of interaction needed to bond a large group.

1. Weddings provide a ritual opportunity to bring together the large circle of friends and relatives known to the human couple.

2. In humans, conversation replaced grooming as the main way of making relationships, providing a means of bonding larger social groups together.

Friends and acquaintances

Although humans live in country groupings that can number hundreds of millions of individuals, real human social groups, as defined by the number of people that any one individual knows well enough to call a friend, are much smaller. In fact, it seems that each of us has on average about 150 acquaintances that we can claim to know reasonably well. Calculations suggest that monkeys or apes living in groups of this size would have to spend around 40 percent of their day in social interaction in order to bond through grooming alone. In fact, no non-human primate spends more than 20 percent of its time in social interaction, mainly because of the demands imposed by foraging.

A new interaction

Our ancestors found a solution to their social dilemma when language use evolved. Unlike grooming, conversation allows us to interact with several individuals simultaneously (a speaker can converse coherently with up to three listeners, but no more). Language also allows us to exchange information about our social network, something that monkeys and apes, whose knowledge is limited to what

3

4

they see, cannot do. However, in evolving language to solve one problem, our ancestors inevitably created another. Grooming works as a bonding device for monkeys because the pinching and pulling that it involves are good at stimulating the brain to release opiates. These chemicals, which are similar to opium and morphine, play an important role in controlling pain. They are also released whenever the body is stroked or stimulated, like during grooming. They give monkeys and apes a mild opiate "high," which causes them to find the activity pleasurable and relaxing. This enjoyment probably helps bond grooming partners.

Although humans often engage in physical grooming, like stroking and petting, and gain the same opiate-induced pleasure from it as monkeys, such behavior tends to be confined to our more intimate relationships, which often rely more on physical contact than on language. In contrast, our less intimate interactions with acquaintances use conversation as the main means of social interaction. However, since conversation does not have the physical force needed to stimulate opiate production, it lacks the mechanism that makes grooming so effective for bonding in non-human primates.

Getting high on humor

How did our ancestors overcome this chemical gap in our social world? It seems that the answer may have have been by evolving laughter. Laughter is virtually unique to humans. Even if chimpanzees have sometimes been claimed to laugh, they do not laugh as readily or as often as humans. Laughter makes the face and chest muscles work hard, so opiates are released to reduce the muscular stress involved, and we gain a high from the activity. This seems to be why we devote so much time to trying to make each other laugh during conversations. It might also explain why conversations with people who will not joke or laugh seem unrewarding.

3. Smiling and laughing are unique to humans. The rush of opiates triggered by them helps make us feel well disposed to those we interact with.

4. This relaxed session of grooming is typical of primate social life. Although grooming helps keep fur clean, its most important role is in creating the sense of intimacy that bonds two individuals.

The toolmaker arrives

Around 2.5 million years ago, during a sudden drying and cooling of Earth's climate, a new, more lightly built and bigger-brained ape appears in the East African fossil record. With the appearance of *Homo erectus*, the first certain member of the second phase of our story, we see a dramatic change in the manufacture of tools. For the first time, carefully crafted stone implements called "handaxes" appear in the fossil record.

By primate standards, *Homo erectus* was a hugely successful species. It survived for more than 2 million years and became the first great ape to leave Africa and colonize Europe and Asia since the ancestors of the orangutan had made the same journey 15 million years earlier. *Homo erectus* lived until surprisingly recently, only becoming extinct in China and the Far East 50,000–100,000 years ago.

Yet these species showed surprisingly little anatomical or even cultural change during their long time span. The similarity in the size and design of stone handaxes over the period has astonished archaeologists. This constancy suggests that *Homo erectus* was well adapted to its particular niche. It was a niche that, probably for the first time, included a diet with a significant amount of meat. Although chimpanzees are hunters, meat contributes only a small amount to their overall diet. The australopithecines probably hunted in much the same way. However, it seems likely that meat became an increasingly important part of the *Homo erectus* diet, perhaps because the deteriorating climate forced *erectus* to range further out into the woodlands and savannas.

OUR TOOL-MAKING ANCESTORS

A beautifully symmetrical Acheulian-style European handaxe from around 250,000 years ago.

Our hominid ancestors have been making and using tools almost since they first appeared in the fossil record 4 million years ago. The earliest tools used by the australopithecines were probably not too different to the hammer stones of the Taï chimpanzees. However, it is not always clear whether the pebble tools of the australopithecines are in fact manufactured tools or just naturally broken bits of rock. It is not really until the appearance of *Homo erectus* ("upright man"), the earliest unquestionable member of our own genus, around 2.5 million years ago, that we begin to find deliberately manufactured tools. Among these were the "handaxes," large, shield-shaped stones with carefully chipped surfaces.

The function of these handaxes remains obscure. Were they used to crack open bones in search of marrow, to throw at prey animals, or to dig for roots? Some archaeologists have even questioned whether handaxes were tools at all. They suggest that the axes were just the cores of stone left behind after stone flakes had been chipped off for use as razors when cutting up animal carcasses. Perhaps this might explain why these "tools" remained virtually unchanged for nearly 2 million years.

It is not until the so-called Upper Palaeolithic Revolution a mere 50,000 years ago that we find a dramatic improvement in both the variety and quality of artefacts. Suddenly, new kinds of tools, such as needles, awls, and arrowheads, appear, and they are now finely made. Items of pure ornamentation like brooches, and even toys in the form of doll-like figures, appear for the first time, and cave paintings follow soon after.

Neanderthals had the largest brains of all primates, at around .72 cubic inches. They were significantly larger than those of modern humans, whose brains average .48 cubic inches.

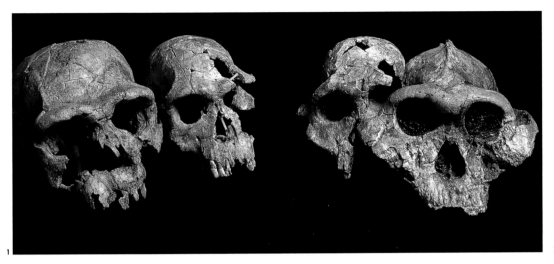

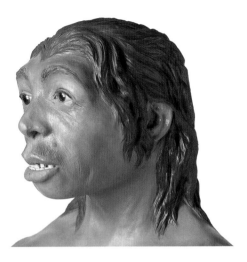

The Neanderthal puzzle

In 1856, quarrymen in the Neander Valley in Germany discovered what appeared to be a human skeleton tucked away in the back of a cave. The anatomists of the day were puzzled by its heavy form and beetle-browed face, and concluded that it was an unfortunate village idiot crippled by rickets, or perhaps a wounded Cossack soldier who, returning from the Battle of Waterloo, had crawled into the cave to die. Later, after the discovery of similar fossils and the publication of Charles Darwin's book *On the Origin of Species* in 1859, it became clear that the Neanderthals, as they had come to be known, might be our ancestors.

A Neanderthal might not have attracted a second look dressed in a suit on a modern city street, but matters would be different if we saw him or her naked. Then we would see someone with a heavy and stocky build, short, thickset arms and legs, and a jutting face with a bulbous nose and no chin. Neanderthals had powerful jaw muscles that allowed the mouth to be used as a vice. The stocky build was an adaptation to the cold climate of Europe during the ice ages, as was the large nose, which appears designed to warm the cold European air before it entered the lungs. Neanderthals were well adapted to Europe's cold climate.

Ancestors or cousins?

For many years, scientists believed that Neanderthals were our direct ancestors. However, genetic studies have finally ended that theory. A few years ago it became possible to extract DNA from tiny fragments of cells on the original Neander skeleton. When this was analyzed, it turned out that the DNA signature was too different from that of modern humans for Neanderthals to have been our direct ancestors, even though some limited interbreeding might have occurred. In all likelihood, they were the descendants of previous populations of early *Homo sapiens* that had colonized Europe several hundred thousand years ago. Modern humans, it turned out, were descended from another branch of early humans that had remained in Africa. The Neanderthals were a side branch on our family tree, not our direct ancestors.

The Neanderthals survived for around 100,000 years in Europe, and toward the end of their history they coexisted with our own ancestors. The last of the Neanderthals finally died out a mere 30,000 years ago, barely 1000 human generations before our time. Why they perished remains a mystery. An inability to cope with the warming climate and changing wildlife of Europe has been suggested, but this seems unlikely because they had previ-

1. Fossil hominids from Lake Turkana, northern Kenya. From left to right they are: *Homo erectus*, a gracile australopithecine, and two robust australopithecines.

2. Reconstruction of a Neanderthal woman based on a 41,000-year-old skeleton from Tabun, Israel.

ously been so successful in adapting to changing conditions. Extermination by the invaders from Africa is a favorite theory, but genocide on this scale is equally implausible without modern weapons. Most likely, the Neanderthals died out for the same reason that most modern native populations have been almost wiped out following the arrival of colonists from elsewhere: disease. There have been spectacular cases of genocide perpetrated by invaders in historical times, such as the extermination of the Moriori people of the Chatham Islands in 1835 by the Maoris of New Zealand, but the populations of most native peoples, from America to Australasia, have collapsed because they lacked resistance to diseases that invaders brought with them.

Out of Africa

Some 70,000 years ago, a new wave of migrants crossed the land bridge that connects Africa to Europe, and spread rapidly through the new continent and into Asia. These people, the Cro-Magnons, were of African origin and were anatomically identical to modern humans, though perhaps a little taller. They were our direct ancestors. They brought with them a new and more sophisticated culture, because soon after their appearance we begin to find finely crafted tools and ornaments in the archaeological record. A little later come the cave paintings of France and Spain that are so evocative of life 30,000 or so years ago.

The Cro-Magnons were extremely successful. Within less than 30,000 years of their emergence from Africa, they had colonized the whole of Europe and spread east through southern Asia to China, the islands of Southeast Asia, and Australia. Perhaps 15,000 years later they walked across the Bering Strait, then exposed by low sea levels, crossing from Asia into Alaska. They swept down through the Americas, taking only a few thousand years to find their way into South America.

⭐ Until as recently as 30,000 years ago, there was always more than one human species in existence.

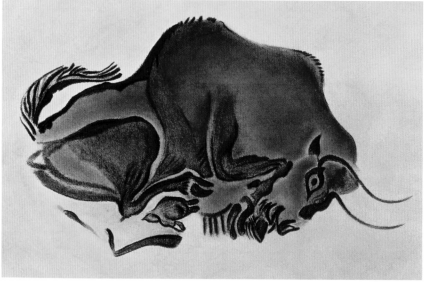

1. The Venus of Willendorf, Austria, a fertility symbol carved in stone around 25,000 years ago.

2. A cave painting of a bison from Altamira, Spain, dated around 13,000 BC.

THE HUMAN ANIMAL

While the fate of the great apes hangs in the balance, that of our own species could hardly be more different. In a matter of 70,000 years, humans have spread across the globe and colonized every continent. We have even ventured beyond the confines of our planet to land on the moon, and have sent unmanned spacecraft to investigate neighboring planets. Across our planet, we have diversified and adapted to different conditions, and we have triumphed over environments and climates that have defeated all other species. We might be excused for viewing ourselves as somehow special.

Human diversity

The world's human population includes a far greater variety of forms than is seen in any other ape. In Africa we find dark-skinned, tall, lean people as well as short pygmies. In Eurasia there are tall, blonde forms as well as short, brown-skinned people with wavy hair, and in the Americas, there are bronzed, dark-haired people. Alongside this diversity of physical forms is a bewildering array of cultural and linguistic forms. Modern humans speak 6,000 recognizably different languages, pray to gods of astonishing variety, and arrange themselves in social groups as diverse as all the mating systems found among our primate cousins.

Yet all this diversity is only skin deep. All modern humans are descended from a common ancestor who lived in Africa only 150,000 to 200,000 years ago, and the common ancestor of Europeans, Asians, Australians, and native Americans lived only about 70,000 to 100,000 years ago. Those differences in stature, skin color, facial form, language, and social habit have all evolved within a few tens of thousands of years. Some

were rapid adaptations to the local environment, and some were adaptations to other evolutionary pressures. The pale skin and blonde hair of northern Europeans, for example, evolved as adaptations to the weak sunlight of high latitudes, since human skin needs sunlight to make vitamin D, but the pigment in dark skin slows this process down. The ancestors of Scandinavians left Africa some 70,000 years ago as dark-skinned people. A mere 3,500 generations later their descendants are white skinned and blonde.

Some genetic adaptations have arisen with even greater speed, such as the ability to digest milk in adulthood. Although every human is reared on milk as a baby, most cannot digest milk as adults because the body stops producing the milk-digesting enzyme, lactase, after weaning. In most humans, milk can cause diarrhea, severe debilitation and even death in older children and adults. However, several races, including most Caucasians and some of the cattle-herding peoples of northeastern Africa, drink milk as

3. Inuits, or Eskimos, are short and squat, a physique that minimizes loss of body heat in the snow-bound Arctic.

4. The tall, thin Masai are typical of peoples adapted to the hot climates of Africa's tropical grasslands.

5. In most human races, milk is ideal for babies but cannot be digested by adults.

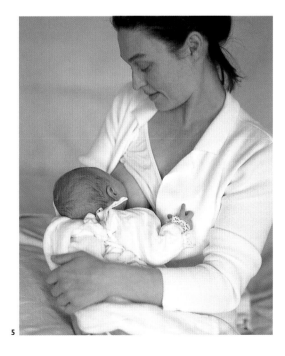

EVE'S DAUGHTERS

Evidence that Cro-Magnons underwent a massive expansion, colonizing Europe, Asia, Australia, and the Americas, after their emergence from Africa some 70,000 years ago comes from studies of human DNA. Advances in molecular genetics now allow us to compare the exact sequences of the genetic code in the chromosomes of two different individuals. We can determine just how different the sequences are and, from this, how long ago the individuals shared a common ancestor.

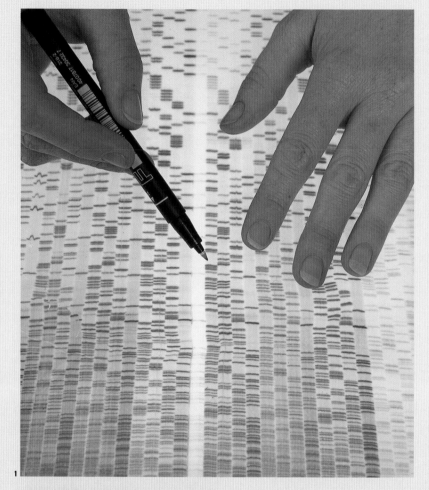

Maternal DNA

Some DNA comparisons have been made using genetic material from cell parts called mitochondria. These tiny "energy pumps" are contained in every cell, but because their DNA is not part of the chromosomal complement in the cell's nucleus, it is inherited only through the female line because the embryo develops from a fertilized maternal cell, the ovum. Therefore, similarities in mitochondrial DNA reflect maternal relatedness. The relationships they trace are all mother–daughter lineages.

Out of Africa

When geneticists compared the mitochondrial DNA from modern peoples, they were astonished to find that all living humans shared similar DNA. The patterns of similarity in mitochondrial DNA suggest that all modern Europeans, Asians, Australians, native Americans, and some northern Africans shared a common ancestor as recently as 70,000 to 100,000 years ago. Since this more

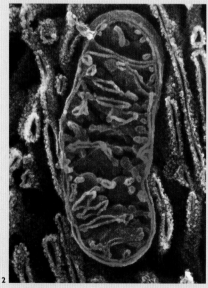

1. When looking for similarities and differences in the barcode patterns of DNA from different individuals, each column represents a single individual's genetic code in a tiny part of one chromosome.

2. A mitochondrian supplies the energy for a cell. It was probably bacteria that successfully invaded cells, since mitochondria are inherited only through the female line.

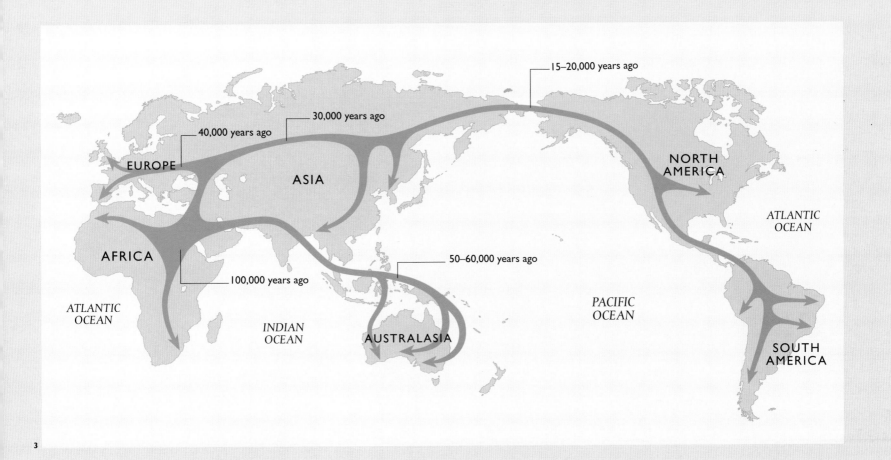

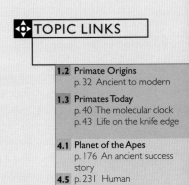

or less common set of DNA is a subset of the variation seen in modern Africa, it suggests that the common ancestress of all modern humans had lived in Africa some time between 100,000 and 200,000 years ago. Although there was no single "Eve" from whom we are all descended, estimates of the size of the ancestral population required to produce the amount of diversity in modern DNA suggest that it was very small. Only about 5,000 females contributed to the ancestry of all modern humans. It is likely that even fewer men did, since the kinds of polygynous mating systems that characterize most human societies mean that fatherhood is much less evenly distributed in populations than motherhood. The last common male ancestors were either many fewer in number or more recent than their female counterparts.

Survivors

Those 5,000 Eves who lived 150,000 or so years ago in Africa need not all have belonged to one social group, or even have lived in the same part of Africa. Rather, what these calculations imply is that, irrespective of how large the human population might have been at that time, only the descendants of those 5,000 Eves survived the winnowing of nature's sieve in the millennia that followed.

The ravages of famines, plagues, and other natural disasters that swept through the populations in Africa and Eurasia resulted in many lineages dying out, until only the descendants of a handful of women survived. Since this must represent only a tiny fraction of all the women alive at that time, this suggests that we are here by the skin of our ancestors' teeth.

3. The origin of modern humans is captured in their rapid dispersal out of Africa around 70,000 years ago. In a mere 50,000 years, they had colonized every continent except Antarctica.

◆ TOPIC LINKS

1.2 Primate Origins
p. 32 Ancient to modern

1.3 Primates Today
p. 40 The molecular clock
p. 43 Life on the knife edge

4.1 Planet of the Apes
p. 176 An ancient success story
4.5 p. 231 Human

1. Tribal society extends into the soccer stadium. These Borussia Dortmund soccer fans display membership of their tribe with specially designed clothing.

adults with no ill effects. These people are predominantly cattle herders, so it seems that their unusual ability to tolerate milk in adulthood evolved to help them get the most out of their herds. Yet cattle-keeping is barely 7,000 years old, and the evolution of milk-tolerance must post-date that.

But despite these and other examples of rapid adaptation, humans remain a more genetically uniform species than most other primates. The genetic distance between the two subspecies of gorilla, for example, is greater than that between chimpanzees and humans. The differences between the various human races barely warrant a second glance, genetically speaking.

While the process of evolving into separate species was no doubt underway in humans, thanks mainly to their remarkable geographical dispersal, any prospect of different species emerging in the future has now been obliterated by the flow of genes that followed the invention of the boat and the airplane.

Genuine speciation requires the isolation of populations for hundreds of thousands of years. That could only happen now if total global economic collapse made travel between different continents impossible.

Tribal badges

Culture has been the hallmark of humanity for more than 50,000 years. Its diversity is nowhere better reflected than in the astonishing array of languages spoken around the world today, and even these must be a mere fraction of all the languages ever spoken, for languages have an extraordinary capacity to change. French, Spanish, Italian and Romanian, for instance, are largely mutually incomprehensible, yet all descend from Latin spoken by the Romans only 2,000 years ago.

Languages, unlike skin colors, are not adapted to local environmental conditions. Rather, they are adapted to maximize group cohesion by drawing clearly recognizable

distinctions between different populations of closely related peoples. Languages and dialects are badges of group membership that identify those who are born into a particular community, and who can therefore be expected to share significant numbers of genes.

Badges of this kind can take many forms besides language. They can include the design of clothing, beliefs about the world, and the peculiar forms of worship and social organization that go with them. The speed at which language changes over time seems to be related to the need to ensure that different groups can be easily recognized, and that false claimants to group membership can be quickly identified. Recognizing local group differences through dialect seems to have an ancient history. In the biblical Book of Judges, the defeated Ephraimites were identified and put to death by the Gileadites by the simple strategy of asking them to pronounce the word *shibboleth*, because the Gileadites could not pronounce *sh-* sounds.

Identifying members of the same clan is important because, like all primate groups, human tribes and clans are cooperative solutions to the problems of successful survival and reproduction. Yet our large groups make us especially susceptible to cheats and free-riders who accept our help and generosity but later decline to pay us back. Mechanisms designed to distinguish group members, who should be helped, from non-group members, who should be treated more cautiously, have been of such evolutionary concern that the human psyche now possesses many. Not least among these is the in-group/out-group distinction that occurs in every human culture. Members of the in-group are treated as brothers and sisters to be afforded unstinting aid, while members of the out-group may be robbed and killed with impunity.

Cain's children

Because languages gradually change into new forms over time, similar languages can be grouped together into families that reflect the ancestry of different peoples. Anthropologists have made some surprising discoveries by studying these language families to investigate how ancient peoples spread around the world thousands of years ago. One finding is that invasion followed by extermination seems to have been a more common pattern than cultural absorption.

An example is provided by the Basques, whose homeland lies in the western Pyrenees between France and Spain. Basques speak a language quite different from any other European language, and analysis of their genes suggests they are unrelated to other Europeans. The Basques almost certainly

⭐ More than 650 languages, 10 percent of the world's total, are spoken on the island of New Guinea.

LANGUAGES OF EUROPE

Indo-European family
- Germanic group (e.g. English, German)
- Romance group (e.g. French, Italian)
- Balto-Slavic group (e.g. Serbo-Croat, Russian)
- Celtic group (e.g. Gaelic)
- Albanian
- Greek

Other families
- Altaic (e.g. Turkish)
- Uralic (e.g. Finnish, Estonian, Hungarian)

Other languages
- Basque

2. Most modern European languages belong to a single family, the Indo-European group, which includes the languages of Iran and India. The exceptions are the native languages of Hungary and Finland, which belong to a separate family of Asian languages, and Basque, which is unrelated to any other modern European language.

represent the last surviving remnant of the people that inhabited Europe before the Indo-Europeans, the immediate ancestors of most modern Europeans , swept in from the east.

The similarities between European languages, except Hungarian and Finnish, indicate that they are part of a large family known as Indo-European languages. This family also includes Farsi, the language of Iran, and all the north Indian languages descended from Sanskrit. The ancestors of Indo-Europeans appear to have been a tribe of horse-riding herders who once lived to the north of the Black Sea. Around 6,000 to 8,000 years ago, they underwent a sudden explosion in numbers and spread rapidly into Europe and Asia, displacing the inhabitants of these regions as they went. In Europe, only the Basques survived, because they were able to retreat into their mountain stronghold.

Such dramatic events seem to be characteristic of recent human history. An equally dramatic population expansion led to the colonization of the entire Pacific between 1000 BC and AD 1000 by seafaring folk from the region around New Guinea and the South China Sea. This migration eventually led to the discovery and colonization of even remote island chains such as Hawaii and New Zealand. Part of this expansion led to the colonization of Madagascar, whose modern inhabitants still speak an Indonesian rather than an African language. Both Madagascar and the Pacific islands were unpopulated at the time of these invasions, and the colonizers found themselves in a virtual paradise where their numbers could rapidly expand.

Elsewhere in the world, invaders encountered resident human populations, just as the Indo-Europeans did in Europe and India. While some invasions no doubt came to grief on the beaches and died out, some proved successful and simply swept aside the resident populations. In much the same way, European populations would later sweep aside the native inhabitants of Australia and the Americas.

1. Tasmanian aborigines, like the man in this 1841 painting by Benjamin Duterreau, were eventually exterminated by white colonists.

2. This 700-year-old New Zealand rock carving depicts the kinds of canoe that brought the Maoris' ancestors across the oceans from the north.

FAMILY PORTRAITS: APES

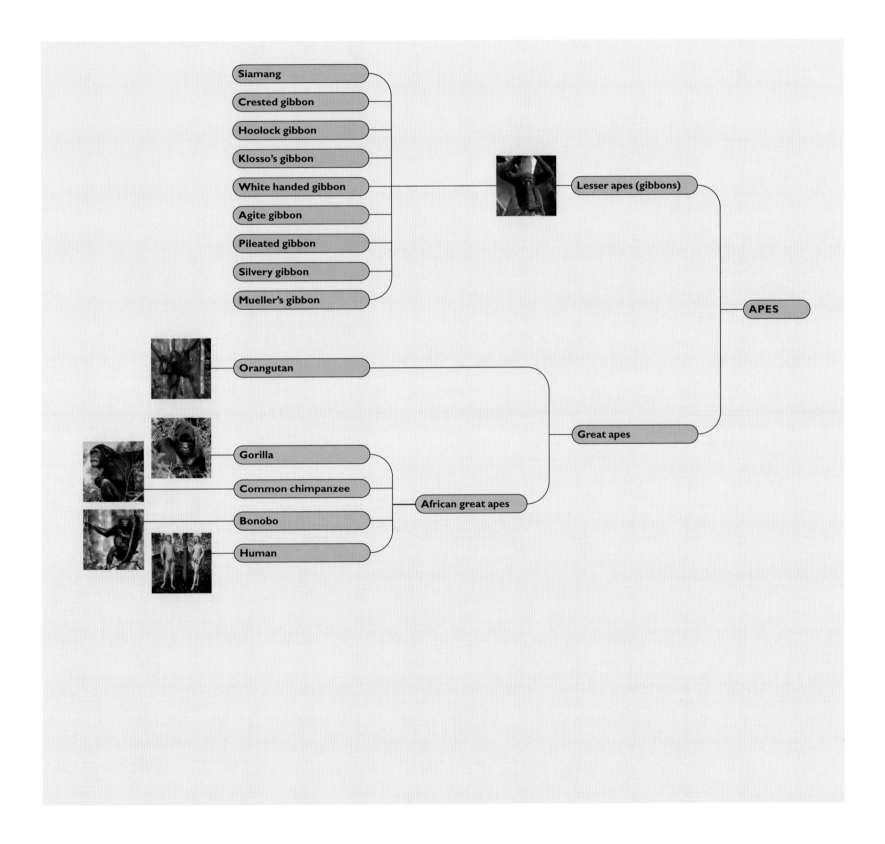

Siamang

Crested gibbon

Hoolock gibbon

Klosso's gibbon

White handed gibbon

Agite gibbon

Pileated gibbon

Silvery gibbon

Mueller's gibbon

Lesser apes (gibbons)

Orangutan

Gorilla

Common chimpanzee

Bonobo

Human

African great apes

Great apes

APES

GIBBON

The gibbons, or lesser apes, are graceful inhabitants of the upper canopy of Southeast Asian forests. Light bodied and gangly in appearance, they are superb acrobats. Gibbons are divided into two main groups, the siamang and the others. Siamangs are larger than the other gibbons, since they are leaf-eaters and tend to inhabit higher altitudes than the smaller, fruit-eating gibbons. Where the siamang is widely distributed on both the islands and mainland of Indo-China, the smaller gibbons tend to be more restricted in their range, with a different species on each island.

Gibbons are normally monogamous and defend territories of about 50–120 acres (0.2–0.5 sq. km). The female's "great call," which advertises the fact that her territory is occupied, is a haunting crescendo of howls accompanied by a spectacular aerobatic display through the treetops. While male and female gibbons differ slightly in body size, the sexes may be different colors in some species. Newborn babies are typically light in color.

The smallest of the apes, gibbons are the acrobats of Southeast Asian forests.

⊕ WHERE IN THE WORLD?

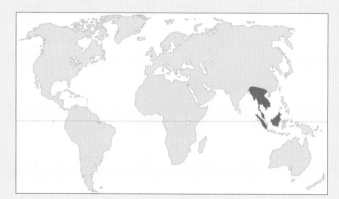

Once widespread throughout Eurasia, gibbons now have a restricted distribution.

FACT FILE

Distribution	Southeast Asia
Species	Siamang (*Hylobates syndactylus*) 8 species of lesser gibbons
Body weight	Siamang: 24-26 lb (11–12 kg) Lesser gibbons: 12-17 lb (5.5–7.5 kg)
Activity pattern	Tree living; day active (diurnal)
Habitat type	Forest
Reproduction	First birth at 9 years, then every 3 years; 1 offspring per litter
Average group size	3–5
Grouping type	Monogamous pairs plus dependent young
Maximum lifespan	32 years
Conservation status	Not currently endangered, but threatened by habitat destruction

ORANGUTAN

Methodical and pensive, the red ape, or orangutan, is the most endangered of the great apes.

Instantly recognizable by its red fur, the orangutan is the only great ape now living outside Africa. As recently as 10,000 years ago, it could be found on the Chinese mainland, but now it is confined to the island forests of Indonesia and Borneo. Like all apes, the orangutan is a fruit eater, and spends its day quietly and often solitary while foraging for food. Although it is typically alone in the wild, the orang is, in fact, sociable and can be kept in captivity in social groups.

As they age, males develop large fleshy flanges around the face, and a long, trailing cape. Their massive body size makes it difficult for them to swing through trees because they cannot easily cross the thin outer branches where trees meet. Instead, they tend to come to the ground and travel between feeding sites on foot. Females, who are only about half the males' body weight, usually remain in the trees with their dependent young, and rarely come to the ground. Males can become highly territorial, defending their ranges in heavyweight contests against rivals who trespass into their space.

FACT FILE

Distribution	Sumatra and Borneo
Species	orangutan (*Pongo pygmaeus*) 2 subspecies
Body weight	Females: 79 lb (36 kg) Males: 170 lb (78 kg)
Activity pattern	Tree-living, occasionally ground-living; day-active (diurnal)
Habitat type	Forest
Reproduction	First birth at 10 years, then every 3 to 4 years; 1 offspring per litter
Average group size	1–2
Grouping type	Mainly solitary, except during mating; dependent young accompany mother
Maximum lifespan	50 years
Conservation status	Endangered: seriously threatened by habitat destruction

⊕ WHERE IN THE WORLD?

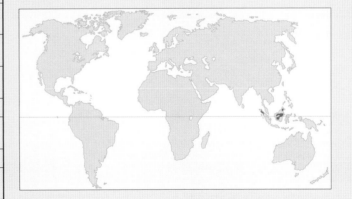

Orangutans are now confined to the islands of Sumatra and Borneo.

◈ TOPIC LINKS

1.3 Primates Today
p. 41 Old World anthropoids

4.1 Planet of the Apes
p. 174 The Apes
p. 178, 179 Recent history
p. 183 Ape anatomy

4.2 Life in Dispersed Society
p. 187 Ape lifestyles
p. 190 Male attachments
p. 193 Nest-makers
p. 194 Reasons to be Faithful
p. 196 Sex and the social whirl

GORILLA

The largest of all the living primates, the gorilla is a gentle giant that does not deserve its fearsome reputation. Although gorilla males can make frightening charges against humans when disturbed, and may even occasionally have ferocious battles with each other, their generally placid nature lends a quiet dignity to their daily life.

There are now three recognized subspecies: the endangered mountain gorilla of the Rwandan volcano region whose population is now approximately 450, the eastern lowland gorilla of the eastern Congo, and the more abundant western lowland gorilla of West Africa. Mountain gorillas are more terrestrial and leaf eating than lowland gorillas, which tend to be tree-living and fruit eating.

Gorilla groups are small by primate standards, travelling only about 1 km during the course of the day's foraging. While not openly territorial, gorillas respect each other's territories. The groups are dominated by a 'silverback' male, who does most of the breeding, but some groups may have a younger 'blackback' male, who might take over the group after the older male's death. Female gorillas are much smaller than the males.

The gentle giants of the African forests are undemonstrative, more inclined to melt away into the forest than to stand and fight.

WHERE IN THE WORLD?

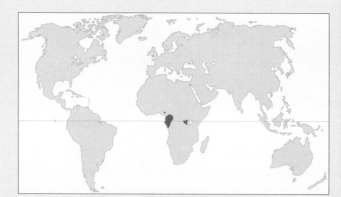

The three subspecies of gorilla occupy separate parts of Africa and have probably been separated for a long time.

FACT FILE

Distribution	Central Africa
Species	Gorilla (*Gorilla gorilla*) 3 subspecies
Body weight	Females: 156-216 lb (71–98 kg) Males: 352-385 lb (160–175 kg)
Activity pattern	Ground dwelling; day active (diurnal)
Habitat type	Forest
Reproduction	First birth at 10 years, then every 4 years; 1 offspring per litter
Average group size	7–10
Grouping type	One-male groups with 2–3 adult females and their young; some groups have 1 or more young adult follower males (blackbacks)
Maximum lifespan	39 years
Conservation status	Endangered: all species threatened by habitat destruction, and the mountain gorilla also by poaching

CHIMPANZEE

Life in a chimpanzee community is fast and furious.

Chimpanzees are the smallest of the great apes, with female chimpanzees somewhat smaller than the males. They are also the most widely distributed, living in woodland and forest habitats throughout much of central and West Africa, except for the Congo River basin, where they are replaced by the bonobos. Chimpanzees are the most intelligent of the great apes and have a life that is rich in social scheming. Unlike other apes, female chimpanzees signal the imminence of ovulation by large red swellings on their bottoms.

Chimpanzees are active and travel up to 3.1 mi (5 km) a day searching for food. They live in communities that can number up to 100 individuals, but average around 55. Their home ranges, of up to 19 sq mi (50 sq km), are vigorously defended by male brotherhoods, groups of closely related males, who occasionally mount expeditions into neighbouring ranges to find and kill rival males. Although chimpanzee communities are large, the relative poverty of their habitat means that they often forage in smaller groups, or sometimes even alone. Feeding-party size varies with the seasonal availability of fruits, but can be large when giant trees, such as the fig, are in fruit. Some populations may also hunt monkeys and small antelope on a regular basis.

FACT FILE

Distribution	Central and West Africa
Species	Chimpanzee (*Pan troglodytes*) 3 subspecies
Body weight	Females: 75-100 lb (34–46 kg) Males: 95-132 lb (43–60 kg)
Activity pattern	Tree living and ground-living; day active (diurnal)
Habitat type	Forest
Reproduction	First birth at 11–12 years, then every 4 years; 1 offspring per litter
Average group size	Community 20–100; foraging party 3–11
Grouping type	Mixed multi-male, multi-female groups
Maximum lifespan	45 years
Conservation status	Not currently endangered, but threatened by habitat destruction

⊕ WHERE IN THE WORLD?

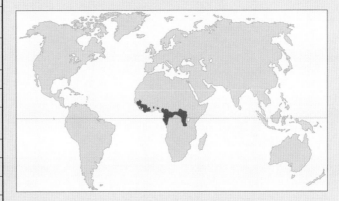

Chimpanzees are confined to the forested habitats of East and West Africa.

✦ TOPIC LINKS

1.1 What Is a Primate?
p. 14 A rather ordinary mammal
p. 16 Defining the species

1.2 Primate Origins
p. 32 Ancient to modern

1.3 Primates Today
p. 40 Old World anthropoids

3.2 Group Living
p. 128 Friends and enemies

4.1 Planet of the Apes
p. 176–185 (throughout)

4.1 Life in a Dispersed Society
p. 186–197 (throughout)

4.1 Apes with Intellect
p. 198–209 (throughout)

BONOBO

The bonobo (or pygmy chimpanzee) is about the same size as its cousin, the common chimpanzee, although perhaps more slightly built. Bonobos are found only in the dense forests of the Congo River basin, and their distribution does not overlap with that of the common chimpanzee. Although the behavior and lifestyle of the two species are very similar, bonobo society is characterized by a more relaxed and friendly atmosphere. As bonobos live in a richer forest habitat than the typical environment of common chimpanzees, their feeding parties tend to be larger and include proportionally more members of the community.

Perhaps because their social groups are larger, bonobos seem to be more actively socially than other chimpanzees. Sexual relations (between all members of the group) are used as both a greeting and a way of reinforcing friendships. Female bonobos have sexual swellings throughout most of the menstrual cycle, possibly in order to facilitate and encourage the high levels of sexual activity. Bonobos are sometimes thought to be more similar to humans than other chimpanzees in many aspects of both their anatomy and behavior.

Bonobos are renowned for their peaceful social groups in which sex is used much as humans would use conversation.

WHERE IN THE WORLD?

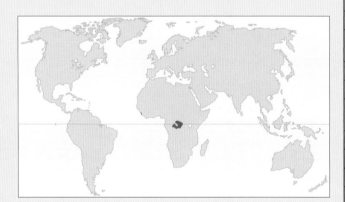

Bonobos are confined to the forests of central Africa.

FACT FILE

Distribution	Congo
Species	Bonobo (*Pan paniscus*)
Body weight	Females: 73 lb (33 kg) Males: 99 lb (45 kg)
Activity pattern	Tree-living and ground-living; day-active (diurnal)
Habitat type	Forest
Reproduction	First birth at 10 years, then every 4 years; 1 offspring per litter
Average group size	Community 10–40; foraging party: 3–13
Grouping type	Mixed multi-male/multi-female groups
Maximum lifespan	Not known
Conservation status	Not currently endangered, but threatened by habitat destruction

HUMAN

Adam and Eve by the sixteenth-century painter Cranach the Younger. The bipedal ape depicted here has been the most successful and the most destructive of all the primates.

Humans are the most intelligent and highly social of all the apes, and are unique in communicating in language based on speech. They also differ from the other great apes in being less dependent on forests and having an upright bipedal style of locomotion. Humans live in monogamous or polygynous family units, forming communities (such as villages or clans); polyandrous marriages occur in a few cases. The females are slightly smaller than the males, and are sexually receptive at all times.

Prior to the development of agriculture about 10,000 years ago, humans lived as hunter-gatherers (in some cases, as specialized fishermen), and successfully colonized every kind of habitat on Earth. The discovery of cultivation meant that many human populations changed to a more sedentary life based on villages; some populations, however, opted to become pastoralists, and managed nomadic herds of domestic animals. In agricultural and modern industrial societies, communities often band together into larger political units, the largest of which (nation-states) can number hundreds of millions of individuals. Kinship relationships are especially important in human societies; in agricultural communities, for example, land is passed down through the generations, usually via the male line.

FACT FILE

Distribution	Worldwide
Species	Human (*Homo sapiens*)
Body weight	Females: 92-160 lb (42–73 kg) Males: 103-172 lb (47–78 kg)
Activity pattern	Ground-living; day-active (diurnal)
Habitat type	All habitats
Reproduction	First birth at 15–20 years, then every 4 years in traditional societies; 1 offspring per litter
Average group size	Large
Grouping type	Monogamous pairs or one-male harems plus dependent young, usually associated together in large social groups
Maximum lifespan	90 years
Conservation status	Not endangered

⊕ WHERE IN THE WORLD?

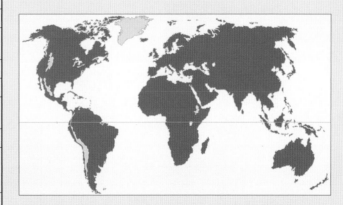

In less than 70,000 years, humans have managed to colonize every continent on the planet.

◈ TOPIC LINKS

1.1 What Is a Primate?
p. 16 Defining the species

1.2 Primate Origins
p. 32 Ancient to modern

1.3 Primates Today
p. 40 The molecular clock

4.1 Planet of the Apes
p. 178 Recent history
p. 182 Flat-chested
p. 197 An obsession with sex

4.3 Apes with Intellect
p. 199 The social brain
p. 201 Mind-readers
p. 203 Conversational apes

4.4 An Ape on Two Legs
p. 210–224 (*throughout*)

Afterword

The primates are remarkable animals, and we are privileged as a species to belong to their family. Who we are and what we do is very much a result of our being a member of that family. We share with our primate cousins a long and eventful history, one in which survival has hinged more than once on a knife's edge. Our achievements have been possible only because of the quirks of history that have produced our prosimian and ape ancestors. These sometimes surprising developments at particular moments during the past 65 million years have not in any sense been the deliberate choice of any particular species. Evolution is a blind process that has no final objective at which it aims. It is not progressive in any sense. Instead, the course of evolutionary history lurches first one way, and then another, as the powerful forces of climate change and ecological competition drive populations inexorably from one near catastrophe to another. We are here because of those accidents of history.

Our shared history gives us a special affinity with our primate cousins, an affinity that brings with it special responsibilities. Our great evolutionary achievement has been our intellect. We can use that intellect, and undeniably have done so, for both good and bad. We have singlehandedly been responsible for setting in motion the greatest ecological disaster to engulf the planet in the last 65 million years. It is our responsibility to find solutions to the dilemmas of this mass extinction. While we should not overlook our obligations toward all the other forms of animal and plant life with whom we share our planet, it is perhaps appropriate that we should view our cousins as family, for that is what they are.

Robin Dunbar and Louise Barrett

June 2000

Further Information

Byrne, R., *The Thinking Ape: Evolutionary Origins of Intelligence* (Oxford University Press, 1995). A very readable guide to brain evolution and social cognition in primates and humans.

Cheney, D. L. and Seyfarth, R. M., *How Monkeys See the World* (Chicago University Press, 1980). Well-written account of some classic experiments and observations on free-living vervet monkeys in Kenya.

Cowlishaw, G. and Dunbar, R.I.M., *Primate Conservation Biology* (Chicago University Press, 2000). A comprehensive, up-to-the-minute survey of the state of primate conservation, but a difficult read for beginners.

Deacon, T., *The Symbolic Species: The Co-evolution of Language and the Human Brain* (Allen Lane, 1997). A wide-ranging overview of the primate and human mind, and the origins of language.

Dunbar, R.I.M., *Primate Social Systems* (Chapman and Hall, 1988). A classic overview of primate social behavior.

Dunbar, R.I.M., *Grooming, Gossip and the Evolution of Language* (Faber and Faber and Harvard University Press, 1996). Primate behavior and the origins of language for the non-specialist reader.

Fleagle, J. G., *Primate Adaptation and Evolution* (Academic Press, 1999). The authoritative guide to primate evolutionary history.

Foley, R., *Humans Before Humanity* (Blackwell, 1995). Human evolution for the non-specialist reader.

Garbutt, N., *Mammals of Madagascar* (Pica Press, 1999). A pictorial guide to Madagascar's mammals, including the lemurs.

Goodall, J., *In the Shadow of Man* (Collins, 1971). The book that started it all...

Goodall, J., *The Chimpanzees of Gombe: Patterns of Behavior* (Harvard University Press, 1986). The definitive guide to the most famous chimpanzees in the world.

Harcourt, C. S., Crompton, R. H. and Feistner, A.T.C. (eds), *The Biology and Conservation of Prosimians* (Karger, 1998). A report on the complete range of issues in the study and conservation of prosimians.

Kummer, H., *In Quest of the Sacred Baboon* (Princeton University Press, 1995). A personal account of studying monkeys in the Horn of Africa.

Macdonald, D. (ed.), *Encyclopedia of Mammals*, 2nd edition (Unwin, 2000). Contains a lengthy and definitive summary of the primates, their taxonomy, ecology and behavior.

McGrew, W. C., Marchant, M.C. and Nishida, T. (eds), *Great Ape Societies* (Cambridge University Press, 1996). The most recent overview of the apes.

Richard, A., *Primates in Nature* (W. H. Freeman, 1985). A classic textbook on primate behavior and ecology.

Rowe, N., *The Pictorial Guide to the Living Primates* (Pogonias Press, 1996)

Smuts, B. B., Cheney, D. L., Seyfarth, R. M., Wrangham, R. W. and Struhsaker, T. T. (eds), *Primate Societies* (Chicago University Press, 1987). A definitive summary of primate biology, with useful chapters on individual families of primates.

Strier, K. B., *Primate Behavioral Ecology* (Allyn and Bacon, 2000). The newest textbook on primate behavior and ecology.

Struhsaker, T. T., *Ecology of an African Rain Forest: Logging in Kibale and the Conflict Between Conservation and Exploitation* (University of Florida Press, 1997). A hard-hitting analysis of the problems of primate conservation by a leading wildlife biologist.

de Waal, F., *Chimpanzee Politics: Power and Sex Among Apes* (Unwin, 1982). The classic account of the drama of power politics between Yeroen, Luit and Nikkie at Arnhem Zoo, Holland.

de Waal, F., *Peacemaking Among Primates* (Harvard University Press, 1989). An exploration of how primates manage their relationships with each other.

Walker, A., *The Wisdom of Bones: In Search of Human Origins* (Alfred Knopf, 1996). The story of human origins for beginners.

Wrangham, R. W. and Peterson, D., *Demonic Males: Apes and the Origins of Human Violence* (Houghton Mifflin, 1996). A personal account of field work on chimpanzees.

WEBSITES

American Society of Primatologists
http://www.asp.org

International Primate Protection League
http://www.ippl.org/index.html

International Primatological Society
http://indri.primate.wisc.edu/pin/ips.html

Jane Goodall Institute
http://www.janegoodall.org/index.html

Primate Conservation
http://www.primate.org

Primate Society of Great Britain
http://www.ana.ed.ac.uk/PSGB/home.html

Fauna and Flora International
http://www.ffi.org.uk

Picture credits

BBC Worldwide would like to thank the following for providing photographs and for permission to reproduce copyright material. While every effort has been made to trace and acknowledge all copyright holders, we would like to apologise should there have been any errors or omissions.

Anthro-photo pages 145 *top* (Sarah Blaffer Hrdy) & 202 (Herbert Terrace); **Ardea** pages 58 (M. Watson), 76 *right* (Peter Steyn), 118 (Jean-Paul Ferrero), 156 *left* (M. Watson), 184 (Jean-Paul Ferrero), 189 (Ferrero-Labat), 191 *bottom* (Parer-Cook), 195 Jean-Paul Ferrero) & 206 *right* (Adrian Warren); **Art Archive** page 224 *top* (Queen Victoria Museum); **Louise Barrett** pages 154 & 156 *right*; **Miles Barton** pages 140 *bottom* & 158 *top*; **BBC Natural History Unit Picture Library** pages 4–5 (Anup Shah),17 *right* (Anup Shah), 23 (Ian Redmond), 33 (Richard du Toit), 37 (Pete Oxford), 41 (Anup Shah), 42 (David Shale), 44 (Anup Shah), 54 (Pete Oxford), 59 *left* (Bruce Davidson), 61 (Pete Oxford), 65 (Pete Oxford), 73 *top* (Nick Garbutt), 98 (Pete Oxford), 99 (Richard du Toit), 112 *top* (Pete Oxford), *bottom left* (Miles Barton), 123 *top* (Richard du Toit), 124 (Anup Shah), 125 *bottom* (Mike Wilkes), 127 (Anup Shah), 137 *left* (Miles Barton), 138 (Vivek Menon), 143 *top* (Anup Shah), *bottom* (Dietmar Nill), 144 (Pete Oxford), 158 *bottom* (Miles Barton), 161 (Nick Gordon), 174 (Anup Shah), 179 *top* (Anup Shah), 187 Neil P.Lucas), 188 *bottom right* (Anup Shah), 192 Bruce Davidson) & 229 (Anup Shah); **Simon Bearder** page 70; **Bridgeman Art Library** pages 218 *left* (Ali Meyer/Naturhistorisches Museum, Vienna), 218 *right* & 231 (Edith A. & Percy S. Strauss Collection, Museum of Fine Arts, Houston, Texas); **Bubbles** pages 201 (Amanda Knapp) & 203 *bottom* (Loisjoy Thurston); **Bruce Coleman Collection** pages 2 (Janos Jurka), 22 *bottom* (Gerald Cubitt), 56 *left* (Alain Compost), 60 (Rod Williams), 64 (Konrad Wothe), 66 *bottom* (Konrad Wothe), 74 Rod Williams, 84 *right* (Konrad Wothe), 92 *left* (Konrad Wothe), 96 (Konrad Wothe), 102 (J. P. Zwaenepoel), 105 (Jorg & Petra Wegner), 107 Gunter Ziesler, 108 *bottom* Luiz Claudio Marigo), 109 *top* (Luiz Claudio Marigo), 117 *top* (Trevor Barrett), 119 (Steven C. Kaufman), 123 *bottom* (Ingo Arndt), 130 (Ingo Arndt), 135 (Konrad Wothe), 136 (Ingo Arndt), 145 *bottom* (Rod Williams), 146–7 (Ingo Arndt), 160 (Rod Williams), 165 (Luiz Claudio Marigo), 185 *top* (John Cancalosi) & 194 *right* (Rod Williams); **Frans de Waal** page 209 *both*; **Robin Dunbar** page 149; **Michael & Patricia Fogden** page 20; **Werner**

Forman Archive page 224 *bottom*; **Fortean Picture Library** page 178 *top* (Copyright 1968 Dahinden, *photo* Patterson/Gimlin) & *bottom* (Tony Healy); **Nick Garbutt, Indri Images** pages 59 *right*, 66 *top*, 71, 78 *right*, 84 *left*, 85, 87, 88–9, 91 & 97; **Michael A.Huffman** page 205; **The Jane Goodall Institute**, **UK** page 199 *bottom*; **S. & R.Greenhill** page 214 *left*; **Images Colour Library** pages 10, 45 *bottom* & 215 *left*; **Melanie Krebs** page 128 *both*; **Linnean Society of London**, by kind permission, page 16 *left*; **Magnum** pages 185 *bottom* & 203 *top* (*both* Michael Nichols); **Florian Mollers** pages 112 *bottom right* & 129; **Natural History Museum, London** pages 25 *both*, 26, 30, 216 & 217 *right*; **Network** pages 214 *right* (Olivier Martel/Rapho) & 222 (Ellerbrock/Bilderberg); **NHPA** pages 14 *right* (Steve Robinson), 19 (Orion Press), 21 (Martin Harvey), 46 (Jany Sauvanet), 55 *left* (Peter Pickford), 77 (Martin Harvey), 79 (Martin Harvey), 92 (Martin Harvey), 94 (Martin Harvey), 101 (Ivan Polunin), 114 *left* (James Carmichael Jr), 115 *right* (Christopher Ratier), 116 *right* (Nigel J.Dennis), 126 (Nigel J. Dennis), 132 (Stephen Dalton), 133 (Iain Green), 139 (Gerard Lacz), 142 (Daryl Balfour), 151 *bottom* (E. A. Janes), 153 *bottom* (Martin Harvey), 155 (Kevin Schafer), 162 (Kevin Schafer), 169 (John Shaw), 173 (Martin Harvey), 177 (Nigel J.Dennis), 179 *bottom* (Martin Harvey), 182 *top* (Martin Harvey), 188 *left* (Nigel J. Dennis) & 204 (Steve Robinson); **Oxford Scientific Films** pages 14 *left* (David Curl), 22 *top* (David Cayless), 29 (Alan Root/Survival Anglia), 35 (Stan Osolinski), 43 (Bob Campbell/Survival Anglia), 48 (David Curl), 52 (Michael Leach), 53 (Densey Clyne/Mantis Wildlife Films), 56 *right* (David Haring), 63 Des & Jen Bartlett/Survival Anglia), 67 (Mark Pidgeon), 69 (David Curl), 75 (Mark Pidgeon), 76 *left* (David Haring), 78 *left* (David Haring), 86 (Doug Allan), 106 (Nick Gordon), 113 *top* (Stan Osolinski), 115 *left* (John Chellman/Animals Animals), 116 *left* (Stan Osolinski), 117 *bottom* (Konrad Wothe), 121 *top* (Warwick Johnson), 122 (Michael Fogden), 125 *top* (Zig Leszczynski), 131 (Belinda Wright), 140 *top* (Jan Teede/Survival Anglia), 150 (Mickey Gibson/Animals Animals), 152 *top* (Mike Birkhead), 157 (Tom Ulrich), 164 (Edward Parker),

166 (Alan & Sandy Carey), 167 (Stephen Mills), 168 (Alan & Sandy Carey), 171 (Michael Dick/Animals Animals), 180 *right* (Edward Parker), 182 *bottom* (Mike Birkhead), 188 *top right* (Dieter & Mary Plage), 190 *left* (Konrad Wothe), 191 *top* (Mike Birkhead), 194 *left* (Clive Bromhall), 197 (Martyn Colbeck), 200 *bottom* (Martyn Colbeck), 206 *left* (Clive Bromhall), 207 *left* (Clive Bromhall), 208 (Clive Bromhall), 227 (Mike Hill), 228 (Daniel J. Cox) & 230 (Martyn Colbeck; **Photofusion** page 219 *right* (Clarissa Leahy); **Planet Earth Pictures** pages 1 (Anup Shah), 13 (Elio della Ferrera), 15 (K.Jayaram), 16–17 *left* (Julian Partridge), 18 (Ned Middleton), 28 (M. & C. Denis-Huot), 47 *top* (K.& K. Ammann), 51 (Ken Lucas), 55 *right* (Rod Williams), 73 *bottom* (Rod Williams), 80 (Peter Lilja), 81 *both* (Nick Garbutt), 95 (Nick Garbutt), 100 (Rod Wiiliams), 108 *top* (Brian Kenney), 109 *both bottom* (Claus Meyer), 111 (Jonathan Scott), 113 *bottom* (K.& K.Ammann), 114 *right* (Anup Shah), 121 *bottom* (Jonathan Scott), 141 *left* (Ken Lucas), *right* (M. & C. Denis-Huot), 151 *top* (Michael McKinnon), 152 *bottom* (John Downer), 153 *top* (John Downer), 163 (Ken Lucas), 170 (Jonathan Scott), 170 (Jonathan Scott), 172 (Brian Kenney), 183 (Anup Shah), 196 (Jonathan Scott), 215 *right* (Jonathan Scott), 219 *top left* (B. & C.Alexander), *bottom left* (Jonathan Scott), 226 (Robert Franz), 232 (Elio Della Ferrara), 235 (Anup Shah) & 236 (Peter Lilja); **Science Photo Library** pages 32 (John Reader), 40 (Carolyn Iverson), 45 *top* (CNES/1989 Distribution Spot Image), 181 (Jacques Langoux), 199 *top* (D. Roberts), 211 (John Reader), 212 (Petit Format/Nestle), 213 (John Reader), 217 *left* (John Reader), & 220 *top* (Simon Fraser), *bottom* (P. Motta & T. Naguro); **Still Pictures** pages 47 *bottom* (Yves Lefevre), 83 (Roland Seitre), 137 *right* (Xavier Eichaker), 180 *left* (Mark Edwards), 190 *right* (Schafer & Hill) & 193 (Michael Gunther); **University of Louisiana** page 200 *top* (Donna T. Biershwale/Institute of Cognitive Science); **Bernard Walton** page 9.

The photograph on page 207 *right* is taken from *The Mentality of Apes* by Wolfgang Kohler, 1925.

Index